ABOLITION AND ITS AFTERMATH

LEGACIES OF WEST INDIAN SLAVERY

Lectures and conference papers given during the William Wilberforce 150th anniversary celebrations at the University of Hull, July 1983

OUT OF SLAVERY
Abolition and After
Edited by Jack Hayward

ABOLITION AND ITS AFTERMATH
The Historical Context 1790–1916
Edited by David Richardson

DUAL LEGACIES IN THE CONTEMPORARY CARIBBEAN
Continuing Aspects of British and French Dominion
Edited by Paul Sutton

THE CARIBBEAN IN EUROPE
Aspects of the West Indian Experience in Britain, France and The Netherlands
Edited by Colin Brock

ABOLITION AND ITS AFTERMATH

The Historical Context, 1790 – 1916

Edited by
DAVID RICHARDSON
University of Hull

FRANK CASS

First published 1985 in Great Britain by
FRANK CASS AND COMPANY LIMITED
Gainsborough House, Gainsborough Road,
London, E11 1RS, England

and in the United States of America by
FRANK CASS AND COMPANY LIMITED
c/o Biblio Distribution Centre
81 Adams Drive, P.O. Box 327, Totowa, N.J. 07511

British Library Cataloguing in Publication Data

Abolition and its aftermath : the historical
context, 1790–1916
1. Slavery—History
I. Richardson, David
306′.362 HT867

ISBN 0-7146-3261-9

Typeset by Williams Graphics, Abergele, Clwyd
Printed and bound in Great Britain by
A. Wheaton & Co. Ltd., Exeter

CONTENTS

PREFACE

With the exception of Barbara Bush's contribution, all the papers and commentaries contained in this volume were presented at a conference at Thwaite Hall, University of Hull, 26–29 July 1983. The conference was organised to commemorate the 150th anniversary of the abolition of slavery in the British Empire, and was attended by over eighty scholars from Britain, Western Europe, the USA and the Caribbean. The holding of such a conference at Hull was particularly appropriate, for the passing of the abolition bill coincided almost exactly with the death in July 1833 of William Wilberforce, the most celebrated member of the so-called 'Clapham Sect' that had done much to initiate and promote the cause of black emancipation. Born in Hull in 1759 and M.P. for the City in 1780–84, Wilberforce subsequently became M.P. for Yorkshire and later Bramber, a pocket borough in Sussex, before retiring from Parliament in 1825. Devoting much of his forty-five year parliamentary career to the task of overthrowing first the slave trade and then slavery in Britain's colonies, Wilberforce came to be regarded by most of his contemporaries, white and black alike, as the inspiration and leader of the British abolitionist movement.

During the first century after abolition, the British anti-slavery movement was largely seen through the speeches, letters and diaries of abolitionist leaders. As a result, the Act of 1833 tended to be interpreted as a triumph of selfless morality and humanitarianism over materialism and vested self-interest. In Sir Reginald Coupland's words, the Abolition Act was 'the noblest measure' in the history of the House of Commons. Given this background it was not surprising, as Professor Drescher reminds us in his introduction to this collection, that the 1933 celebration of the centenary of abolition focused unhesitatingly on the 'Saints', and in Hull's case, on William Wilberforce.

A cursory glance at the essays included in this, the first of a three-volume collection of the conference proceedings, reveals that historical interpretation of abolition has changed in fundamental ways since the centenary celebrations. Stimulated by seminal studies by C.L.R. James and Eric Williams, West-Indian born scholars who challenged the essentially élitist, Anglo-centric and humanitarian approach to abolition of their British contemporaries, historians have recently subjected anti-slavery and its consequences to searching re-appraisal. Seeking to reflect current research interests, the essays in this volume focus on three main themes. These are, first, the contribution made by the slaves themselves to their own emancipation; second, the connections between the British and Continental abolitionist movements; and third, the adjustment of Caribbean labour systems to slave emancipation. In examining these themes, these essays offer important new insights and interpretations of British abolition and its impact in Western Europe and the Caribbean, and help to put into firmer historical perspective the significance of British anti-slavery. In particular, they remind us that abolition was more than just a British movement and that the slaves were not simply passive observers of events in Britain. Furthermore, by drawing attention to the social and economic adjustments to slave emancipation in the Caribbean, including the resort to indentured labour, they underline the very real limitations of the abolitionists' achievement in 1833.

The Hull conference was arranged in three sections dealing with the historical context of abolition, its long-term impact on the Caribbean and its legacy to Britain since 1945. General responsibility for organising the conference, which was marked by the conferment of an honorary Doctorate of Letters on C.L.R. James by the Chancellor of the University, Lord Wilberforce, lay with the University's Wilberforce Sesquicentenary Committee. In my capacity as the arranger of the historical section and editor of the papers relating to it, I wish to thank two members of this committee in particular, Jack Hayward and Paul Sutton, for their help in organising this part of the conference. Financial support for the conference was generously provided by the Commonwealth Foundation and the British Academy. I am also grateful to all those who contributed to the historical panels of the conference for their punctual submission of original and revised versions of their papers. Finally, I am indebted to Irene Baldwin for her invaluable assistance in both producing copies of papers for the conference and preparing them for publication.

David Richardson

NOTES ON CONTRIBUTORS

H. McD. Beckles is a Lecturer in History, University of the West Indies, Mona, Jamaica.

Barbara Bush is a research student of the Department of Economic & Social History, University of Sheffield and a tutor for the Open University.

Serge Daget formerly taught at the University of Abidjan, Ivory Coast and is Maître de Conférences to U.E.R. of Sciences Historiques at the University of Nantes.

Seymour Drescher is Professor of History, University of Pittsburgh, Pennsylvania, and Secretary of the European Program of the Wilson Center, Smithsonian Institution Building, Washington, D.C., U.S.A.

P.C. Emmer is Lecturer in History, the Centre for the History of European Expansion, University of Leiden, The Netherlands.

S.L. Engerman is Professor of Economics and History, University of Rochester, New York, U.S.A.

David Geggus is Associate Professor of History, University of Florida at Gainesville, U.S.A.

W.A. Green is Professor of History, Holy Cross College, Worcester, Massachusetts, U.S.A.

S.W. de Groot is Lecturer in History, Historisch Seminarium, University of Amsterdam, The Netherlands.

K.O. Laurence is Professor of History, University of the West Indies, St Augustine, Trinidad.

W.K. Marshall is Professor of History, University of the West Indies, Cave Hill, Barbados.

J.P. Siwpersad was formerly a Lecturer in History in Surinam. He is currently resident in Holland.

Mary Turner is Associate Professor of History, Dalhousie University, Halifax, Nova Scotia, Canada.

PART A

Introduction

1

The Historical Context of British Abolition

SEYMOUR DRESCHER

I

Some one hundred and fifty years ago in 1833 the Parliament of Britain legislated the end of slavery in the British colonies.[1] The Act of 1833 was more than a massive manumission. To those who celebrated the event in Britain, and to observers abroad, it was a decisive step in the elimination of the institution throughout the world.

The context of an event is not fixed once and for all in human memory or historical discourse. It is an ever-shifting current, sometimes clear and placid, sometimes churning up long-forgotten or never noticed debris from far upstream.

For a century after British emancipation its historical context was virtually unchanged. The centenary of 1933 was solemnly celebrated as a national and imperial triumph. The City of Hull, as the home-town of William Wilberforce, was the designated centre of the event. The commemoration focused on the life of the 'liberator' who had died just as the emancipation bill cleared its last parliamentary hurdles. *The Times* accurately headlined the Hull events: 'Centenary of Wilberforce'. A great civil procession led by Hull's Lord Mayor, a host of dignitaries and descendants of Wilberforce filed past the liberator's birth-place and his brightly wreathed statue, past his grammar school and its assembled students. The proceedings were consecrated by the Archbishop of York and accompanied by hymns and spirituals. The flags of fifty nations simultaneously unfurled before a crowd of twenty thousand.[2]

For the celebrants, as for the nation at large, there was little ambiguity about the significance of the Act of 1833. The reigning historians of England and of Abolition, George Macaulay Trevelyan for *The Times*, and Reginald Coupland at Hull, agreed that emancipation had elevated all mankind to a higher moral plane. The national memory was refreshed by a roll call of the gallant band of Saints led by their incomparably English hero. The beneficiaries were also remembered: West Indians who devoutly assembled on the hilltops to await the sunrise of freedom, and natives of Africa, unaware that British penetration henceforth entailed the end of slavery in 'the heart of darkness'.[3]

Except for the clearly imperial emphasis on Africa, Coupland and Trevelyan made little change in the ideological frame of reference laid down by those who had celebrated emancipation a century before: a corrupted nation was roused by a band of prophets who provided humanity with a decisive victory over materialism, avarice, and exploitation. Here, if anywhere in Anglo-American historiography, lay the watershed of the 'Whig' interpretation of history. Anti-slavery's progressive political narrative core was fleshed out with religious and economic history. British emancipation was the purest evidence of human progress. Historians never wearied of repeating Lecky's verdict on abolition as 'among the three or four perfectly virtuous pages ... in the history of nations'.

In short, the story was dramatic, the motives clear, the ending happy. In 1833 Britain was safe for reform, the West Indies for freedom and Africa for penetration.

Now consider this collection of papers first presented at a conference fifty years later. A casual observer might note that both the principal scene of the centenary and its leading actors have virtually vanished. There are no papers devoted specifically to British abolitionism, nor to its statesmen, nor to its Saints, not even a single paper on Hull's own hero. One is reminded of William Cobbett's little list of things that would not be missed when he was forced to leave England in 1816. Cobbett's ultimate consolation, you may recall, was: 'No Wilberforce! think of *that*! no Wilberforce!'

What has happened? First, as the Whig interpretation's holy of holies, abolitionism almost begged for an iconoclast. For a budding generation of West Indian scholars in the 1930s, the imperial abolitionist tradition represented a filiopietistic case of selective recall.

In 1938 C.L.R. James arrestingly returned the focus to history's most dramatic example of slave self-liberation – the St Domingue revolution. *The Black Jacobins* was the very anti-model of the modern major historians.[4] The event was supremely violent. It succeeded in the teeth of British military intervention. It was not orchestrated by eighteenth-century evangelicals or by great metropolitan statesmen.

A second major challenge to the traditional perspective was also inspired by James. *The Black Jacobins* observed that British policy toward St Domingue and slavery was dominated by material interests. Another West Indian scholar, Eric Williams, expanded that perspective into a global attack on the idealistic tradition of British historiography. His *Capitalism and Slavery*, in 1944, asserted the primacy of economic determinism.[5] He tied every phase of the rise and fall of British slavery to specific phases of capitalist development. Slavery, like some mercantilist Dr Frankenstein, created an industrial capitalist giant which destroyed its creator with a toxic dose of laissez-faire. Lecky's three or four 'pure pages' of sacred history had suddenly vanished. With almost biblical speed the great deluge of conscience called up by the Saints shrank to a small cloud guided by Adam Smith's invisible hand.

Since James and Williams, an explosion of empirical research has expanded and pluralized the historical context of British abolition. Scholars are hard pressed to stay abreast of development. Three years ago a comprehensive teaching bibliography on slavery listed over 3,200 entries, most published since the 1960s. Supplements have since increased the total to 4,000.[6] If British America is still over-represented within slavery studies, African, Asian and pre-modern varieties are now an integral part of a truly global framework. Cross-cultural and cross-temporal tabulators now move easily across space and time.

Economists, demographers and anthropologists also rediscovered slavery. Scholars have developed economic models to explain fluctuations of slavery in the British colonies which were unclear or invisible to contemporaries.[7] A surge of demographic interest swept over a subject which was one of the first to invite mathematical speculation two centuries ago. Newly uncovered long-range processes, what Bernard Bailyn has called 'latent events', present historians with a new background to the history of slavery.[8] We have begun to re-order our sense of scale. For example, the most recent collective volume on the abolition of the slave trade contains essays on Afro-Asian as well as Euro-American dimensions of abolition.[9] There is now far more emphasis on the differential impact of abolitionist policies over the long term.

However, even the broadest extensions of context have not yet altered one element, the Anglo-centrism of the emancipation process as a whole. There is a difference between showing that the destruction of slavery was not just a sequence of British initiatives and denying that Britain forms the single most important piece in the puzzle. Without that piece the essays contained in this volume are still three peripheries in search of a core. After all allowances for local social forces, scholars usually take note of exogenous British pressure throughout the century of emancipation between the 1780s and 1880s.

Recent historiographic extensions of the boundaries of British culture actually enhance the case for regarding Britain as the abolitionist core. In America, the Civil War and its racist aftermath prevented emancipation from becoming an element of consensual nationalism throughout the nineteenth century. In the British slave colonies too, abolition was hardly a consensual symbol during the nineteenth century.

Britain occupies a similar core position in relation to the European Continent. There is a clear distinction between the national, mass-based and aggressive British abolitionism, and the more in-bred, timid and erratic movements of its neighbours.[10] In terms of resources expended or forgone for abolitionist ends the British stood out, from the early mass boycotts and petitions, to the culminating election of 1832, when colonial slavery became a national campaign issue for the first and last time in European history.

From the early nineteenth century, and certainly before Waterloo, Britain was clearly identified as the premier abolitionist nation. By then abolitionism in France was correspondingly identified with domestic cataclysm, colonial disaster and British maritime hegemony. After 1815 waves of nationalist resentment often accompanied Continental defiance of British abolitionist policies.[11] Foreign suspicions nurtured a persistent undercurrent of cynicism which also characterizes the history of British abolition.

There was, of course, one major interruption to this historical geography of abolition. The initial British lead in the 1780s was pre-empted during the decade of the St Domingue and French Revolutions. If France's emancipation decree of 1794 was largely reactive to Caribbean events, Britain actively sought to restore slavery.[12] Significantly, Britain lost control of the pace of abolition during moments of maximum popular mobilizations in France and the Antilles.

These French and other Continental cases provide new comparative dimensions with which to assess the significance of economic, political and cultural variables in British abolition. In the last half century, this 'ecology' of British anti-slavery, and the assignment of weights to background factors, has generated the most fruitful and intense controversy.

II

The torrent of cross-cultural and cross-disciplinary scholarship allows us to fit the varieties of slavery more precisely into world history. We have moved away from some connotations of the 'peculiar' institution. The slave market may still be designated as an 'uncommon' market in that its principal objects were human beings, but not because its sellers, buyers or more remote participants behaved differently from those in other markets.[13] Their actions, like their profits, were far more normal than previous generations cared to imagine. Here, too, the twentieth century has rediscovered the banality, not of evil, but of most human actors.[14]

As the economic patterns of slavery become clearer, what of anti-slavery historiography? At the moment we have developed far more powerful models to account for the expansion than for the end of slavery.[15] The nice fit between economics and slavery's rise was at first logically extended to its demise. Eric Williams launched an account of a 'decline' phase of British slavery by designating specific economic and ideological forces behind every shift in the downward slide of the British West Indies after 1776. He explained abolition as a measurable result of declines in profits, of a relative commercial devaluation and of a rise of hostile economic interests. Subsequent research has so far failed to sustain his timing or his complex of economic forces. The world economic conditions which encouraged the growth of British slavery before 1775 were still clearly operative when Britain abolished its slave trade in 1807, its slave system in 1833, and colonial apprenticeship in 1838. The fundamental characteristics which had driven the Atlantic economy for three centuries – New World demand for labour and capital, temperate zone demand for tropical staples and African demand for Euro-American commodities – remained intact, while British emancipation was forced on its own slave-holders and abolition was pressed on foreigners. The further one proceeds into the age of abolition the more the rhythm of the slave trade and slavery is dominated by political action. For example, Anglo-American abolition in 1808 resulted in a dramatic shift of the slave trade toward Ibero-America. But even regarding Brazil's nineteenth-century boom, David Eltis calculates that the British navy accounted for far more of the annual variation of Brazilian slave imports from 1825 to 1850 than did coffee exports or slave prices.[16]

Williams' economic approach also reasonably focused on a 'revolution' in British political economy. Here, Williams developed a new anti-slavery dimension to the old Imperial school's general turning point of 1776. West Indian slavery supposedly went down with mercantilism, under the combined impact of American Independence and Adam Smith. However, another of our many recently-eroded turning points has been 1776 and all that. Cain and Hopkins have cogently argued that Britain's shift toward laissez-faire did not occur until fifty years after American Independence. Moreover, between 1783 and 1833 a policy of real free trade, including a free trade in slaves, would have given a boost to British colonial slavery. So the argument that British slavery was phased out in tandem with a declining mercantilism is doubly flawed.[17]

On the micro- as well as on the macro-economic level, we have also moved away from the abolitionist assumptions which dominated historiographical discourse from Thomas Clarkson through Williams. We now recognize a deep conflict between free labour and maximized staple output in nineteenth-century Caribbean conditions.[18] At this micro-economic level it seems that the 'irrational' planters of the Whig–to–Williams tradition were more rational predictors of *economic* outcomes than their abolitionist antagonists. The vow that one would have free labour and cheaper sugar too was a *tour de force*, a metropolitan marriage of convenience in order to defend the central philosophical premise that nothing so bad could be good or long enduring.

Forty years of economic history after Williams launched his arresting attack on the fuzzy-minded idealists of the Centenary we stand at a very curious cross-disciplinary crossroads. The economic historians, indeed their cliometric phalanx, begin to wax bold with the conclusion that economic factors and interests cannot explain the attack on the slave trade and slavery. Indeed, one has also waxed metaphoric, if not poetic, at the discovery of an 'altruistic interest' in the heart of economic starkness. Donald McCloskey noted that in anti-slavery cliometricians discovered a point where 'irrationality leaves footprints in the snow of informed selfishness'.[19] To this one need only add that in measuring those footprints we have been able to reconstitute a fair-sized humanitarian mammoth, woolly-minded though its economic thinking may have been.

It is unsatisfactory to retreat to the bland formulation that purely economic factors alone do not explain abolition. This still leaves the misleading impression that economic historians have discovered a compound of economic factors that played a strong role in the destruction of slavery. So far no work has demonstrated such a balance of economic forces with the same degree of conviction with which we can now account for the expansion of slavery.

Have we thus come full circle on this fundamental question? Not quite. Almost all serious scholars (and this was Williams' major contribution) now ground themselves in the observation that it was surely 'no accident' that British abolition coincided with the industrial revolution. This orientation has opened up new lines of argument, but there are discordant notes here too.

As already indicated, historians recognise that industrialisation actually encouraged the expansion of the slave trade and slavery in Africa and America. Given this positive and direct impact of industrialisation, attention has swung away from economic interests toward economic ideology. One form of this argument, by no means entirely new, is that industrialisation breeds antagonism by capitalists to slavery as an inefficient form of work discipline. Factory and coerced plantation labour are incompatible and technological development thus doomed slavery. This hypothesis has run into a number of challenges based on nineteenth-century case studies. The twentieth century created even stronger cases for the primacy of non-economic factors in modern emancipations and revivals of coerced labour. For example, in 1920 the Soviet Union had the same per capita level of industrial output as did Britain shortly after 1800. In its next generation of industrialisation Britain dismantled slave labour in its islands. The Soviet Union correspondingly created a whole new forced labour archipelago. Moreover, a full century after British emancipation, one of Europe's most mature industrial capitalist societies developed one of the largest coerced labour systems in history.[20] If the Nazi slave labour system turned out to be a curtailed nightmare, both examples revealed new possibilities of revivals of forced labour, in certain *political* contexts, in both developing and mature industrialised economies. Therefore historians cannot permit premises about attitudes supposedly mandated by technological or economic imperatives to carry the burden of accounting for British emancipation.[21]

A second approach is more indirect but therefore more difficult to verify. It focuses on changing elite attitudes toward the labour force generally in the eighteenth century, culminating in a 'free labour ideology'. One version of this argument emphasises the British 'discovery' that the supply curve of labour is not necessarily backward bending (i.e. that workers would continue to work beyond minimum subsistence or custom-bound accumulation) and that voluntary labour was more efficient than coerced labour.[22] Another version of changing elite attitudes sees British anti-slavery as arising from fear of, rather than confidence in, free labour. In this variant, abolitionism was a capitalistic reaction to the intensification of class discipline and of labour's exposure to an unbuffered market. Mobilisations against slavery psychologically 'screened out' the social havoc being wrought by industrialism in England itself.[23] These two approaches, 'optimistic' and 'pessimistic', obviously differ on the operative variables within the industrialisation process. They also both present historians with similar chronological difficulties. Optimistic free labour ideology arrived too early. It emerged just when Britain was starting to *expand* its slave empire. The pessimistic counter-ideology also seems to have emerged too early – the 1780s and early 1790s – to have been a nation-wide elite reaction to the dark satanic mills or other localized manifestation of industrialisation. There is no time here to explore other methodological difficulties of verification. At the moment these 'ideological' approaches represent the most recent and subtle linkage between abolition and industrialisation.

At this stage the urge to elicit a causal connection between British economic development and abolition invites certain provisional reflections. First, and most definitively, Williams' suggestion of a general front of economic interests against slavery has not been substantiated. Some scholars turned toward a primarily ideological strategy. The vocabularies appropriate to social psychology and symbolic analysis have replaced the interplay of economic interests. The forms of group self-deception and false consciousness now occupy a much larger role in such historical analyses than the logic of economic man.[24] Sir Reginald Coupland's assertion of the primacy of pure idealism has been succeeded not by Williams' antithesis of impure interests, but by variations on the primacy of *impure* idea. Historians must remain aware that this economic-ideological approach subtly sets the agenda of historical investigation. It both designates *economic* ideology as the really crucial development in the attack on slavery, and implies that anti-slavery was generated by those who had attitudes toward labour, from outside, above, or against it.

This elite-oriented perspective coincides with another recent trend in Euro-American historiography, a devaluation of the humanitarian and democratic achievement of the age of emancipation. Much of modern social change is critically analysed as the zero-sum substitution of one form of coercion or surveillance for another. Historians, including those of anti-slavery, who employ this concept, emphasise the ability of political and cultural elites to hegemonically dominate the masses. According to Michel Foucault, the most famous, and most popularised, proponent of this general perspective, the age of reform re-emerges as an age of confinements of the masses – in the prison, the workhouse, the poorhouse, the madhouse, even the schoolhouse.

As with analyses based on economic ideology, abolition, at best, fits only *indirectly* into this age of surveillance. In the colonies emancipation clearly weakened one of the most ruthless institutions of surveillance and confinement invented by Western culture. None of the ruling groups who inherited fragments of the masters' institutional authority – magistrates, planters and clergy – regained the degree of control destroyed by emancipation. Authority itself was fragmented. Colonial emancipation can again be re-interpreted *dialectically* as a quasi-liberating movement which 'displaced' capitalist anxieties about increasing industrial and bureaucratic discipline in the metropolis itself.[25]

For the metropolis, applied hegemony theory has simply assumed that anti-slavery ideology resulted in a net gain for domestic hierarchy and the political establishment. On the contrary, British anti-slavery always remained a double-edged sword to be turned against the economic or political status quo. The main weakness of this social control model is that it relies more on the plans and rhetoric of the putative hegemonisers than on measured outcomes.[26]

This conception of slave emancipation as a world made by bourgeois and bureaucrat represents only one strand of recent scholarship. A number of historians are more impressed by the coincidence of abolition with new forms of religious and political organisation than with the concomitant arrival of the factory, the poorhouse and the penitentiary. The late Roger Anstey, an heir of the evangelical tradition, skilfully elaborated the links between anti-slavery and evangelical theology in Britain.[27] But others have attempted to locate evangelicalism and abolitionism more precisely within the economically dynamic areas of industrialising Britain and to extract some of the latent social content of this development. Historians of abolition are also now more apt to note that large segments of evangelical Christianity remained indifferent to or tolerant of slavery in some areas of British culture. One need only expand the frame of reference to mainland Europe to illustrate the fact that Protestant theology did not generate mass abolitionism elsewhere in Northern Europe. They apparently lacked the requisite political and economic environment of Anglo-America. From the British case, moreover, we now recognise that anti-slavery was not confined to evangelicalism or nonconformity. It also found enduring support in democratic secular movements.

The connection between anti-slavery and the expansion of mass political activity is one of the most striking correlations of the age of abolition. It has been seriously explored only in the last decade of this generation's historiographical explosion.[28] The first ripple of British abolition in the late 1760s and 1770s coincided with the political ferment in Anglo-America following the Seven Years War. The second abolitionist wave coincided with pressures for parliamentary reform in Britain and the early stages of the French Revolution. The passage of Emancipation in 1833 was clearly related to the passage of the Reform Bill.

If popular, metropolitan abolitionism has only begun to receive its due, the same is as true of the colonial popular context. Fifty years ago historians of anti-slavery might make passing reference to slave revolts during the last years of British slavery. But the continuity of that resistance during the whole history of slavery was rarely recognised. The standard narrative of emancipation was a story without slaves, or of the slaves reacting spasmodically to metropolitan stimuli. Likewise the flight and independence of maroons, and the haemorrhage this represented to plantation slavery, was never integrated into mainstream narratives. Scholars of the present generation have undertaken intensive studies of slave resistance in the British colonies, pressing their investigations back to Indian and European labourers who often preceded the Africans.[29] The impact of these revisionist approaches to the history of slavery has been clear and dramatic. Their impact on abolition is less certain. The occurrences of maroonage in British slavery have been meticulously documented. But as long as they could be relatively isolated within particular regions they were 'factored' into plantation systems as bearable, overhead costs of frontier slavery. Maroon communities could even act as backfires, setting limits to further flight or revolt. Even in the case of St Domingue we must weigh its crushing trauma to the French system and the wave of panic it engendered elsewhere against the enormous impetus the destruction also gave to the expansion of slavery in the circum-Caribbean. Despite the enormous disruption of the French Revolutionary wars the decade of the St Domingue revolution accounted for the second highest African slave displacement in the entire history of the slave trade. On the other hand an entirely different dynamic of Caribbean popular mobilisation developed in the nineteenth century in tandem with popular metropolitan anti-slavery. The uprisings in Barbados in 1816, in Demerara in 1823 and in Jamaica in 1831 were based on slave assessments of the eroding political position of the West Indian plantocracy in the metropolis after the abolition of the slave trade.

It is striking that the combination of social phenomena which induced Anglo-America to make the decisive breakthroughs to popular politics and industrialisation also served as the background to anti-slavery. This does not mean that industrialisation or broadened political participation caused the destruction of colonial slavery. They ensured that anti-slavery could more easily overcome the network of vested interests in an economy developing rapidly with free labour, and with a historically high level of autonomous religious and political associations. Emancipation also emerged in a culture which had trans-oceanic links between whites and blacks unmatched elsewhere in Europe.

III

Another set of issues revolves around the impact of emancipation. The Centenarians were content to describe the first rays of the rising sun that brought freedom to the West Indian slaves. Their attention then turned to the unfinished business of the African slave trade and slavery. Their premise of a radical discontinuity between slavery and freedom allowed them to bring the West Indian story to an end with emancipation or apprenticeship.[30] Historians are now less content to leave the scene of the crime at the moment of redemption. We are also analytically concerned with differential outcomes, which cast light on what is assignable to slavery, what to the plantation system, what to racism, what to the imperial system, and above all what to variations of context within each system.

For the colonies as a whole, perhaps the most obvious continuity of post-emancipation society was the persistence of tropical trade patterns. The economics of comparative advantage did not disappear with emancipation. The sugar market became more complex with the addition of new beet and cane producers, but North Atlantic demand remained dynamic throughout the age of emancipation. The vitality of the plantation was demonstrated in the revival of older areas and the emergence of new staple frontiers in the Americas, Africa and Asia.

While the great flood of European immigration to the Americas surpassed the African diaspora just after the end of the British apprenticeship, the tropics continued to rely on an influx of non-European bound labour.[31] Ironically this wave of indentured servants offers proxy evidence of the potential British colonial slave demand for generations after the closing of the slave trade. Three quarters of the world's indentured labourers after 1838 moved to the British colonies, especially to frontier colonies acquired at the height of British slavery early in the nineteenth century. The British colonial system which was producing two-thirds of the North Atlantic's sugar in 1815 hired two-thirds of the world's indentured servants during the 'long' nineteenth century.[32] The indentured servants of Asia displaced what would have been the final victims of the slave trade. On the other hand the resurgence of indentured labour clearly came too late to enable the British system to regain ground lost between abolition in 1808 and the end of the apprenticeship thirty years later. In this respect the indentured labour flows to non-British areas are equally interesting. One colony after another seems to have sprung to life, clamouring for indentured labour in the wake of emancipation.

Emancipation must be viewed from a wider perspective than through the continuities of the plantation system. The end of apprenticeship was followed by non-pecuniary gains for freedom. Female and child labour was reduced or withdrawn. On one plantation with continuous records for a century and a half, the female proportion of its labour force dropped by fifty per cent during the century after emancipation. But two-thirds of that reduction occurred within the first two decades.[33] Individual choices of housing, dress, education and consumption were still further from direct planter control. Despite attempted constraints on labour following emancipation, freedom widened the collective choices of freedom in the religious, communal and political spheres.[34] It seems to have been easier for both indentured Africans and Asians to preserve their local cultural inheritance intact than it was for victims of the slave trade.

Given differences in access to cheap land between Britain and most colonies there were once and for all gains to ex-slaves relative to British workers, and for a decade after emancipation the British consumer subsidised both the profits and wages of West Indian free sugar. In this sense, freedom also enhanced metropolitan susceptibility to both conservative and radical images of inefficient black labour in the colonies. Victorian racism may ironically have been encouraged by the economic aftermath of emancipation.

In one important way the generation after apprenticeship stands in sharp distinction to its predecessor. British abolitionism could no longer so directly control the direction of colonial social development. After 1838, anti-slavery could not outdraw all others as a petition issue.[35] The movement fragmented over economic and strategic issues. The earlier broad division between economic and non-economic interests was blurred. The end of apprenticeship brought divisions between the interests of free metropolitans and freedmen. The export performance of the sugar colonies did not fulfil the abolitionists' generally high expectations of sustained and enhanced output with an unsupplemented free labour force.[36] New tensions arose between planters and their workforce from the conditions of physical mobility, family autonomy and property rights in land.

However much the outcome of emancipation deviated from abolitionist expectations the Imperial Parliament still placed severe general constraints on the conditions of colonial development. British legislation exposed the colonies to slave-labour competition and to the general world sugar depression of the late 1840s and 1850s. This abrogated much of the material boost most ex-slaves enjoyed immediately after apprenticeship.[37]

Abolitionists who had staunchly deflected evidence against the free labour ideology before emancipation found themselves hard-pressed to resist full integration of the colonies into Britain's laissez-faire Empire after 1840. Most abolitionists joined their fellow Britons in considering the survival of the plantation important. From a Caribbean perspective it might appear that they were committed to keeping the colonies tied to the international economy because of an overriding belief in laissez-faire. However, the most significant context for British abolitionism after apprenticeship was not the West Indies but the Atlantic world.

Whatever attraction a peasant solution might have had for many ex-slaves, the strategic audiences for abolitionists were the political classes of Europe and the Americas. Anti-slavery priorities were limited by the distribution of power in societies beyond their control and by the increasingly competing claims of British economic interests. From an even broader perspective, Ralph Austen has shown that the same conflict between ideological and economic goals which occurred in the struggle over British policy in the Atlantic re-appeared in the Indian Ocean economy during the later nineteenth century.[38]

Instead of ending the battle against slavery with an apotheosis, historians have therefore measured with ever increasing subtlety the balance sheet of emancipations, the degrees of freedom, the racial restrictions which inhibited the freedmen's choices, and the new system of bonded labour which limited the economic power of ex-slaves even when it enhanced the pre-migration situation of the indentured. From a number of perspectives the traditional concept of abolitions as dramatic transformations of human relations has been challenged. Old forms of slavery shifted to foreign areas and new forms of constrained labour arose in the old British colonies. There has also been some ideological devaluation of the abolitionist transformation because it was a core-led non-violent social change. This clashes with the prominent role of armed struggle in many national liberations of the last fifty years.[39] Because of the emotional appeal of armed *self*-liberation as the means of social change, we must be wary of the implicit corollary that major social change is not obtained without an appeal to mass violence. Some historians deal with the aftermath of British emancipation as just another hegemonic sleight-of-hand, perpetrated by ruling classes on slaves and non-slaves alike. We must fully incorporate into our historical consciousness the continuity of violence, resistance, deception and contempt which made it so difficult to achieve a society of free equals in emancipated societies. In contrast to the historiography of slavery, we have yet to develop a broad comparative framework, using post-revolutionary as well as post-emancipation societies which will enable us to make a more accurate assessment of the age of emancipation.

IV

Whether or not humanity ascended to a higher plane one hundred and fifty years ago we are still justified in recognising one kind of discontinuity between the world the slaveholders made and the world which unmade them. Even in its narrowest terms abolition produced a new set of political constraints and forced major new welfare components into an earlier political economy. Older views about whom a state was called upon to consider, or how a national interest was to be calculated were changed, at least for the age of emancipation.

Neither the problems nor the context of abolition can be the same for an international gathering of historians in 1983 as they were for Coupland and Trevelyan. They celebrated the event as the point of departure for another century of British imperial hegemony and as a step forward in the history of morals. Yet when they wrote the Empire was a bare generation from its own disintegration. And a turning point of European moral history was even closer. At the same moment that the flags of fifty nations were unfurling before 20,000 at Hull, tens of thousands were preparing to march under quite other banners at the first Nuremberg rally of National Socialist Germany. The same *Times* issues which serenely reported the festivities at Hull carried accounts of Jews forced into the streets of Germany to perform degrading tasks. The fifty years which followed have hardly diminished our sense of the depths of human brutality. Our rising tolerance for cynicism may reflect the bitter experience of the recent past as much as deeper insights into a more distant past. In Britain, half a century ago, the slaveholder was a stranger from the periphery whose disappearance reinforced the Western world's sense of its superiority to the most dazzling achievements of antiquity. Few today feel such comfortable distance from wielders of instruments of degradation and coercion; the libertarian civil order imposed on the periphery could not be sustained at the core. We are so awash with evidence of brutality and of indifference to human suffering that we are almost embarrassed by evidence of humanitarian achievement.

This is one new reason to study the annihilation of slavery. One form of systematic coercion was mastered by a collective human effort over a century. To understand the process requires looking beyond the brutal or indifferent or simply profit-seeking people who created and sustained the institution. Those who persist in tying abolition to combinations of economic interests, elite manipulation and functional deceptions may be creating new blind alleys for historical understanding.

In one way British emancipation is more striking in the perspective of our twentieth century upheavals than when it was complacently viewed as the harbinger of the whole future. Even on the less significant level of collective biography, historians need no longer be distracted by abolitionists' redemption claims for a multitude of sins or by their odour of sanctity. As Orwell wrote of Gandhi, compared with most leading political figures of their century or ours, how clean a smell they managed to leave behind.

But moral assays of the liberators (including the slaves) are of far less moment than the political achievement itself. Emancipation was a hundred years war in which men and, to an unprecedented extent, women, black and white, on both sides of the Atlantic destroyed an institution of millennial assurance. Less than a decade after 1833 that very unutopian Frenchman, Alexis de Tocqueville, observed that the world had just witnessed something without precedent in recorded history – slavery abolished at one legislative stroke, not through generations of mitigated bondage, nor insensibly modified by a multitude of unrecorded private decisions. British emancipation was not a 'latent' fact, detected only centuries after the event. Nor had it been torn in blood and terror from a master class by isolated and desperate slaves. Three quarters of a million freedmen and women were welcomed by free men and women from social death to life. 'If you pore over the histories of all peoples', concluded de Tocqueville, 'will you find anything more extraordinary?'[40]

What impressed an outsider like de Tocqueville in the 1840s was the transformation, not the motives of its agents. Slavery was primarily an institution not a moral category. British abolition was therefore historically significant in the way that British industrialisation or the British social movement was. The British happened to be first, not intrinsically superior or pure. In the long view it seems to have been an extraordinary and peculiar use of world primacy. In 1683 Britain was what she is again today, a small island at the edge of the Eurasian landmass. Between then and now she became the centre of a world empire and a world economy. And just midway upon this imperial passage, she also legislated the destruction of slavery throughout her colonies, and surely accelerated the destruction of chattel slavery throughout the world.

From the perspective of the late twentieth century David Brion Davis echoes de Tocqueville's judgement. However drawn out and compromised its benefits appeared, the process of emancipation still 'seems one of the most extraordinary events in history'.[41] We are not misguided in taking stock of a turning point in one of the long revolutions which changed the shape of human relations. Our expansions of temporal and spatial scale, our multi-disciplinary corings, may enable us to draw a more valuable legacy of comprehension from the history of emancipation than could the celebrants who preceded us. But this can be so only if we do not allow the constraints of cynicism or of ideological predestination to shackle our historical imaginations.

NOTES

1. The emancipation act of 1833 did not extend to India.
2. See *The Times*, 29 July 1933 esp. pp. 13–14; also *ibid.*, 4, 5 May; 24, 25 July; 2, 4, 5, 9, August.
3. *Ibid.*, 24 July 1933. Reginald Coupland, 'The Memory of Wilberforce' (address at the Guildhall, Hull, 25 July 1933), *The Hibbert Journal*, 32, no. 1 (October, 1933), pp. 93–103.
4. C. L. R. James, *The Black Jacobins: Toussaint l'Ouverture and the St. Domingo Revolution* (London, 1938); Herbert Aptheker, *American Negro Slave Revolts*

(New York, 1943); Raymond and Alice Bauer, 'Day to Day Resistance to Slavery', *Journal of Negro History*, 27 (1942); Kenneth Stampp, *The Peculiar Institution* (New York, 1956); H. O. Patterson, 'Slavery and Slave Revolts: A Socio-Historical Analysis of the First Maroon War, Jamaica, 1655–1740', *Social and Economic Studies*, 19 (1970), pp. 289–335; essays by Richard Frucht, M. C. Campbell, L. F. Manigat, Angelina Pollak-Eltz, S. W. de Groot, O. D. Lara, and Michael Mullin in Vera Rubin and Arthur Tuden (eds.), *Comparative Perspectives on Slavery in New World Plantation Societies, Annals of the New York Academy of Sciences*, vol. 292 (1977); and most recently E. D. Genovese, *From Rebellion to Revolution: Afro-American Slave Revolts in the Making of the Modern World* (Baton Rouge, 1978); and Michael Craton, *Testing the Chains: Resistance to Slavery in the British West Indies* (Ithaca, 1982).

5. Eric Williams, *Capitalism and Slavery* (Chapel Hill, N. C., 1944). Two major bibliographical surveys regard *Capitalism and Slavery* as the point of departure for modern historical scholarship on the British Caribbean. See W. K. Marshall, 'A Review of Historical Writing on the Caribbean since 1940', *Social and Economic Studies*, 24 (1975), pp. 271–87, and bibliography; W. A. Green, 'Caribbean Historiography, 1600–1900: The Recent Tide', *Journal of Interdisciplinary History*, 7 (1977), pp. 509–30.
6. J. C. Miller, *Slavery: A Comparative Teaching Bibliography* (Crossroads, 1977). See also J. C. Miller and D. H. Borus, 'Slavery: A Supplementary Teaching Bibliography', *Slavery and Abolition: A Journal of Comparative Studies* (Cass), 1 (May, 1980), pp. 65–110; J. C. Miller, 'Slavery: A Further Supplementary Bibliography', *Slavery and Abolition*, 1 (September 1980), pp. 199–258; Miller's supplements bring the number of titles to over 4,000. As an illustration of the acceleration of scholarly productivity more than 90 per cent of the twentieth-century publications on slave resistance and abolition in this bibliography have appeared since 1945 and more than 60 per cent during the 1970s alone. On recent historiographical and anthropological trends see also D. B. Davis, 'Of Human Bondage', a review of Orlando Patterson's *Slavery and Social Death* in the *New York Review of Books*, 17 Feb. 1983, pp. 19–22; and Igor Kopytoff, 'Slavery', *Annual Review of Anthropology*, 11 (1982), pp. 207–27.
7. A. H. Conrad and J. R. Meyer, *The Economies of Slavery and Other Studies in Econometric History* (New York, 1964). See also Donald McCloskey, 'The Achievements of the Cliometric School', *Journal of Economic History*, 38 (1978), pp. 13–28; A. H. Conrad and J. R. Meyer, 'The Economics of Slavery in the Ante Bellum South', *Journal of Political Economy*, 66 (1958), pp. 95–130; S. L. Engerman, 'Coerced and Free Labor: Property Rights and the Development of the Labor Force' (forthcoming) *Annales: Economies, Sociétés, Civilisations* (typescript kindly furnished by the author). A most ambitious comparative analysis of a large number of slave systems is Orlando Patterson, *Slavery and Social Death: A Comparative Study* (Cambridge, Mass., 1982).
8. On the significance of emergent 'latent events' see Bernard Bailyn, 'The Challenge of Modern Historiography', *American Historical Review*, 87 (1982) pp. 1–24; on the switch to African slave labour see inter alia, D. W. Galenson's survey of the literature in *White Servitude in Colonial America* (New York, 1981), pp. 141–68; for a summary of the demographic literature see R. W. Fogel, *Without Consent or Contract: The Rise and Fall of American Slavery* (forthcoming), Chapter VI: 'Population and Politics', kindly sent by the author in typescript. On the timing of the switch to African slave labour, see R. N. Bean and R. P. Thomas, 'The Fishers of Men: The Profits of the Slave Trade', *Journal of Economic History*, 34 (1974), pp. 885–914; H. A. Gemery and J. S. Hogendorn, 'The Atlantic Slave Trade: A Tentative Economic Model', *Journal*

of African History, 15 (1974), p.225; R.C. Batie, 'Why Sugar? Economic Cycles and the Changing of Staples in the English and French Antilles, 1624–54', *Journal of Caribbean History*, 10 (1976), pp.8–9; H.A. Gemery and J.S. Hogendorn, 'Elasticity of Slave Labour Supply and the Development of Slave Economies in the British Caribbean: The Seventeenth Century Experience' in Rubin and Tuden (eds.), *Comparative Perspectives, op. cit.*; H.McD. Beckles, 'The Economic Origins of Black Slavery in the British West Indies, 1640–1680: A Tentative Analysis of the Barbados Model', *Journal of Caribbean History*, 16 (1982), pp.36–56.

9. David Eltis and James Walvin (eds.), *The Abolition of the Atlantic Slave Trade* (Madison, Wisc., 1981).
10. Seymour Drescher, 'Two Variants of Anti-Slavery: Religious Organization and Social Mobilization in Britain and France, 1780–1870', in Christine Bolt and Seymour Drescher (eds.), *Anti-Slavery, Religion and Reform* (Folkestone, 1980), pp.43–63.
11. See, for example, Serge Daget, 'France, Suppression of the Illegal Trade, and England, 1817–1850', Eltis and Walvin (eds.), *op. cit.*, pp.193–217; L.C. Jennings, 'The French Press and Great Britain's Campaign against the Slave Trade, 1830–1848', *Revue Française d'Histoire d'Outre-Mer*, 67 (1980), pp.5–24.
12. David Geggus, *Slavery, War and Revolution: The British Occupation of St Domingue, 1793–98* (Oxford, 1981).
13. See, inter alia, H.A. Gemery and J.S. Hogendorn (eds.), *The Uncommon Market: Essays in the Economic History of the Atlantic Slave Trade* (New York, 1979).
14. See McCloskey, 'Achievements of the Cliometric School', *op. cit.*; Gavin Wright, *The Political Economy of the Cotton South: Households, Markets and Wealth in the Nineteenth Century* (New York, 1978).
15. See, inter alia, Bean and Thomas, 'Fishers of Men', *op. cit.*, pp.885–94; E.P. LeVeen, 'The African Slave Supply Response', *African Studies Review*, 18 (1975), pp.9–28; Galenson, *White Servitude, op. cit.*; R.S. Dunn, *Sugar and Slaves: The Rise of the Planter Class in the English West Indies, 1624–1713* (New York, 1973), pp.68–74.
16. David Eltis, 'Free and Coerced Trans-Atlantic Migrations: Some Comparisons', *American Historical Review*, 88 (1983), pp.251–80, esp. p.265n.
17. P.J. Cain and A.G. Hopkins, 'The Political Economy of British Expansion Overseas, 1750–1914', *Economic History Review*, 2nd series, 33 (1980), pp.463–90; Seymour Drescher, *Econocide: British Slavery in the Era of Abolition* (Pittsburgh, 1977), ch.10.
18. See Engerman, 'Coerced and Free Labor', *op. cit.* For a survey of some general implications, see David Eltis & S.L. Engerman, 'Economic aspects of the abolition debate', in Bolt and Drescher (eds.), *op. cit.*, pp.272–93. Thus the issue is not whether economic universals exist. We must all, abolitionists included, produce, buy, sell or steal goods, services or ideas. The problem is how shaping and constraining were the economic universals that have been or can be specified and, equally important, in which direction? So far no one has come close to demonstrating that they can account for either the differences in anti-slavery intensities from one cultural area to another or the fact that anti-slavery rose at a specific moment in any one area. David Eltis has an excellent summary of the economic paradoxes of abolition in his forthcoming work on the abolition of the slave trade.
19. McCloskey, 'Achievements of the Cliometric School', *op. cit.* We do not imply that all metropolitan areas do not fit into the economic paradigm. For example,

Magnus Mörner suggests that Spanish humanitarian legislation at the end of the eighteenth century was carefully attuned to economic conditions: 'Thus, the horrifying "super-exploitation" of slaves in Cuba around 1800 is perfectly compatible with the gradual breaking up of the slave institution in some other Spanish American territories at approximately the same time'. (From 'Slavery, Race Relations and Bourbon Reorganization in Eighteenth Century Spanish America', kindly sent in typescript by the author.)

20. Engerman, 'Coerced and Free Labor', *op. cit.*, p. 24.
21. See, inter alia, Tandeter Enrique, 'Forced and Free Labour in Late Colonial Potosi', *Past and Present*, 93 (1981), pp. 98–136. Using the dynamic Cuban case, Rebecca Scott has subtly challenged Manuel Moreno Fraginals' thesis about the incompatibility of slave labour and industrialisation (in *El Ingenio: Complejo económico social cubano del ayúcar*, 3 vols. (Havana, 1978), II, p. 27) and that mechanisation entailed abolition. See R. J. Scott, 'Explaining Abolition: Contradiction, Adaptation, and Challenge in Cuban Slave Society, 1860–1886', a paper drawn from her unpublished Ph.D. dissertation, 'Slave Emancipation and the Transition to Free Labor in Cuba, 1868–1895' (Princeton University, 1982) and presented in Santo Domingo, 11–13 June 1981. Fred Bateman and Thomas Weiss, *A Deplorable Scarcity: The Failure of Industrialization in the Slave Economy* (Chapel Hill, 1981), p. 4; R. S. Starobin, *Industrial Slavery in the Old South* (New York, 1970), p. 189. Slavery was apparently quite compatible with the technology of sugar in the British West Indies in 1830 or in Cuba in 1860 or with the technology of both agriculture and industry in the American South. See also Paul Bairoch, 'International Industrialization Levels from 1750 to 1980', *Journal of European Economic History*, 11 (1982), pp. 269–333.
22. Engerman, 'Coerced and Free Labor', *op. cit.* Howard Temperley, 'The Ideology of Anti-slavery', in Eltis and Walvin (eds.), *op. cit.*, pp. 21–36 also roots anti-slavery in a broader range of everyday experience than free labour.
23. D. B. Davis, *The Problem of Slavery in the Age of Revolution, 1770–1823* (Ithaca, 1975); C. D. Rice, *The Scots Abolitionists, 1833–1861* (Baton Rouge and London, 1981), pp. 27, 31.
24. See Davis, *op. cit.*, and Howard Temperley, 'Capitalism, Slavery and Ideology', *Past and Present*, 75 (1977), pp. 94–118.
25. See Lawrence Stone, 'Madness', *New York Review of Books*, 16 December 1982, pp. 28–36. For specific linkages with the factory and the poorhouse, see Davis, *op. cit.*, pp. 357–66, 381–5, 459–66; and for the prison in 'The Crime of Reform', *New York Review of Books*, 26 June 1980, p. 14.
26. Seymour Drescher, 'Cart Whip and Billy Roller: Anti-Slavery and Political Symbolism in Industrializing Britain', *Journal of Social History*, 15 (1981), pp. 3–24. On social control and reform in Britian, see F. M. L. Thompson, 'Social Control in Victorian Britain', *Economic History Review*, 2nd series, 34 (1981), pp. 189–208. See also D. D. Laitin, 'Capitalism and Hegemony: Yorubaland and the International Economy', *International Organization*, 36 (1982), pp. 687–713.
27. Roger Anstey, *The Atlantic Slave Trade and British Abolition, 1760–1810* (London, 1975), pp. 184–93; Roger Anstey, 'Slavery and the Protestant Ethic', in Michael Craton (ed.), *Roots and Branches: Current Directions in Slave Studies* (Toronto, 1979), pp. 157–72. See also the important reservations by Emilia Viotti da Costa in *ibid.*, pp. 173–7.
28. Most recently, James Walvin, 'The Public Campaign in England Against Slavery, 1787–1834', in Eltis and Walvin (eds.), *op. cit.*, pp. 63–79; Seymour Drescher, 'Public Opinion and the Destruction of British Slavery', in James

Walvin (ed.), *Slavery and British Society 1776–1846* (London, 1982), pp. 22–48; James Walvin, 'The Propaganda of Anti-Slavery', *ibid.*, pp. 49–68; Betty Fladeland, 'Our Cause Being One and the Same: Abolitionists and Chartism', *ibid.*, pp. 69–99; Patricia Hollis, 'Anti-slavery and British Working Class Radicalism in the Years of Reform' in Bolt and Drescher (eds.), *op. cit.*, pp. 294–315.

29. See inter alia, the essays on the Caribbean by Richard Frucht, M. C. Campbell, L.F. Manigat, S.W. de Groot, and O.D. Lara in Rubin & Tuden (eds.), *Comparative Perspectives, op. cit.*, part VI; Genovese, *From Rebellion to Revolution, op. cit.*; Craton, *Testing the Chains, op. cit.*; H.McD. Beckles, 'Rebels and Reactionaries: The Political Responses of White Labourers to Planter-Class Hegemony in Seventeenth-Century Barbados', *Journal of Caribbean History*, 15 (1981), pp. 1–19.
30. In addition to the essays by Coupland and Trevelyan, cited above in notes 2 and 3, see G. M. Trevelyan, *British History in the Nineteenth Century and After* (London, 1922); Reginald Coupland, *The British Anti-Slavery Movement* (London, 1935) and the similar works by F. J. Klingberg, *The Anti-Slavery Movement in England* (New Haven, 1926), C. M. McInnes, *England and Slavery* (Bristol, 1934) and H. A. Wyndham, *The Atlantic and Slavery* (London, 1935).
31. Eltis, 'Trans-Atlantic Migrations', *op. cit.*, p. 256, Table 1.
32. Based on S. L. Engerman, 'Servants to Slaves to Servants: Contract Labor and European Expansion' (typescript kindly sent by the author), Table II.
33. S. L. Engerman, 'Economic Aspects of the Adjustments to Emancipation in the United States and the British West Indies', *Journal of Interdisciplinary History*, 13 (1982), pp. 191–220, which actually ranges beyond these two regions.
34. See, inter alia, R.L. Ransom and Richard Sutch, *One Kind of Freedom* (Cambridge, 1980) and W. A. Green, *British Slave Emancipation: the Sugar Colonies and the Great Experiment* (Oxford, 1976); W.K. Marshall, 'Commentary', in Craton (ed.), *Roots and Branches, op. cit.*, pp. 243–7, summarises much of the recent literature.
35. Howard Temperley, *British Anti-Slavery, 1833–70* (London, 1972); E.I. Pilgrim, 'Anti-Slavery Sentiment in Great Britain: Its Nature and Decline, 1841–1854', unpublished Ph.D. thesis, Cambridge University, 1952.
36. Engerman, 'Adjustments to Emancipation', *op. cit.*; David Eltis, 'Abolitionist Perceptions of Society After Slavery', in Walvin (ed.), *Slavery, op. cit.*, pp. 195–213.
37. Green, *British Slave Emancipation, op. cit.*
38. Much of the resistance of European governments to the abolition of slavery explicitly derived from the fact that the levels of labour productivity and reliability were regarded as the least successful outcomes of British emancipation. See L. C. Jennings, 'French Perceptions of British Emancipation: A French Observer's Views on the post-Emancipation British Caribbean' (typescript kindly sent by the author); Alexis de Tocqueville, 'On the Emancipation of Slaves', in Seymour Drescher (ed.), *Tocqueville and Beaumont on Social Reform* (New York, 1968), pp. 137–73; R. A. Austen, 'From the Atlantic to the Indian Ocean: European Abolition, the African Slave Trade, and Asian Economic Structures', in Eltis and Walvin (eds.), *op. cit.*, pp. 117–29.
39. Craton, *Testing the Chains, op. cit.*, p. 323.
40. de Tocqueville, 'On the Emancipation of Slaves', in Drescher (ed.), *op. cit.*, p. 138.
41. D.B. Davis, 'British Emancipation as a New Moral Dispensation', *Rice University Studies*, 67 (1981), pp. 43–54.

PART B

Slaves as Agents of Their Own Emancipation

2

Towards Emancipation: Slave Women and Resistance to Coercive Labour Regimes in the British West Indian Colonies, 1790–1838

BARBARA BUSH

Popular stereotypes of slave women have portrayed them as passive and downtrodden work-horses who did little to advance the struggle for freedom. The 'peculiar burdens' of their sex allegedly precluded any positive contribution to slave resistance.[1] Many Europeans, however, declared that women were more troublesome than men and contemporary accounts frequently refer to 'bothersome' domestic servants and 'female demons' who thwarted the overseer in the field.[2] Through an examination of women in the formal and informal plantation economy this paper will argue that women were primary agents in the emancipation of the slave community. It will explore women's position in the plantation occupational hierarchy and their reactions to punishment and coercion. In showing how women constituted the 'backbone' of the slave labour force, it will illustrate how their non-cooperation at work helped to nourish the general spirit of resistance during the troubled transitional period from slavery to abolition when economic uncertainty and planter indebtedness arguably intensified exploitation.

I

In slave society 'black women produced ... brown women served and ... white women consumed'.[3] Within the complex occupational stratification which developed with sugar monoculture during the eighteenth century, women generally occupied a less favourable position than men. As William Beckford noted:

> A Negro man is purchased either for a trade, or the cultivation of the different processes of the cane – the occupations of women are only two, the house with its several departments and supposed indulgencies, or the field with its exaggerated labours. The first solution is the most honourable, the last the most independent.[4]

Apart from the midwife, doctoress or chief housekeeper (who was often a privileged mulatto mistress),[5] the slave elite consisted almost solely of men. Women were generally restricted to the lower ranks.

In his analysis of the occupational pattern of Roaring River estate, Jamaica, in 1756 Richard Sheridan found that of the 92 women on the estate, 70 were field workers whereas of the 84 men, only 28 worked in the field and 19 were skilled tradesmen. Women not engaged in field work had a variety of occupations. In the house there were two cooks, two 'house wenches' and a washerwoman. Several older women had lighter jobs, carrying water to quench the thirst of field negroes, acting as drivers to the 'Piquino' gang or supervising the labour of small children. There were also two doctoresses (or traditional healers). A similar occupational pattern existed on the Worthy Park and Mesopotamia plantations in Jamaica in the 1790s. At Worthy Park 70 women out of 162 worked on the land compared with only 29 men from a total of 177.[6]

From the earliest days of the slave trade African women were regarded by Europeans as eminently suited to field work because of their perceived 'drudge' status in polygynous marriages. A large part of the labour on sugar estates consisted of digging holes for canes, hoeing and weeding – tasks generally accepted in slaving circles as 'women's work' in Africa.[7] To conceal the degree of exploitation of slave women and to defend themselves against the abolitionists, planters alleged that they preferred male slaves and supported this argument by citing the high ratio of males to females on sugar estates.[8] Contemporary evidence tends to contradict their figures and indicates that they may have been exaggerating for propaganda purposes. The plantation lists for Roaring River and Worthy Park, Jamaica cited above and figures given for Barbadian plantations reveal a fairly even balance of the sexes. As Dunn points out, if a slight imbalance had existed before 1800, according to evidence from Jamaican plantations this disappeared between 1800 and 1818.[9]

The most important class of slaves comprised 'the most robust of both sexes' whose work consisted of 'preparing and planting the soil, cutting the canes, feeding the mill and aiding the manufacture of sugar and rum'.[10] The importance of women in the formal plantation economy (as opposed to the informal economy such as peasant cultivation and marketing activities) is reflected in the fact that planters valued prime female slaves only slightly less than males. Between 1790 and 1807, before the ending of the slave trade, the approximate purchase price of a 'new' male slave was £50 to £70 while a healthy female brought from £50 to £60. Prices of creole slaves were roughly 20 per cent higher though skilled tradesmen could command up to 100 per cent more.[11]

Men and women were often sold together in 'jobbing gangs'. A Jamaican advertisement in 1827, for instance, offered a 'small gang of effective and well-disposed Negroes', 17 males and 17 females.[12] At work in the field a rough equality of the sexes existed and the labour regime ensured that women shared the same backbreaking work, miseries and punishments as their menfolk. Slaves were turned out of their quarters at 6 a.m. and worked until sunset (6 to 7 p.m.) or later in crop-time and had little time to call their own.[13] Field work was hard, monotonous and degrading and resulted in a low rate of productivity. Michael Craton, for instance, has estimated that at the end of the eighteenth century Jamaican slaves cut only a fifth as much at crop-time as the equivalent modern-day wage earners.[14] In the last years of slavery conditions on the plantations deteriorated despite new welfare legislation introduced under abolitionist pressure. Planters were forced to squeeze a profit out of increasingly uneconomical estates and slaves may have been more harshly used than in the early period before the plantation system matured when they were sometimes treated better than white indentured servants.[15]

Despite their economic value, field workers were treated as part of the capital stock of the plantation and maintained at bare subsistence level. Though they performed the hardest labour, their living conditions were far inferior to the more privileged house slaves and elite craftsmen and they suffered from greater ill-health and a far higher death-rate.[16] In addition they were the frequent victims of physical punishments which ranged from savage whippings to confinement in the stocks. Though domestic slaves were not immune to European cruelty, punishment of field slaves was a common occurrence as profit could only be extracted through physical punishment.

Such measures were justified by planters in view of 'the savage, intractable humour' of slaves and the 'many acts of violence' they committed. Without the constant use of the whip, they argued, it was impossible to work the large estates.[17] When slaves reacted to harsh work conditions through non-cooperation or outright insubordination they were punished. Planters like Edward Long tried to play down the degree of cruelty involved but he was forced to admit that some planters did 'at times' exhibit 'inhuman tempers'.[18] Rather than subdue the slaves, however, physical punishment only served to heighten their resentment. As William Beckford noted, 'the whip ... does not correct but multiply faults'.[19] Slaves, both male and female, were thus caught up in a vicious spiral of punishment and resistance.

As women were valued first and foremost as units of labour rather than childbearers few concessions were made for pregnant women or mothers with young families. If anything, women were less compliant workers than men. 'Monk' Lewis, the liberal Jamaican planter, having tried 'every method to satisfy his slaves and render them happy and secure' discovered that the only slaves he was obliged to punish were two women whose behaviour in the field was 'aggressive' and uncooperative. When the first legislation forbidding the whipping of black women was introduced in Trinidad in 1823 planters strongly objected on the grounds that female slaves were 'notoriously insolent' and only kept in some 'tolerable order' through the fear of punishment. One colonial official stated that female slaves more frequently merited punishment than males.[20]

Under the overseer's whip 'neither age nor sex found any

favour'. One critic of slavery described the procedure for formal punishment of both male and female offenders in Jamaica in 1824 as follows:

> The posterior is made bare and the offender is extended prone on the ground, the hands and feet being firmly [held] by other slaves ... the driver, with his long and heavy whip, inflicts under the eye of the overseer, the number of lashes, which he may order.[21]

For women in particular the degradation inflicted by this act was compounded by the fact that the whippings were carried out by black drivers who, eager to retain their privileged position, showed no lenience.[22]

In respect of outright sadistic cruelty, female domestics, because of their closer proximity to their masters and mistresses, were perhaps in a more vulnerable position than field workers. They often fell victim to personal caprice. As a house guest in Jamaica, the Reverend Henry Coor recalled the master having nailed the ear of a house wench to a tree because she had broken a plate.[23] White mistresses were notoriously cruel, reflecting perhaps their underlying jealousy of attractive female slaves who were also expected to perform 'unofficial' duties as concubines.[24] The precarious and contradictory position of domestic slaves often cancelled out their apparent comforts and privileges. At any time, moreover, they could be relegated to field work, regarded by whites as the ultimate punishment.

Pregnancy did not guarantee a reprieve from this harsh regime. Women were expected to work in the fields and house until at least six weeks before delivery and return to work no later than three weeks afterwards.[25] In practice this consideration was rarely afforded and, in consequence, women on West Indian plantations had an excessively low birth rate and suffered from numerous gynaecological complaints.[26] As slave prices rose in the late eighteenth century in response to plantocratic anxiety over the threatened abolition of the slave trade, measures were introduced in an effort to give better care to pregnant women and mothers and promote 'a healthy increase'. However, as Beckford noted, such measures were often negated by the pressures on the planter or, in his absence, his manager to yield a profit.[27] The black birth-rate failed to show any significant increase until after Apprenticeship had ended in 1838.[28]

If pregnant women complained, they risked a flogging. One abolitionist observer recalled the following incident on a Jamaican plantation in the 1820s:

> Two [pregnant] women desired to quit the field during the rain ... The overseer refused them permission. They went to complain to a magistrate, but were stopped on their way by a neighbouring overseer and [were] thrown into the stocks until he sent them back to their own overseer who [again] put them in the stocks and had them flogged.[29]

After 1807, some provisions were made to exempt women from floggings but even as late as 1826, Jamaican laws limiting the number of lashes which could be inflicted on individual slaves made no special concessions for women, pregnant or not. Slaves could receive up to 10 lashes except in the presence of an overseer when 39 lashes could be administered. A second punishment could not be administered until the culprit was 'entirely recovered' from the former one under a penalty of £20.[30]

Jamaican planters were renowned for their callous indifference to the special needs of pregnant women. One doctor related the salutary tale of how one woman, confined to the stocks for 'misconduct' and liberated only a few days before delivery, subsequently died of puerperal fever. Monk Lewis, on the basis of several adverse reports, concluded that white overseers and book-keepers '[kicked] black women in the belly from one end of Jamaica to another', harming both the women and their unborn children.[31] Lewis was genuinely concerned about the welfare of his female slaves but, in times of economic uncertainty, women constituted for most planters too valuable a labour unit to be accorded preferential treatment.

Resistance to punishment itself demanded great courage and was harshly dealt with for, as Beckford remarked, 'the indolent only and the ill-disposed encounter punishment'.[32] Women were often regarded as 'ill-disposed' or even dangerous and punished commensurately, particularly in the final years of slavery when unrest was widespread and whites uneasy and nervous. In St Lucia in 1828, for instance, some women slaves were charged with 'discontent and mutiny'. As punishment, in place of the collar which had been banned in 1826, the accused were hung by the arms to a peg, raised so high above their heads that the toes alone touched the ground, the whole weight of the body resting on the wrists of their arms and the tips of their toes.[33]

Unfortunately, little evidence exists which records the reactions of women to such treatment or provides any solid indication of the frequency and extent to which it occurred. It was in the interests of planters to conceal the degree of cruelty towards women and written records can provide only a limited insight into the punishment regimes experienced by female slaves or the degree of resistance they generated. The slim evidence available suggests that if women did complain or physically resist they received additional, harsher punishment. Cooper, for instance, referred to one particular woman who, when placed in the stocks by her overseer, complained to the attorney and in consequence received 39 lashes from the same overseer. Accounts of ex-slaves from the ante-bellum South, where conditions were arguably less Hobbesian, indicate that women often resisted floggings, despite the threat of further reprisals.[34]

The West Indian slave laws sanctioned the punishment of slaves. The fundamental concern of the plantocratic Assemblies which devised the slave codes was the protection of property and the social control of an unwilling work force. Though 'protective' as well as 'policing' clauses existed to ensure minimum welfare standards, these were frequently abused in the absence of any effective methods of enforcement. Before 1790, British slave laws, unlike the French *Code Noir*, offered little or no protection for women or for slave family life in general. For most of the slavery era, masters had complete control over the lives of their slaves who were legally defined as chattels rather than human beings.[35]

Amendments to the laws were made as socio-economic conditions changed. However, even after ameliorative legislation was introduced in response to abolitionist criticisms, the British slave codes retained their essentially repressive, punitive emphasis. Special clauses were introduced to protect pregnant women and promote family life,[36] but as was stressed above, there is little evidence to suggest that they were adhered to in practice. Though in theory slaves could plead their cases in front of an attorney or magistrate, slave testimonies were non-admissible as evidence against whites.[37] Thus, despite the increasing intervention of the British government after 1807, the new laws became 'specious in words and inoperative in practice'. Under pressure from metropolitan circles planters had introduced them 'grudgingly and of necessity'.[38] They did little to improve the working conditions of women or to reduce the degree of resistance to the system.

As Bryan Edwards noted, it was only possible to govern slaves through fear-based enforcement of a punitive legal code.[39] In resisting the system slaves clearly challenged their given legal status and proved that they were human beings possessed of free will. Repression tended to be counter-productive – the harsher the system, the greater the insubordination of slaves. The more this insubordination threatened the legitimacy of thc system, the more violent was the white response. Both master and slave were thus trapped in this reactive process, but the slave, in taking conscious actions to resist and assert his or her essential humanity, ultimately challenged the whole moral basis of slavery. On the more mundane, everyday basis they simply made it unworkable.

In the fields women experienced the harshest labour and punishment regime on the plantation, but, as Beckford noted above, they also retained the greatest independence and cultural autonomy. According to Goveia, field slaves were allowed to retain Africanisms to underscore their inferiority.[40] Women were in the vanguard of the cultural resistance to slavery which helped individuals survive the slave experience. Their important contribution to the 'private' lives of slaves – the reconstitution of the family and the building of a viable black community life – has been analysed elsewhere.[41] It was this cultural strength, however, which helped women resist the system in their more 'public' lives as workers. In the fields cultural defiance was expressed through language and song. Language in particular was an important element in black identity and cultural unity, a major form of defence against dehumanisation.[42] Women field hands were experts in the use of the rich creole language which, with its *double-entendres* and satire, was frequently employed as subtle abuse of whites.[43] Through such channels women helped to generate and sustain the general spirit of resistance.

Accounts of plantation life from varied sources confirm that women gave their labour unwillingly and were a source of constant frustration for managers and overseers. They habitually shirked work, used verbal abuse, feigned illness and were accused of lying, stealing and inciting unrest. A revealing source of information is plantation journals and punishment lists. Data from the records kept on the estates of the London merchants, Thomas and William King, for the period from the early 1820s to the beginning of the Apprenticeship period, chart the deep level of everyday resistance sustained by female slaves.[44]

The Kings owned plantations in Grenada, British Guiana and Dominica. As absentee landowners they left the day-to-day running of their estates to attorney/managers who were required to keep meticulous records. In plantation journals they entered all punishments meted out to individual slaves, the reasons why they were carried out, the names of the persons who administered and witnessed them and the place and date. If the culprits were female, the manager had to note 'the nature and extent of punishment' in a special column. This was obviously to comply with the legislation introduced throughout the British West Indian colonies in the 1820s which forbade the whipping of female slaves. Thus while male offenders received an average of 15 to 20 'stripes' or lashes, the common *recorded* punishment for women was a varying period of time in the stocks or solitary confinement.

Women were far more often accused of insolence, 'excessive laziness', disobedience, quarrelling and 'disorderly conduct' than were male slaves. Individual women were regularly punished for defiant behaviour. On Friendship Sarah Plantation in British Guiana in 1827, for instance, a female slave named Katherine was punished on 11 and 30 November for insolence to the overseer and quarrelling respectively. Another slave, Henrietta, had to spend a day and a night in the stocks for 'continually omitting to comply with her task'.[45]

On the Kings' other plantation in British Guiana, Good Success, where out of 211 slaves, 93 were female, there was a number of consistently troublesome women. From January to June 1830, Quasheba was punished repeatedly for 'refusing to go to work when ordered by the doctor'. Another habitual offender, Caroline, was punished on 4 May for 'abusing the manager and overseer and defying the former to do his worst'. During the same period one particular woman, Clarissa, was reported three times for poor work and malingering. In the first instance she was accused together with another woman, Lavinia, of leaving work unfinished, 'assigning no cause' for so doing. On another instance, she refused to work because of a cut on her finger and when ordered to do so by the doctor, used 'abusive language' to the manager. Though her punishments increased in severity from 12 hours solitary confinement to 60 hours in the stocks, her spirit to resist remained undiminished.[46]

From the different plantation records an overall pattern emerges of women as persistent offenders. On average, they were punished more frequently than men. For instance, on the Friendship Sarah Plantation in the six month period from January to June 1827, out of a total of 171 slaves on the plantation, 34 were punished of whom 21 were women.[47] The threat of punishment had little deterrent effect though many methods employed were only marginally more 'humane' than the whip. Women still had to suffer the degradation and discomfort of the 'hand and foot' stocks or solitary confinement, sometimes with the additional debasement of wearing a collar. In contrast to the whip which was short and sharp, substitute punishments lasted from a few hours up to three days and in very serious cases a longer period was recommended. Sunday, the only free day, when slaves cultivated their own plots, was the favourite date for confinement. All punishment involved public humiliation as it was administered by slaves, witnessed by white employees and usually took place 'before the House' or in the hospital.

Faced with the intransigence of black women which ran to more serious crimes such as running away, attempts to poison their masters, and 'exciting discontent in the gang', hard-pressed managers argued that the whip was the only means of keeping females in order. Official records may indeed have conveniently 'overlooked' harsher punishments. Even in the 1820s on certain plantations, the whip was still used on women occasionally. For instance, under 'general observations' for 1823, the manager of Baillies Bacolet Plantation, Grenada, noted that Eliza had received 20 lashes for 'violent behaviour in the field ... and for excessive insolence to myself when reprimanding her in the presence of the gang'. On the same plantation as late as 1833 another woman, Germaine, was given 15 lashes for 'wilfully destroying canes in the field' and general neglect of duty.[48]

Though not so overtly rebellious, domestic servants, the majority of whom were women, also used subtle tactics to frustrate their white masters and mistresses. They may have superficially accommodated to slavery, adopting the habits and dress of the Europeans who they served and lived with, but in the opinion of contemporary observers they were a constant source of irritation. Arguably, their impact on whites was all the more intense than that of field hands because of their constant and close physical presence. Emma Carmichael was sorely tried by the domestic slaves under her supervision on her husband's Trinidadian estate. Minor thefts were a common occurrence, always denied by the suspects. Her washerwomen never carried out their work properly and 'used generally more than twice the quantity of soap, blue and starch' required by washerwomen in England. They also had a tendency to 'lose' articles of clothing and, of all the 'troublesome' Carmichael establishment, were the most 'discontent, unmanageable and idle'. From their arrival in Trinidad, the Carmichaels were harassed by the grumbles, lies and uncooperative nature of female slaves in particular and cited their insubordination as one of the reasons the estate was sold prior to emancipation.[49]

Other contemporary observers made similar comments. Long felt that the 'propensity to laziness' was chiefly conspicuous in house servants and Lewis complained of their inefficiency and refusal to correct faults. For John Stewart, female domestics were so 'refractory, vicious and indolent' that in managing them the white women became 'a greater slave than any of them'.[50] Of all slaves, domestics exhibited the greatest duality of behaviour and were in the most contradictory position. Though outwardly they were obliged to conform more than field slaves to European culture and values, they employed covert and subtle means to retain their cultural integrity and to protest their enforced enslavement.

According to planters, women of all classes employed ingenious strategems to avoid work and frequently feigned sickness and a multitude of 'female complaints'. One enterprising female on the Carmichael estate miraculously exhibited a different coloured tongue on each visit to the plantation doctor. When the fraud was exposed she received a flogging, the standard punishment for 'shamming and idling'. When weaning houses were introduced in Jamaica to cut down on the extended suckling of slave infants which was regarded as another form of female malingering, women strongly resisted this early separation from their babies. According to Lewis the main reason for this 'obstinacy' was their wish 'to retain the leisure and other indulgencies ... of nursing mothers'. Planters even went so far as to accuse their female slaves of 'wilfully' infecting their children with yaws in order to be released from labour for a time.[51]

Occasionally, women actually mutilated themselves to avoid work or as part of their rejection of slave status. After one of Monk Lewis' female slaves was injured at work, she was allowed a week off to recover. When ordered by the doctor to return to work, however, she was found to be still unfit as she had tied 'pack thread' around her healing wounds which cut deep into the flesh, rubbed in dirt and nearly produced 'mortification' in her fingers. One female Jamaican runaway, known as Phibba or Cuba, was described in an advertisement as branded 'A.W.' on both shoulders which were 'raised in lumps' from endeavouring to remove the brand.[52]

Individual women sometimes committed grave offences which were punishable by death. On a visit to a Slave Court in Kingston, Monk Lewis witnessed the trial of a 15-year-old servant girl, Minetta, accused of attempting to poison her master. In her testimony, she admitted to infusing 'corrosive sublimate' into some brandy but denied that she knew it was poison and alleged she had only administered it on her grandmother's orders. According to Lewis, her story was a complete fabrication. She lied blatantly and he was appalled by her 'hardened conduct' throughout the trial. On being condemned to death she heard the sentence pronounced 'without the least emotion' and was seen to laugh as she was escorted out. For planters like Beckford such behaviour confirmed the slaves' 'lack of gratitude and respect' ('most noticeable' in those who had been the most 'indulged'), but for the individual slave it was an assertion of free will which demanded much resolution and courage.[53]

But where women were intransigent in their formal work roles, their contribution to the informal economy, the cultivation of slave provision grounds, higgling and marketing, reflected a considerable degree of energy and enterprise. For instance, on the Carmichael estate there was one particular domestic slave who, although she was a 'clever and superior person with not a disagreeable countenance' was 'next to impossible to manage'. When relegated to field work for insubordination, she made such a 'commotion' that she was placed in the stocks. As this failed to subdue her rage, the driver conceded to Mr Carmichael that she would never work for him 'or any other Massa'. Outside her formal role, however, this same woman worked extensive provision grounds which were kept in 'beautiful order' and ran 'a complete huckster's shop' on the estate. She held dances at her house from which she reputedly made a great deal of money; supper, liquor and music were provided by her with each slave paying 'half a dollar' admission.[54] Thus, in contrast to her negative attitude to working for her white master, her role in the slave community was positive and dynamic. In addition, her activities gave her a degree of economic independence and self-reliance which contrasted sharply with the inferior position of European women like Mrs Carmichael who were completely dependent on their husbands.

This informal economy was separate from the externally-orientated plantation economy which was linked to the international mercantile system, and provides an illustration of the dual response to slavery. In the external or 'public' sphere, controlled by and for the benefit of whites, slaves proved 'irascible', indolent, dishonest and 'artful', the stereotype of the inferior black. This contrasted sharply with the 'private' sphere of their lives where, 'beyond the ken' of their masters, they sought to create a viable family and community life. The informal internal marketing system, created primarily by the slaves themselves and in which women played a prominent role, was fundamental to the creation and integration of creole slave society and constituted a positive adaptation to slavery.

The existence of an economy controlled by blacks stemmed from the reluctance of West Indian planters to provide slaves with sufficient food. From early times, slaves were encouraged to supply their own food needs. Each adult slave was allocated a plot on marginal estate lands on which to grow provisions. By the late eighteenth century masters were legally bound to appoint a 'sufficient quantity' of land for each of their slaves, male and female, and to allow them enough free time for cultivation of this land.[55]

For one and a half days each week, Saturday afternoon and Sundays, the slaves were freed from formal plantation labour to work their provision grounds or 'polinks' (as distinct from the tiny plots or yards close to their houses). As the rewards of their labour were their own, not their masters', they expended much effort to produce vegetables, ground provisions, roots and herbs. Any surplus could be exchanged at the Sunday market for money or other necessary articles, thereby offering an additional strong incentive.[56] If owners failed to respect these customary rights or attempted to sell slaves, they met with strong resistance. Slaves became very attached to their cottages and lands and if taken from them often developed 'habits of heedlessness and indolence' which rendered them worthless to their owners. This had serious implications in the late period of slavery when estates more frequently changed hands and owners sold off slaves as 'stock' with callous disregard for the family bonds or community attachments of individual slaves.[57]

Paradoxically, the reluctance of West Indian planters to supply slaves with the basic necessities of life was instrumental in developing a degree of independence and resilience in Caribbean slaves denied their counterparts in the southern states of the USA where a more intrusive paternalism existed. By 1800, slaves had come to dominate the internal marketing system of the West Indian colonies which was indispensable to black and white alike. As Bryan Edwards noted, the gardening and marketing activities of the slaves were beneficial to both slave and planter. The former earned extra money and the latter did not need to feed his slaves.[58]

The focal point of these 'informal' economic activities was the Sunday market which was important from the very beginning of slavery. By 1819 it had become an institution where 'several thousands of human beings ... principally negroes, were busily employed in all kinds of traffic in the open streets'.[59] The market was so central to creole community life that the stringent laws restricting the mobility of slaves were relaxed to allow them to engage in such activities. A clause in the 1826 *Laws of Jamaica*, for instance, stated that no slave could travel about without a ticket 'specially worded and signed' by his or her owner *except* if going to market.[60] This worked against the plantocracy, as it facilitated communication between the plantations and the coordination of slave plots.

Women slaves were prominent as marketeers and 'higglers' (middlemen), a reflection of their African cultural heritage and successful adaptation to new circumstances in which they found themselves in the New World. In West Africa, women were entitled to sell any surplus from their own farm plots as well as the products of their special skills such as baskets and prepared foods. They were allowed to keep the entire profit from these transactions which gave them a degree of economic independence that was accepted by the community as an integral part of their ascribed role. Though many changes have occurred in both West Indian and West African societies since the slavery era, black women have retained their economic independence and still tend to dominate local markets.[61]

Regardless of the hardship encountered in their formal work-life, slave women were energetic and resourceful in the cultivation of their own provision grounds. Whites had mixed feelings about such activities. Whilst recognising their economic importance, planters were worried by the entrepreneurial independence they fostered. Market women were often described as clever, cunning and untrustworthy. An advertisement for a runaway Kingston woman placed in the *Jamaica Mercury* in 1779 accused her of absconding from her owner with money she had received from the sale of provisions. In the same town in 1827, a similar advertisement appeared for three runaways, an 'elderly black woman of the Mundingo (Mandingo) country' and her two daughters. All were described as 'well-known' higglers who were 'very artful' and likely to pass themselves off as free persons.[62] Participation in the informal economy thus not only offered women independence from black men but a way to freedom from white masters.

After the abolition of slavery, the internal marketing system developed by the former slaves and free coloureds became the basis of the West Indian free peasantry and urban petit-bourgeoisie. During the slavery period, these economic activities gave meaning and purpose to an otherwise bleak and depressing existence. Whole families were involved in the cultivation of provision grounds and this fostered a sense of communal solidarity essential to survival. Women made a major contribution to this slave 'underlife' over which the whites had little control. In addition to contributing to the independence of mind noted by contemporary European observers, the relative freedom of movement allowed to women in their marketing activities enabled them to make an important contribution to organised slave resistance, the collective action which complemented the 'day to day' individual resistance or non-cooperation discussed above.

Women were active in organised slave uprisings from the very earliest days.[63] Until the last years of slavery, these uprisings were largely inspired by African forms of collective resistance.[64] With the creolisation of slave society and the spread of Christianity and literacy, the character of slave rebellions began to change. After 1800, the influence of the European abolitionist movement and the ideas of the French Revolution became more marked in slave unrest. The example set by Toussaint Louverture in leading the slaves to freedom in Saint Domingue acted as an inspiration to blacks in the British Caribbean who began to articulate their grievances in the context of the egalitarianism of the French revolutionaries.

One of the main contributions made by women to the generalised slave unrest in the turbulent years which preceded abolition was the use of verbal abuse or satire to inspire other slaves to revolt. Following the example of Saint Domingue, for instance, women on a Trinidadian plantation intimidated their master by singing an old revolutionary song. As they walked along a path balancing plantation baskets on their heads they rattled *chac-chac* pods and danced in rhythm to this chorus:

> Vin c'est sang beque (Wine is white blood)
> San Domingo
> Nous va boire sang beque (We shall drink white blood)
> San Domingo.[65]

Sometimes, women extended their lack of cooperation in the fields to actual physical assault on whites with the intention of fomenting unrest among their fellow slaves. In the vicinity of Monk Lewis' plantation in Barbados in 1812, an overseer was murdered and a slave plot subsequently exposed. Before the imprisoned ringleaders of this plot were executed, an overseer on an adjacent estate had occasion to find fault with a female field hand belonging to a hired gang. In response to his criticism, she flew at him 'with the greatest fury', grasped him by the throat and invited her fellow slaves to kill him. The suddenness of this attack 'nearly accomplished her purpose' and the overseer was only saved by his own slaves who came to his assistance. The woman was executed.[66]

Individual women were accused of being the ringleaders of revolts. During the Barbados slave revolt in 1816, a woman named Nanny Grigg was implicated. According to the confession of Robert, a slave from the Simmons plantation, this woman had informed the blacks that she had read in the newspapers that they would all be freed on New Year's Day. She was 'always talking about it', he said, and told the slaves they were all 'damned fools' to work. When the blacks had not been freed by New Year, she declared that the only way they could achieve freedom was to fight for it by setting fires 'the way they did in Saint Domingo'.[67]

As emancipation became more of a concrete reality, promised by 'Massa Buxton' and his friends in England, the slaves' concept of freedom changed. No longer did they seek to overthrow the whites and establish carbon-copy African kingdoms, as they had during the earlier failed rebellions, but they envisaged their freedom within the established framework of the existing society. Creolisation played an important part here. By the 1820s, the vast majority of slaves had been born in the West Indies and had been more exposed to European ideas through, for instance, the new nonconformist missionary activity.[68]

Another important factor affecting the relationship between master and slave was the diversification of the plantation system as the economic link between the West Indian colonies and the metropolitan economy was re-defined. Class relations developed and changed and the capitalist basis of the plantation system became firmly established as more and more plantations fell into the hands of absentee English merchants through indebtedness and mismanagement. It was during the last years of slavery that the essential socio-political structures which characterised the free West Indies were elaborated and reinforced. As mercantilism was superseded by capitalism, which established labour in a free contractual relationship to capital, social relations between master and slave began to change.[69]

In the economics of slave production, slaves were classed as capital not labour. This definition proved increasingly archaic and restrictive as the British economy moved towards free trade. The debate over free versus slave labour intensified as emancipation approached and the concept of free, waged labour formed the basis of the 1833 Abolition Act. During the Apprenticeship period both planter and slave had to adapt to the new system of free collective bargaining which, guided by the 'hidden hand' of the market place, was to determine the wages of 'free' labour. In so doing freed blacks first encountered the limitations of the new wage labour system as the planter sought to control his 'free' labour force. By 1838 planters were arguably won over to the idea that they could more cheaply cultivate their land with free rather than slave labour. Though obliged to pay wages they had been released from other responsibilities for the welfare of their labour force.[70]

These important economic and social changes affected the resistant strategies employed by blacks. During the 1830s organised unrest was more in the character of European peasant uprisings than African armed resistance. The proletarianisation of the slave population sharpened the desire for complete emancipation. Many of the slaves' grievances centred on the expected difficulties surrounding the transition to peasant/rural proletariat status. Because of their pivotal economic role on slave plantations, women were intimately involved in these changes. After emancipation in 1833, for instance, former enslaved mothers regarded it as a great insult that overseers should ask their free children to work without money wages and loudly protested any attempts to do so.[71]

In the final years of slavery, blacks were active agents in securing their own freedom. A number of serious revolts occurred which reflected the disaffection of the mass of slaves. A contemporary account of the 1831 rebellion in Jamaica described how whole families fled the plantations. This was an archetypal creole uprising, known by whites as the 'Baptist revolt' because of the alleged encouragement the slaves were given by the fundamentalist teachings of radical Baptist preachers. The revolt was triggered off by rumours that freedom had already been granted by the British Parliament. Work on the plantations ceased and slaves joined the rebels in vast numbers, hiding in the woods and taking with them 'whatever weapons, ammunition or food they could collect'. Not a soul was to be seen on the estates excepting the old, sick and disabled.[72]

In these later uprisings women adapted their tactics to meet the changing conditions. Records indicate that they were verbally aggressive, acted as go-betweens, participated in subversive activities and joined in physical confrontations with the colonial authorities. When the Jamaican militia went into the hills to squash the 1831 revolt, they initially tried to extract information from women, assuming they would be more amenable to white authority. Most of the women, however, prevaricated so much that it was obvious they were concealing information. One woman attempted to lead a militia party straight into a rebel ambush. Another woman apprehended by the militia was discovered to have been acting as guide to a rebel foraging party as she was well acquainted with the provision grounds in the area. Because of their physical mobility as higglers and market sellers, women were ideally placed to act as spies and messengers without attracting too much suspicion.[73]

When the resistance was finally broken, the slaves returned to their plantations. But, as with similar unrest in other islands, there had been serious economic dislocation and the slaves were uncowed in their opposition to the existing regime. During the subsequent Apprenticeship period, planters found it increasingly difficult to control their work-force at a time when they were under pressure to extract the maximum profit from their estates.[74] These were worrying times for the European population and the fear and insecurity inspired by the restless and potentially dangerous black population have been vividly evoked in Jean Rhys's novel, *Wide Sargasso Sea*.

Conditions of labour remained one of the major issues for the newly-freed blacks. Many former slaves had 'betaken themselves to other occupations more profitable than field labour' and planters and estate managers had great difficulty securing a steady and continuous flow of labour.[75] Abolition had raised black aspirations and discontent was expressed not only in reluctance to work but also in mass protests. Again women played a prominent role. In St Kitts in 1834, for instance, mob action was taken during a general protest against work conditions. A British official who observed this 'turbulent and rebellious' resistance to the law stated that few men were involved and the crowd consisted largely of women and children. After the general unrest was suppressed 16 rebels, including two women, were put on trial for 'sedition and mutiny' and inciting others to rebel.[76] Women in Trinidad during this same period had a similarly notorious reputation and white observers made strong remarks about their insubordinate nature.[77] The spirit of rebellion and independence which had sustained women throughout the slave experience and buffered them against the dehumanisation of the plantation labour regime was thus still strongly in evidence in the years immediately after abolition.

II

The evidence presented above suggests that women made an important contribution to both routine non-cooperation with the labour regime and organised slave resistance. Until recently, however, historians have assumed their role to be passive as their sex allegedly precluded any concrete role in active slave resistance. Negative stereotypes of black women focusing on their sexual relationships with white men have proved particularly durable. In discussing modern Caribbean culture, for instance, Peter Wilson has claimed that, because they were treated differently from black men, black women were 'more readily and firmly attached' to the alien society of the whites from the earliest days of slavery. Unlike men, they were able to improve their social standing through concubinage but in so doing were forced to adopt white values and accommodate to, rather than resist, slavery.[78] Though undoubtedly a small minority of women followed this pattern, the indications are that it was far from typical. Women were in the vanguard of cultural resistance to slavery and, despite their alleged advantages, it seems that the majority of women rejected rather than encouraged the sexual advances of white men regardless of the penalties this might incur.[79]

Women's inspiration to resist came primarily from their economic role in the formal plantation economy. As they constituted the 'backbone' of the field labour force and the majority of domestic servants, women were ideally placed to frustrate their masters in numerous ways from everyday acts of non-cooperation – malingering, sabotage, stealing and verbal abuse – to more serious actions such as running away, poisoning and incitement to revolt. If anything women were arguably in a better position than men to co-ordinate subversive activities. This was not solely a result of the mobility they had as market women but a consequence of contemporary European perceptions of women which denied them any positive leadership role and may have initially placed them above suspicion, particularly during the last years of slavery when, on the surface, more slaves had assimilated European cultural values.

Within the general framework of resistance and survival which ultimately guaranteed emancipation, women were primary agents. Despite the threat of frequent, often harsh punishment which included the whip, women fought fiercely against the system. Through their rebellious and insubordinate behaviour, they not only jeopardised the planters' profits but voiced a strong and effective protest against the harsh conditions of their servitude. This assertion of free will challenged the legal definition of slaves as chattels for it underscored the essential humanity of blacks and presented Europeans with moral dilemmas which ultimately weakened one of the basic arguments for the retention of slaves.

In addition to their contribution to general slave resistance, including organised slave revolts, women were crucial in transmitting the spirit and tradition of resistance to their children through song and oral tradition. Caribbean women have been described by Melville Herskovits as the 'primary exponents' of African-derived culture. It was this culture which helped to shield the slaves from dehumanisation and give them the strength to survive servitude.[80] Strong cultural traditions were evident, for instance, in the gardening and marketing activities of slave women. Their vigorous activities in this informal economy helped to foster a spirit of resilience and independence which integrated and strengthened the slave community and prepared slaves for their role as free peasants after abolition.

Contemporary evidence indicates that throughout most of the period of slavery, female slaves in the British West Indies (unlike their counterparts perhaps in the states of the Old South) were valued primarily as workers rather than childbearers. They had a paramount position in both the formal and informal economy and a rough equality of the sexes existed in the 'public' as opposed to the 'private' sphere of slave life. Though abolitionist pressures and practical fears about declining slave birth rates after the ending of the slave trade in 1807 forced planters to introduce measures to protect pregnant women and encourage a stable family life, little change in the status of slave women actually occurred. Planters still relied heavily on female labour and the need to yield profits in an uncertain and rapidly changing economic climate cancelled out any superficial concessions allowed to slave women.

Humanitarian welfare measures were costly and slow to produce results. In Jamaica in 1831, for instance, planters estimated that it cost £112 to rear a child from birth to 14 years, including paying for the lying-in of mothers and compensating for the reduction in labour productivity of slave mothers in general. According to Douglas Hall this constituted an important argument in the debate over the comparative costs of slave versus free labour, for free-born children would not be the planter's responsibility and would therefore cost nothing as replacement labour.[81]

After emancipation, women essentially retained the economic roles they had been allocated during slavery. Many of the socio-economic problems associated with the plantation system and sugar monoculture persisted, hindering constructive development.[82] Black women remained in low status occupations in the externally-orientated cash-crop economy as plantation labourers and seasonal cane-cutters and retained their prominent role in the internal marketing system.[83] They also continued to act as catalysts in the integration of creole society through their continuing contribution to the cultural life of the black community.[84] The high degree of economic and social independence of Afro-Caribbean women which derived from Africa and was reinforced by slavery has enabled them to play a significant role in modern labour struggles and in the continued resistance to colonial and neo-colonial domination, as the active participation of women in the recent Grenadian revolution illustrates.[85]

Before and after emancipation, women's spirit to resist was heightened by the racism implicit in the Caribbean class system. In an elaborate hierarchy based on the interlinked criteria of colour and economic status, black women were in the lowest position. During slavery, racist stereotypes of black women as passive work-horses or scarlet temptresses sought to degrade them and portray them as inferior species. Such negative stereotypes were used to justify and rationalise the economic and sexual exploitation of slave women and proved extremely durable. A reassessment of the existing evidence indicates that, in effect, women did not comply with this stereotyped image. Supported and sustained by their African cultural heritage, they resisted European racism and the essentially exploitative system which it sought to conceal.

The methods of resistance adopted by slave women reflected the ever pervasive influence of their African heritage and the tangible, brutal circumstances of the slave labour regime. At work women showed much courage in refusing to cooperate and in verbal abuse of masters. They also showed considerable industry and enterprise in the informal economy. As the foremost bearers of Afro-Caribbean culture, women transmitted the 'consciousness and practice of resistance' in a system which sought at all times to undermine it. The labour needs of the slave labour regime caused a 'crude levelling' of the sexes and ensured that women shared the same experience as black men. The harsh conditions of life stimulated rather than squashed resistance and strengthened the resolve and independent stance of women. Contrary to popular assumptions, as modern Caribbean writers like Brathwaite and Mathurin have stressed, the black woman's economic role ensured that she was (and still is) as deeply committed to 'the art and act of subversion and liberation' as her kinsman.[86] From slavery through emancipation to the present day, women have been active agents in black liberation struggles and their important contribution should be given fuller recognition.

NOTES

1. European images of slave women are discussed in my *'Lost Daughters of Afrik': Black Women in British West Indian Slave Society* (Ormskirk, 1984), Chap. 1.
2. Emma Carmichael, *Domestic Manners: Five Years in Trinidad and St Vincent*, 2 vols (London, 1833), I, p. 119; M. Lewis, *Journal of a Residence Among the Negroes of the West Indies* (London, 1845), p. 103.
3. Lucille Mathurin, 'The Arrival of Black Women', *Jamaica Journal*, 9, nos. 2 and 3 (July 1975), p. 2.
4. William Beckford, *Remarks Upon the Situation of Negroes in Jamaica* (London, 1788), p. 13.
5. The role of the powerful coloured housekeeper is discussed in my 'White "Ladies", Coloured "Favourites" and Black "Wenches": Some Considerations on Sex, Race and Class Factors in Social Relations in White Creole Society in the British Caribbean', *Slavery and Abolition*, 2 (1981), pp. 253–4.
6. R. B. Sheridan, *Sugar and Slavery: An Economic History of the British West Indies, 1623–1775* (Barbados, 1974), pp. 257–8; Michael Craton and James Walvin, *A Jamaican Plantation: the History of Worthy Park, 1670–1970* (London, 1970), p. 138. See also R. S. Dunn, 'A Tale of Two Plantations: Slave Life at Mesopotamia in Jamaica and Mount Airy in Virginia 1799–1828', *William and Mary Quarterly*, 3rd Series, 24 (1977), p. 32.
7. Bryan Edwards, *The History, Civil and Commercial of the British Colonies in the West Indies*, 3 vols. (London, 1801), I, pp. 540–1, II, p. 76; Edward Long, *The History of Jamaica*, 3 vols. (London, 1774), II, pp. 304, 404; John Adams, *Sketches Taken During Ten Voyages to Africa Between the Years 1786–1822* (London, 1822), p. 8. Contrary to contemporary opinion, women in Africa did not perform all the heavy labour; tasks were divided according to a strict division of labour. See, for instance, Olaudah Equiano, *Equiano's Travels: His Autobiography* (ed. Paul Edwards) (London, 1967), p. 4; M. J. Herskovits, *The Myth of the Negro Past* (Boston, 1941), p. 58.
8. Edwards, *History, op. cit.*, II, pp. 106, 118; Long, *op. cit.*, II, p. 385; John Stewart, *A View of Jamaica* (London, 1823), p. 309.
9. The high male to female ratio referred to by planters and used as an explanation for the low rate of natural increase of slave populations is not reflected in the numerical analyses of Jamaican plantations (see note 6) or the evidence concerning individual Barbadian plantations submitted to the 1789 Select Committee on the Slave Trade (*British Sessional Papers (hereafter B.S.P.), Commons, Report of the Lords of Trade on the Slave Trade*, vol. 26 (1789), 646a, Barbados, ans. no. 23, 36).
10. Robert Dallas, *The History of the Maroons*, 2 vols. (London, 1803; reprinted Frank Cass, 1968), I, p. vii. See also Thomas Cooper, *Facts Illustrative of the Condition of Negro Slaves in Jamaica* (London, 1824), p. 3.
11. Edward Brathwaite, *The Development of Creole Society in Jamaica* (Oxford, 1971), p. 154; Edwards, *History, op. cit.*, II, p. 132; *B.S.P.*, vol. 26 (1789), 646a, Part 3, Jamaica, ans. no. 29.
12. Advertisement dated 18 August 1827, *The Royal Gazette*.
13. Beckford, *Remarks, op. cit.*, p. 44.
14. Craton and Walvin, *A Jamaican Plantation, op. cit.*, pp. 103–4.
15. Richard Ligon, *A True and Exact History of the Island of Barbados* (London, 1657; reprinted Frank Cass, 1970), p. 43.
16. Elsa Goveia, *Slave Society in the British Leeward Islands at the End of the Eighteenth Century* (Barbados, 1965), p. 234; Craton and Walvin, *A Jamaican Plantation, op. cit.*, p. 125.

17. Long, *op. cit.*, II, pp. 270–2; William Beckford, *A Descriptive Account of the Island of Jamaica*, 2 vols. (London, 1790), II, p. 51; John Riland, *Memoirs of a West Indian Planter* (London, 1837), p. 142.
18. Long, *op. cit.*, II, p. 270.
19. Beckford, *A Descriptive Account, op. cit.*, II, pp. 40–1.
20. Lewis, *Journal, op. cit.*, p. 103; P.R.O., Colonial Office Series, CO 295/60, 295/66, Commandant of Chaguanos to Woodford, 20 August 1823, cited in Bridget Brereton, 'Brute Beast or Man Angel; Attitudes to Blacks in Trinidad, 1802 to 1888', Unpublished Paper, St Augustine, Trinidad, 1974.
21. Cooper, *Facts, op. cit.*, pp. 17–18.
22. John Stedman, *Narrative of a Five Years Expedition Against the Revolted Negroes of Surinam, 1772–1777*, 2 vols. (London, 1796), I, p. 117.
23. Henry Coor's evidence in B.S.P., vol. 92 (1791–2), no. 745, p. 34.
24. See, for instance, Stedman, *op. cit.*, I, pp. 77, 179; Bush, 'White Ladies ...', *op. cit.*, pp. 256–7.
25. P. Wright (ed), *Lady Nugent's Jamaica Journal* (Kingston, 1966), pp. 69, 77; William Sells, *Remarks Upon the Condition of Slaves in The Island of Jamaica* (Shannon, 1972 reprint), p. 17.
26. See my discussion of childbirth in the slave community in *Lost Daughters, op. cit.*, chap. 6.
27. For planter views on this problem see Thomas Roughley, *The Jamaican Planters Guide* (Edinburgh, 1823), p. 24; Beckford, *Remarks, op. cit.*, pp. 24–5.
28. See Richard Sheridan, 'Mortality and Medical Treatment of Slaves in the British West Indies', in S. Engerman and E. Genovese (eds.), *Race and Slavery in the Western Hemisphere: Quantitative Studies* (New York, 1973), p. 289. During the period from 1817 to 1832 the slave birth-rate in Jamaica actually declined, a reflection of deteriorating conditions on the large plantations. See B. W. Higman, *Slave Population and Economy in Jamaica, 1807–1834* (London, 1976), pp. 153–5.
29. Cooper, *Facts, op. cit.*, p. 20.
30. 'Abstract of the Jamaican Slave Law, 1826, no. 37', in B. M. Senior, *A Retired Military Officer* (London, 1831), p. 145.
31. John Williamson, M.D., *Medical and Miscellaneous Observations Relative to the Islands of the West Indies*, 2 vols. (Edinburgh, 1817), I, p. 191; Lewis, *Journal, op. cit.*, pp. 174–5.
32. Beckford, *A Descriptive Account, op. cit.*, II, pp. 383–4.
33. John Jeremie, *Four Essays on Colonial Slavery* (London, 1831), p. 6.
34. Cooper, *Facts, op. cit.*, p. 19. For slave testimonies from the Old South see Frederick Douglass, *The Life and Times of Frederick Douglass* (New York, 1883), pp. 51–2; Eugene Genovese, *'Roll, Jordan, Roll': The World the Slaves Made* (New York, 1974), pp. 619 et seq.
35. Elsa Goveia, *The West Indian Slave Laws of the Eighteenth Century* (Barbados, 1970), pp. 25, 48. Jeremie, *Essays, op. cit.*, provides a useful contemporary analysis of the workings of the slave laws.
36. Goveia, *Slave Laws, op. cit.*, pp. 194–6; 'Abstract from the Laws of Jamaica, 1809', 'Abstract from the Leeward Islands Act, 1798' in Edwards, *History, op. cit.*, III, pp. 181–2, 183–5; 'Abstract from the Slave Laws of Jamaica, 1826' in Senior, *op. cit.*, p. 144.
37. Goveia, *Slave Society, op. cit.*, p. 197.
38. *Edinburgh Review*, 55 (April, 1832), p. 148. Goveia draws similar conclusions; see her *Slave Laws, op. cit.*, p. 39.
39. Edwards, *History, op. cit.*, III, p. 36.
40. See note 4; Goveia, *Slave Society, op. cit.*, pp. 244–5.

41. This aspect of women's resistance to slavery is dealt with in my article '"The Family Tree is Not Cut": Women and Cultural Resistance in Slave Family Life in the British Caribbean', in G. Y. Okihiro (ed.), *Resistance Studies in African, Caribbean, Latin American and Afro-American History* (Boston, 1984).
42. The importance of language in black resistance is stressed in Franz Fanon, *Black Skin, White Masks* (New York, 1967), pp. 13–14.
43. Long, *op. cit.*, II, p. 278; *Lady Nugent's Journal, op. cit.*, p. 153.
44. These records may be found in the Atkin Slavery Collection, Wilberforce House, Hull. The main sources used here are the Baillies Bacolet Plantation Returns (Grenada) 1820–1833 and the Punishment Record Books for Friendship Sarah and Good Success Plantations (British Guiana) 1823–1833.
45. Punishment Record Book, Plantation Friendship Sarah, Nov.–Dec. 1827.
46. Punishment Record Book, Good Success, 1830.
47. Punishment Record Book, Plantation Friendship Sarah, 1827.
48. Baillies Bacolet Plantation Returns, 1823, 19 Feb. 1833.
49. Carmichael, *Domestic Manners, op. cit.*, I, pp. 118–19, 256–8, II, pp. 268, 334.
50. Long, *op. cit.*, II, p. 415; Lewis, *Journal, op. cit.*, p. 175; Stewart, *View of Jamaica, op. cit.*, p. 172.
51. Carmichael, *Domestic Manners, op. cit.*, II, p. 202; Lewis, *Journal, op. cit.*, pp. 145–6; Stewart, *View of Jamaica, op. cit.*, pp. 304–5. According to Edwards this practice was in effect a form of mild inoculation used by female Koromantyn slaves; Edwards, *History, op. cit.*, II, p. 69.
52. Lewis, *Journal, op. cit.*, p. 92; *Jamaica Mercury*, 2 Oct. 1779.
53. Lewis, *Journal, op. cit.*, p. 104; Beckford, *Remarks, op. cit.*, p. 13.
54. Carmichael, *Domestic Manners, op. cit*, I, pp. 184–6.
55. Jamaican Assembly decree in *Laws for the Government of Negro Slaves, 1787*, vol. II, cited in F. K. Augier and S. C. Gordon (eds.), *Sources of West Indian History* (London, 1962), p. 169. The general development of this local economy is traced in S. W. Mintz and Douglas Hall, 'The Origins of the Jamaican Internal Marketing System' in S. W. Mintz (ed.), *Papers in Caribbean Anthropology* (New Haven, 1970), pp. 3–26.
56. For a contemporary description of the slave 'polinks' and comments on their significance to the slave community see Dallas, *Maroons, op. cit.*, I, pp. cviii–cix; Beckford, *A Descriptive Account, op. cit.*, II, pp. 151–60, 187; Edwards, *History, op. cit.*, II, p. 137; Long, *op. cit.*, II, pp. 410–11.
57. Edwards, *History, op. cit.*, II, pp. 53–4. See also Jeremie, *Essays, op. cit.*, p. 78; and Beckford, *Remarks, op. cit.*, p. 8 for similar criticisms. During the final years of slavery there were many advertisements for slaves who were to be sold to pay off debts. For instance at a public slave sale at Buff House Court House on 5 Oct. 1827 a woman slave and her son were put up for sale by their owner in payment for taxes to the Government. *The Royal Gazette*, notice issued from the Collecting Constables office.
58. Edwards, *History, op. cit.*, II, p. 131.
59. Bickell cited in Riland, *Memoirs, op. cit.*, pp. 203–5. Many abolitionists regarded the Sunday market as a 'horror' as it violated the Lord's Day. See, for instance, Cooper, *Facts, op. cit.*, pp. 4–8. A detailed description of the Jamaican Sunday market is given in Beckford, *A Descriptive Account, op. cit.*, II, pp. 153–4.
60. 'Abstract of the Laws of Jamaica, 1826, no. 41', in Senior, *op. cit.*, p. 146.
61. For a discussion of the role of women in traditional West African society see Sylvia Leith-Ross, *African Women: A Study of the Ibo of Nigeria* (London, 1939), pp. 124–8; W. M. MacMillan, *Africa Emergent: A Survey of Social, Political and Economic Trends in British Africa* (London, 1938), pp. 38 et seq.

Though little reliable evidence exists from the slave era itself, Equiano refers to 'frequently' going to market with his mother before being snatched away by slavers (*Travels, op. cit.*, p. 7). An interesting insight into the economic activities of modern Nigerian women is provided by Flora Nwapo's *Efuru* (London, 1966). For an analysis of women's role in modern Caribbean societies see Frances Henry and Pamela Wilson, 'The Status of Women in Caribbean Societies: an Overview of their Social, Economic and Sexual Roles', *Social and Economic Studies*, 24 (June, 1975), pp. 165–9.

62. See slave runaway advertisements in *The Jamaica Mercury*, 26 June 1779; *The Royal Gazette*, Oct. 1827.
63. For a discussion of women's role in earlier slave resistance see Barbara Bush, 'Defiance or Submission: the Role of Slave Women in Slave Resistance in the British Caribbean', *Immigrants and Minorities*, 1 (1982), pp. 23–31.
64. See Monica Schuler, 'Ethnic Slave Rebellions in the Caribbean and the Guianas', *Journal of Social History*, 3 (1970), pp. 374–92.
65. Cited in V. S. Naipaul, *The Loss of Eldorado* (London, 1973), pp. 292–3.
66. Lewis, *Journal, op. cit.*, p. 93.
67. *Report from a Select Committee of The House of Assembly Appointed to Enquire into the Origins, Causes and Progress of the Late Insurrection* (Barbados, 1818), appendix D.
68. For an interesting analysis of the creolisation process see E. K. Brathwaite, 'Caliban, Ariel and Unprospero in the Conflict of Creolisation: A Study of the Slave Revolt in Jamaica, 1831–32', in Vera Rubin and Arthur Tuden (eds.), *Perspectives on New World Slave Societies*, vol. 292, *Annals of the New York Academy of Sciences* (1977), p. 41.
69. One of the most thorough discussions of the debate over free labour versus slave labour in the context of abolitionism and the rise of capitalism may be found in D. B. Davis, *The Problem of Slavery in the Age of Revolution, 1770–1823* (London, 1975).
70. Douglas Hall, *Free Jamaica, 1836–65* (New York, 1959), pp. 19–27. For general economic changes in Jamaica post 1800 see Brathwaite, *Creole Society, op. cit.*, pp. 80–95.
71. Joseph Sturge and Thomas Harvey, *The West Indies in 1837* (London, 1968), p. 173.
72. Senior, *op. cit.*, pp. 180, 204–7, 212–16.
73. *Ibid.*
74. Contemporary impressions of this period from the planter perspective are recorded in the letters of Mr and Mrs L. P. Lockhart and Mr B. Lockhart of Dominica to William King, 1825 to 1839. The letters for February to April 1836, for instance, reflect the serious financial difficulties and personal distress of the writers, Atkin Slavery Collection, Wilberforce House, Hull.
75. Resolutions of the House of Commons, 1837, Clauses 5 and 6 cited in K. N. Bell and W. P. Morell (eds.), *British Colonial Policy: Select Documents 1830–1860* (Oxford, 1928), pp. 421–2.
76. 5 Aug. 1834, Fahie to MacGregor, B.S.P., vol. 50 (1835), p. 637; Returns of the Convictions under Court Martials for Offenders, 6–8 Aug. 1834, cited in Richard Frucht, 'Emancipation in St Kitts, 1834', *Science and Society*, 1 (1975), p. 208.
77. Brereton, 'Brute Beast', *op. cit.*, pp. 10–14.
78. P. J. Wilson, *Crab Antics: the Social Anthropology of English-Speaking Negro Societies in the Caribbean* (New Haven, 1973), p. 193.
79. See my *Lost Daughters, op. cit.*, chap. 6.
80. Melville and Frances Herskovits, *Trinidad Village* (New York, 1947), pp. 8–9;

Walter Rodney, 'Upper Guinea and the Origins of Africans Enslaved in the New World', *Journal of Negro History*, 54 (1969), p. 345.

81. Douglas Hall, 'Slaves and Slavery in the British West Indies', *Social and Economic Studies*, 2 (1962), pp. 306–8.
82. See, for instance, George Beckford, *Persistent Poverty: Underdevelopment in Plantation Economies of the Third World* (New York, 1972).
83. W. M. MacMillan, *Warning from the West Indies: A Tract for Africa and the Empire* (London, 1936), pp. 76–80; MacMillan, *Africa Emergent, op. cit.*, p. 83.
84. Martha Beckwith, *Black Roadways: A Study of Jamaica Folk Life* (N.Y., 1969), pp. 160, 168, 172.
85. See, for instance Rhoda Reddock, 'Women's Movements and Organisations in the Process of Revolutionary Transformation: the Case of Grenada' in D. Durham and J. P. Perez-Saintz (eds.), *Crisis y Repuesto in America Latina y del Caribe* (Costa Rica, 1984).
86. Edward Brathwaite, 'Submerged Mothers', *Jamaica Journal*, 9, nos. 2 and 3 (February, 1975), p. 48; Lucille Mathurin, *The Rebel Woman in the British West Indies During Slavery* (Kingston, 1975).

3

The Maroons of Surinam: Agents of their own Emancipation

SILVIA W. DE GROOT

I

Throughout the history of plantation agriculture based on slave labour, planters had to deal with the reactions of their slaves against the system. The origins of black resistance against slavery were rooted in various factors, ranging from the personalities of the slaves themselves to their forcible transport from Africa to the Americas and the brutalised and dehumanising conditions they experienced under New World plantation regimes. The forms of resistance were as varied as their origins, and included acts of passive resistance such as work shyness, more overt forms of resistance such as sabotage, self-mutilation and even suicide, and outright revolt and marronage. Revolts, usually involving groups of slaves, were often accompanied by marronage, as rebels disappeared into the bush or forest, taking with them loot and non-mutinous slaves. Here they developed their own organised guerrilla bands which served to raid plantations for supplies and to protect their own forest settlements and encampments from assault by white patrols. Over time Maroon settlements developed into stable semi-autonomous agricultural communities with their own political and religious organisation; sustaining trading links with white coastal settlements, these communities also cultivated a variety of crops on plots carved out of the forest.

Two of the most important Maroon communities established in the Caribbean during the eighteenth century were in Jamaica and Surinam. Numerous factors contributed to their success as semi-independent settlements but two perhaps deserve particular emphasis. These were the low ratio of whites to blacks in plantation societies and the relatively close proximity of plantation agriculture to substantial tracts of unhealthy and near impenetrable rain forest. As in most Caribbean plantation economies, blacks outnumbered whites by a very considerable margin in both Jamaica and Surinam; a ratio of 20 slaves to one white was normal during eighteenth-century Surinam. Such a ratio made the supervision and control of slave populations extremely difficult and created opportunities for those slaves so inclined to run away or rebel. Runaway slaves in Jamaica and Surinam were assisted also by the existence of tropical jungle which provided not only an immediate haven for runaways but a barrier to white pursuit. Unable to recapture or suppress the Maroons, white colonial authorities were ultimately obliged to negotiate treaties with Maroons in both Jamaica and Surinam, which in the latter instance at least recognised the freedom and autonomy of Maroons.

This paper seeks to explain how the Maroons of Surinam became agents of their own emancipation. Although marronage was a widespread feature of New World societies during the era of slavery, the Maroons of Surinam (and to a lesser degree those of Jamaica) have been the only ones to sustain their existence as a distinct society from the beginning of their struggle for freedom in the second half of the seventeenth century until today. We shall analyse their struggle for freedom in terms of their relationship with the plantation economy during the two centuries before the abolition of slavery in Surinam in 1863. The paper also includes a short description of the main features of Maroon societies in Surinam.

II

Relations between the Maroons and the colonial government in Surinam had constant as well as changing features. In their dealings with each other these features caused different policies and attitudes.

Surinam, situated on the north-east coast of South America, between 2° and 6° North and 54° and 58° West, covers an area

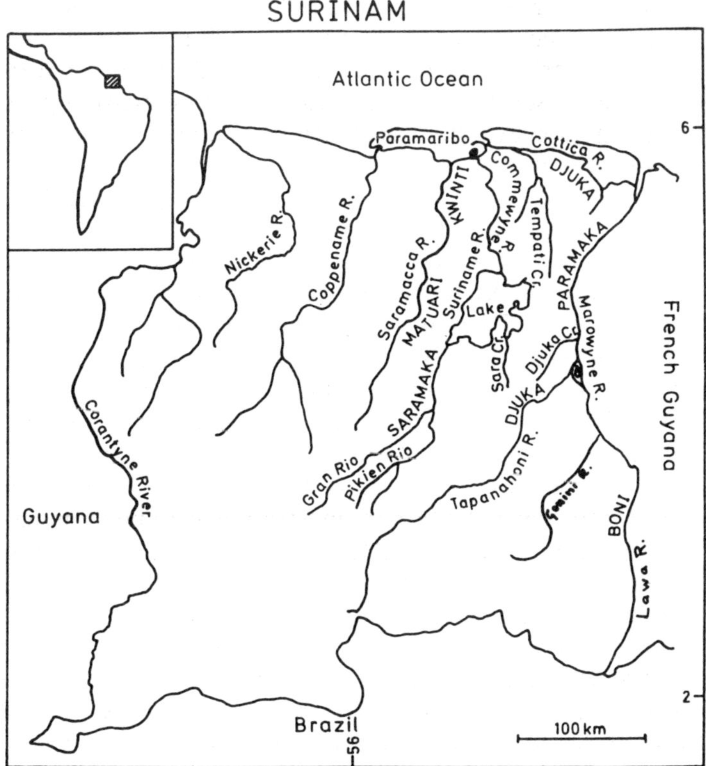

of some 142,822 km² (55,167 square miles). It is a tropical region with an average day temperature of 26°C, an average night temperature of 23°C, and two dry and two rainy seasons. The western frontier is formed by the Corantyn River, the eastern frontier by the Marowyne River. In the south the country borders on Brazil, in the north on the Atlantic Ocean. The Corantyn and Marowyne rivers, as well as the Surinam River and Coppename River, run from south to north; the Cottica, the Commewyne, the Saramacca and the Nickerie run partly parallel to the coastline. The upper reaches of the South–North flowing rivers are difficult to navigate and can only be attempted by dug-outs. The coastal fringe consists of heavy sea-clay, criss-crossed by strips of sand and shell, and is 50 to 100 kilometres wide. This is the agricultural region, traditionally the plantation area, made suitable for this purpose largely by reclamation. Most of the inhabitants of Surinam live here today, with Paramaribo as capital and focal point. To the south of this area stretches a wide belt of savanna and secondary woods, beyond which the jungle starts and the terrain becomes hilly, with several mountain ranges that have peaks rising to a height of 800 to 1200 metres. In this jungle the Maroons and Indians live. The former have settled along the rivers, the latter lead a nomadic or semi-nomadic existence.

Surinam developed into a slave-based plantation colony after 1650. Before 1667 it was under British rule but came under Dutch authority thereafter. Until 1795 Surinam was owned by the Chartered Society, a triumvirate consisting of the Dutch West Indian Company, the City of Amsterdam and Cornelis Aerssen van Sommelsdijk; together they administered the colony under the supervision of the States General. The colony was governed by a Governor, a Political Council and a Criminal Council. Two groups sought to profit from the colony: the Directors of the Chartered Society and the plantation owners. In spite of their often conflicting interests, an unstable equilibrium was maintained and great fortunes were made by them both for more than a century. From 1799 to 1814 Surinam was a British protectorate. From 1816 until 1954 it was a colony of the Netherlands. It then became an autonomous part of the Kingdom of the Netherlands until 1975 when independence was granted.

After a period of prolonged prosperity during the eighteenth century the colony fared badly from the late eighteenth century until the 1860s. The causes of this lay in guerrilla wars with the Maroons, the raising of exorbitant loans, the French Revolution and Napoleonic wars, the prohibition of slave trade and, in 1863, the abolition of slavery.

It has been estimated that the number of slaves imported from West Africa into Surinam was 300,000 to 350,000. Despite this the slave population of the colony remained, as Table 1 shows, below 60,000 throughout the period before abolition. The black population nevertheless exceeded the white by a considerable margin throughout the eighteenth century, outnumbering the white by 25 to 1 in 1738, 15 to 1 in 1786 and 6 to 1 in 1830. As a result plantation owners lived in constant fear of slave uprisings.

Table 1
The Population of Surinam 1680 to 1863

	Slaves	Whites	Plantations	Maroons
1680–1690	2800	800	200	7–800
1690–1700	5100	800		
1700–1710	7500			
1710–1720	18000	1000		
1720–1730	29000	1250		
1730–1740	40000	2100	400	5–6000
1740–1750	50000	2400		
1786–1791	53000	3300	591	7000
1791–1830	53000	8500	451	
1830–1863	33600	16500	162	8000

Source: Richard Price, *The Guiana Maroons* (Baltimore, 1976), pp. 8, 10, 11, 24.

Such fears were far from groundless. In order to cope with life within the plantation system, slaves reacted to their condition in a variety of ways. These ranged from total submission to open resistance, including violence and marronage. Marronage probably occurred from the very beginning of the slave system in Surinam, which originated with the first English colonisation in 1650. Although during the period of English colonisation between 1650 and 1667 some 2000 slaves were imported and marronage occurred, there is no mention of maroon warfare or peace treaties in available sources. When the Dutch took over the colony in 1667, about 1200 slaves were still living there. For the first decade or so of Dutch occupation the colony stagnated but after the take-over by the Chartered Society and the arrival of its first governor in 1683 a serious start was made to develop the plantation system in the colony. The number of plantations and white settlers rose quickly, as did the number of slaves imported and at the same time the number of Maroons. At this point the Indians, who resented the invasion of their country and attempts to enslave them, started to attack the colonists. So did the Maroons. In 1686 the Governor made peace with a group of Indians and Maroons and for the ensuing ten years or so no further large scale attacks occurred.

Some indication of the growth in the Maroon population is provided in Table 1; these estimates are, of course, only very rough and, as Price has suggested are probably inflated.[1] Nevertheless they indicate that the Maroon population may have been some ten percent or more of the black population of Surinam during the eighteenth century, and an even higher proportion during the seventeenth and nineteenth centuries. The Maroons gathered in groups and formed strong military organisations, attacking plantations in order to supply their people with weapons, women, utensils and food. Their operations were often attended with arson and murder.

Initially, the plantation colony reacted strongly to Maroon assaults by employing civil patrols and militia, regular military troops and defensive cordons, and inflicting heavy punishment on captives (including death after 1721). Such measures had only limited success, however, and the colony suffered severely from the regular attacks of the seasoned 'guerrilleros' and was unable to defeat them in their abodes. White soldiers were unused to war in dense tropical woods and swampy savannas. Feelings of frustration and hatred prevailed with most of the colonists, who saw no other solution than complete destruction of the 'runaways, the murderers, the rabble, the hordes, the devil's spawn'.

It is possible to discern a change of attitude on the part of both whites and blacks during the eighteenth century. Feeling bereft of their property, the colonists initially saw their lost slaves as enemies, and as formidable guerrilla-fighters. Their hope was to bring them to submission or to extinguish them. However, it became apparent, although perhaps not consciously admitted at first, that a new free black society had emerged which was unlikely to be suppressed. Some colonists, realising that complete destruction was impossible, thought of making peace with Maroon groups in order that they might try to destroy the rest.

For the Maroons the transition from submission to freedom was deliberately taken and consciously brought about. Their former frustrations vanished and changed into feelings of pride, but also of mistrust and bellicosity. In time however their attitude changed. Their growing numbers, demanding more villages and larger subsistence crops, and the development of more intricate social organisation lessened their mobility. Their search for a more sedate existence was hampered by the constant pursuit of them by white patrols and troops. Consequently the Maroons gradually came to see peace as a solution to the stalemate. Before 1730 two main groups of Maroons had settled along or near two of the large rivers: one on Ponama Creek near the Saramacca River called 'Saramaccan Runaways', the other near the Marowyne River along the Djuka Creek, called 'Djuka Runaways'.

In 1730 a military patrol was sent to the Ponama Creek. It made contact with the Maroons, destroyed some of their palisaded villages and offered a general pardon and immunity from attack on condition that the Maroons leave the plantations alone and refuse to take any new runaways into their group. The offer was refused as the Maroons did not trust the whites. In 1749 a second attempt at peace was made, contrary to the wishes of many of the colonists, but carried through by the governor and his adherents. This time a substantial patrol was sent out to attack once more the Saramacca Maroons. Its orders were to wipe out as many villages and Maroons as possible and then to offer peace. This time the assault met with success and the chief of the Maroons agreed with the terms of peace. A one-year truce was concluded to be followed by a solemn peace negotiated by a new party of whites bearing presents for the Maroons. In the meantime, however, the power of the governor dwindled and only a small, badly protected party started out. On its way it was attacked and massacred by a dissident chief, who seized the presents. Deprived of his expected presents the Saramacca chief assumed the whites had broken their promises and resumed hostilities.

Another ten years of guerrilla activity by the Maroons and white retaliation ensued before the next attempt to establish peace was made. Both parties were now more inclined than ever to come to peace, and one of the Maroon groups, the Djuka, even left written notes with peace offers at the plantations they attacked and looted. A different approach was now decided upon by the whites: they realised that a display of power would be in vain, so they first sent two slaves known to be trusted by the Djuka Maroons, and then a peace party with proposals. The negotiations on these proposals were laborious. The Djuka bartered on every single article before accepting the treaty, but finally the parties came to terms and peace was concluded in 1760. In their joy over this achievement the colonists forgot about their initial intention to induce the pacified Maroons to help them to conquer those still at war and asked the Djuka instead to send out people to investigate the possibilities of renewing peace negotiations with the Saramacca Maroons. This initiative succeeded, for in 1762 peace was made with this group on the same terms as those agreed with the Djuka. In the meantime, however, the Saramacca had moved from the Saramacca River to the Surinam River, leaving behind them a new autonomous group, named after their leaders, Becu-Musinga. This group initially refused to accept peace and continued attacking plantations, but finally in 1767 they were induced by the whites with the help of the Saramacca Maroons to accept peace terms.

All the peace treaties concluded with the Maroons in Surinam during the 1760s were similar to the one concluded by the Jamaican authorities with their Maroons in 1739. Recognising the Maroons to be free people, the treaties allowed them to live in the region 'at present inhabited by them, and all the necessary adjoining land', provided this was no closer than at least two days or ten hours' travelling from any plantation.[2] They were also allowed to bring their products to Paramaribo in groups, not exceeding twelve persons at a time, and were granted autonomy in their own jurisdiction (except for death-sentences). In return, the Maroons agreed to send back any new runaways who came to join them and to help 'exterminate' new runaways, especially those 'banded together between Marowyne and Cottica Rivers'.[3] They further agreed to allow a number of whites to live among them to see that the terms of the treaties were observed and accepted that a number of young Maroons, close relatives of their chiefs, should live among the whites in Paramaribo. The whites unofficially promised to send the Maroons every two years 'presents' in the form of necessities that they requested.

The colonists were initially exulted by these treaties. Official days of prayer and thanksgiving were held. Maroons visiting Paramaribo were received with great pomp by the Governor and the Courts and shown around the city in carriages. As a mark of respect, the Maroons were called Bush-negroes (a name the Maroons in Surinam consider as a name of honour to this day). White settlers were required to give free passage to the Maroons in order to allow them to come to the coastal area. In offical letters they were addressed as 'Beloved Friends'. Parties of whites were allowed to visit the territory of the Djuka Maroons in the first years after the peace and before the official white observers took their place amongst them. Previously the Maroons had never allowed peace negotiators to come near their places of residence, but they received these visitors with hospitality and kindness and showed them their villages. Lieutenant Vieira and ensign Collerus visited the Djuka Maroons in 1760 and in company with a Mr Gregory, who was to design a map of the area, made two further trips in 1761. Their commission required them to deliver presents, to urge the Djuka to send a party to the Saramacca Maroons in order to persuade them to make peace, and to see whether the terms of the peace treaty of 1760 were being operated.

One immediate source of conflict in interpreting the peace treaties lay in the clauses relating to the return of new runaways. The Maroons refused to accept the unconditional return of runaways and sought to differentiate between those runaways who had been maltreated by their masters and those who had murdered or poisoned their masters. They wished to admit the first category of runaways into their society, but agreed to send back the latter to be punished. Furthermore, they also wanted to retain all the women who tried to join them. To these refinements of the treaty the government's deputies refused to consent: they pointed out that the Maroons, after long deliberations, had solemnly accepted the articles of peace, and that their interpretation could not be accepted. The Maroons declared that they would accept the peace, but they urged the government to act against those who used violence against their slaves, claiming that it would be difficult to return those who had been tortured.

In May 1761 Lieutenant Vieira fell ill and immediately the Maroons had him treated by a priest. Collerus described his doings extensively in his journal. Collerus' journal also indicates that he was impressed by Cato, the sister of the Chief Pamo, who was the most important priestess among them, representing the oracle god, and was able to prophesy when entranced by 'one of these people's musical instruments'. 'Experience shows', Collerus records, 'that her prophesies often come true, being somewhat like (without comparison) what we read about Elias, who needed a musician before he could start prophesizing'. Collerus had received during his visit to the Djuka in November 1760 a daughter of Cato as a present. In his journal in 1761 he reported that he wanted to marry her 'as it is usual among whites when peace was made among nations, because by marrying, closer kinship ties would ensure peace more durably'. Unfortunately Cato's daughter was already betrothed to a young Maroon, but Cato offered herself as the bride of Collerus. 'Seeing that she and her company wanted this very much, and that it would enhance their confidence in the whites', Collerus accepted. A daughter of Chief Pamo was also offered to Vieira as a wife. The marriages were concluded without ceremony and afterwards, as Collerus records they 'went to Hoeman Condré where the woman Cato lived and stayed overnight'.

This romance has been described at some length, because it shows in a clear way the difference in attitude between these offical envoys of the government and that prevailing formally in plantation society itself. In the latter intercourse between whites and blacks was frowned upon and was officially the subject of punishment.

The joyful feelings that prevailed in Surinam in the immediate aftermath of the peace treaties soon faded however. In the first place the conditions on the plantations did not change: the relationships between slaves and masters stayed very much the same. In the second place the problem of new runaways continued to exist and worst of all, unpacified Maroon groups had settled in the region near the coast and close to the plantation area. These groups under the leadership of competent and bellicose leaders felt strong enough to attack plantations and from 1765 onwards the story described earlier began to repeat itself: assaults and retaliation, escalating into guerrilla warfare. It took ten years, an army of 1500 soldiers and a tenacious Swiss colonel to force these Maroons, the Boni (named after their main leader), to cross the Marowyne River into French Guyana. The Boni War influenced the relationships between the pacified Maroons and the colonists considerably, sharpening mutual distrust and creating new misunderstandings and friction.

The Djuka Maroons were at first of very little help to the whites in fighting the Boni 'guerrilleros'. Occasionally they put out patrols but these met with limited success. The Saramacca and the Becu-Musinga or Matuari (as they became known) refrained from offering assistance as the war occurred too far away from their abodes. Not until after the Boni had crossed the Marowyne River did the Djuka really begin to take action. As the Boni crossed the Marowyne and slowly moved up the river they threatened the Djuka control over the area. The river was the Djuka's main communication artery with the coastal area where they traded and smuggled, and they objected to its occupation by another people. In October 1777 the Djuka launched an attack against the Boni, seizing 21 prisoners and killing seven. To the dismay of the colony, however, they immediately reached an agreement with the Boni, which lasted until 1791. Although the Djuka sent reassuring messages to Paramaribo that no new actions against the whites would be taken by the Boni, they failed to take action when in 1788 the Boni raided a couple of plantations unexpcctedly.

The Boni, retreating from the heavy attacks of the whites, moved up the river once more, forcing the Djuka to move up as well and threatening their control over the river. The whites did everything they could to play off the two groups against one another. In 1791 war broke out between the Djuka and Boni. After the Boni raided and destroyed the Djuka headquarters, a counter-attack was mounted by the enraged Djuka in which Chief Boni himself as well as another chief were killed. The strength of the Boni Maroons was now completely broken. The final combined struggle of the whites and Djuka against a common foe reassured the colonists, and led to the signing of a treaty in 1793 which placed the Boni under the tutelage of the Djuka. This treaty remained in force until 1860.

III

The new state of peace which had come about after 1793 encouraged new attitudes on the part of both the Maroons and the whites. The Maroons had created a stable society and formed what has sometimes been called a 'state within a state'. The two parties had to deal with each other as independent, or rather semi-independent, entities. However, the white coastal society and the Maroons clearly differed in attitudes and opinions towards each other. These differences were conditioned amongst other things by attitudes towards the peace treaties. The Maroons were convinced that it was they who had forced the whites into negotiations for peace. By contrast, the whites claimed that through military action and retaliation they had forced the Maroons into peace. According to the Maroons the peace treaties regulated freedom and autonomy within their own region. The whites considered the benefit of the treaties to be the prevention of renewed attacks and the reduction in numbers of new Maroons. The Maroons considered themselves entitled to the large amount of presents which were to be sent to them regularly. The white government on their part regarded the distribution of gifts as a special favour. The Maroons feared that the whites would renew hostilities and seek to re-enslave them; the colonists feared that the Maroons, either singly or together, would renew guerrilla activities and thus ruin the colony.

These differences in attitude were reflected in the enforcement of the peace treaty of 1793. As before, the Maroons had their own interpretations of the article of the treaty stipulating that they were to hand over new runaways or help the colonists to hunt them down. Although the whites wanted this provision in particular to be observed, the Maroons always reluctantly acquitted themselves of this duty.

Similar problems arose over the article requiring the Maroons to allow a number of whites or 'postholders' to live among them. Postholders, who usually consisted of a soldier and two assistants, had a far from enviable position. Most of them knew little about the Maroon societies, or their language. The position was quite ambiguous: the whites expected them to ensure that the Maroons adhered to the terms of the treaties, to hand over runaways and to report on the internal policies of the Maroons and their possible relationships with other Maroon groups. The Maroons, on the other hand, regarded them more or less as their hostages. They were fully aware of the roles of postholders in their societies, and they sought to use them as intermediaries to notify their wishes to the government. Their general distrust of the whites was expressed in their attitude towards the postholders. To be able to perform their tasks, the white officials had to be as devious as their hosts, but this was rarely achieved. The first white postholder among the Djuka was a sergeant of

German origin, named Frick, who spoke the vernacular badly, and complained about the difficulty of capturing and confining runaways. As runaways were usually armed and offered resistance to recapture, Frick wrote to the white authorities asking for more help to be sent with the regular provisions and stores. His letter ended with a pathetic cry of distress: 'I cannot believe that it is your Honours' intention to let me go to the dogs here ...'. Frick's popularity with the Maroons quickly declined and they forbade him to send any letters setting forth their wishes and complaints to Paramaribo, 'as they did not help anyway'. They eventually imprisoned him and his two soldiers, and confiscated all his possessions. Although soon released, Frick's relationship with the Maroons was intolerable and he asked to be relieved.[4] His request was granted in 1763, one year only after his appointment as postholder.

Three-quarters of a century later, relations between the whites and Maroons had hardly changed. In 1835, 1837 and 1838 peace treaties were renewed with each of the Maroon groups. The principal articles were again concerned to protect the white colony. The postholder was given more responsibility for observing the Maroons' movements and activities. But the attitudes of the parties towards each other had not changed perceptibly. The fact that part of the Djuka Maroons now chose to live periodically closer to the white plantation area in order to exchange their timber for bananas, rum and implements or to engage in smuggling with both whites and slaves, served only to enhance tensions.

The similarity of the attitudes of the postholders after 1838 to those in 1762 is shown by a letter from a postholder in 1846. Advanced in years, the writer bemoaned his fate in being 'exiled so to speak in the wilderness, among recalcitrant negroes, who are supposed to be human beings, without the solace of God's supreme guidance, left to my own resources, in an external humdrum. So consider, Honourable Sir, the unhappiness arising from this and the great suffering all this is causing a respectable, well-brought-up person'.[5] This letter shows the racial prejudice which was central to all of the whites' attitudes. Yet this same postholder lived with a black slave by whom he had a son he loved dearly, whom he manumitted and gave his own name. Even the 'enlightened' government officials, who in their dealings with the Maroons' chiefs treated them with due respect, showed similar feelings of superiority on many occasions. The Maroons for their part were convinced that the whites' way of living was a threat to their own society. It was quite obvious to them that they were superior to whites in terms of surviving and subsisting in the tropical rain forests. They had, as Price claims, 'a world view rooted in isolationism and in a belief in their moral and military superiority over whites as well as over coastal blacks, whose lack of courage they viewed with disdain'.[6]

IV

Although the French Revolution and the Napoleonic wars had some impact on the Dutch colony, the relationship between masters, slaves and Maroons hardly changed. There was some fear among the planters of an uprising among the slaves, who had been moved by the idea of freedom. But there proved to be no real cause for alarm. The fact that the treaty obligations of the whites to send gifts to the Maroons regularly were neglected strained the relations between whites and Maroons, without causing open conflict.

During the first half of the nineteenth century, however, conditions in Surinam changed considerably. External as well as internal influences brought about the necessity to re-assess colonial policies as well as the ensuing ethnic relationships. One major external factor was the prohibition of the Dutch slave-trade in 1814 and the enforcement of it by law in 1826. From then on, no new slaves were brought into Surinam, and the estimated number of slaves on plantations in the colony decreased. The abolition of slavery, first by Britain in 1833 and then by France in 1848 put increasing pressure on the Dutch authorities to follow suit. The colonists began to realise that not only would they have to treat their slaves carefully but also that in due course slavery would be abolished. In order to keep their plantation economy going, even on a much smaller scale, the planters recognised that they would need manpower, probably in the form of wage-labour. These developments brought about important changes in the whites' attitudes towards the Maroons. They came to see the large number of independent blacks in the interior as an untapped source of potential plantation hands. By 1856 they felt that the number of slave runaways had decreased substantially and that uprisings on plantations or renewed attacks from Maroons were no longer to be feared. As a result all restrictions on the movements of Maroons laid down in the treaties of 1835–8 were abolished. The Maroon chiefs were invited to Paramaribo where they were advised that the government had decided to abolish the restrictions on the movement of people and goods on the river or to Paramaribo as well as a number of military posts established to supervise these restrictions. After revealing these changes, the Governor made a formal speech to the chiefs. This speech in its pompous, paternalistic, self-righteous wording gives a clear indication of the whites' attitudes towards the Maroons. The Governor claimed that in order to

> foster the expectations that the privileges granted them by the Administration may serve as proof to them that the Administration is sincerely desirous of putting its trust in the different Maroon tribes and is well disposed towards them; that they may therefore not only abstain from any kind of behaviour by which they are likely to forfeit the Administration's trust in them, but will also constantly exert themselves to merit the Administration's satisfaction by conscientiously fulfilling all their obligations, being loyal subjects and always behaving well; that the best proof they may give of the desired attitude in order to be worthy of further favours from the Government and be able to enjoy the same rights in all respects as other free citizens will be not only their forgoing of all unacceptable behaviour and their willingness to go properly dressed, as befits civilized men and women, but also their agreeing to freely admit Christian teachers for the purpose of giving them religious instruction and, now that they are given their freedom, that they may freely offer their produce for sale, apply themselves to useful activities to a greater extent than before, and spend their gains thriftily and for useful purposes'.

The Governor for his part assured them that, if they did not disappoint those expectations, they could depend on the administration's full cooperation and willingness to further their interests. All postholders were duly informed of the new regulations, and were given their instructions accordingly.[7]

The expectations the Governor fostered were to be disappointed, however. The Government Secretary entrusted with Maroon affairs remarked in his Colonial Report of 1857 that

As first sign of the favourable influence of the new regulations on the Maroons may be noted the fact that the Aucaners [Djuka] who used to appear formerly in town almost naked, now seem to attach some importance to appearing properly dressed ... For the time being, one should not have too many illusions about their desire to work, as an attempt to employ them as labourers for the improvement of the Saramacca Canal proved a failure.

Two years later in 1859 he referred to them as 'lazy and slothful'. Pursuant to the abolition of the restrictive measures, it was resolved to stop the sending of gifts, since the Maroons would be able to provide for themselves now that they had been granted freedom of movement and offered employment opportunities. To compensate for this, it was felt that the chiefs of the different tribes should be paid a fixed allowance, but that the chiefs themselves should ask for it, so that the Maroons would regard the payment thereof as a favour.[8] The Maroons were not impressed by such suggestions. In their own society they renounced pure generosity, and although accepting that a broad ideal of mutual cooperation existed, assumed that in reality mutual help was largely impossible without payment for every service rendered. While 'the quintessence of morality is generosity', Saramacca Maroons, according to Price, 'presume that [people] are acting to assure their own short-term material gain'.[9] Understandably, therefore, the Maroon chiefs were highly suspicious of the motives of the government, sensing that its real intention was simply to profit financially from the deal.

The new regulations made very little difference to the Maroon way of life. For years they had established a pattern of migrating from the upper river to the coastal area, without paying much heed to the restrictions. The military posts at which they were supposed to report were avoided at will. They sometimes ran into trouble, especially when they came down in unusually great numbers. This happened mainly when crop failure struck their agricultural plots and famine ensued. In these circumstances, their access to the coastal area was occasionally barred by the heads of the military posts, often for days or even weeks.

As far as wage labour was concerned the Maroons simply refused even to consider working on plantations. Lumbering and river transport already formed part of their activities and they only intended to extend their work as they themselves thought fit. They were much annoyed, however, by the abolition of gifts, which they had come to regard as a type of tribute. The Paramount Chiefs continued to be favoured by payment of a salary but the chiefs of other clans who used to share in the distribution of gifts were left without compensation. Finally, although the Saramacca had been allowing Protestant missionaries in their midst since 1765, the appeal of the Governor to admit missionaries and accept 'religious instruction' was flatly refused by the Djuka.

The Governor, believing that the Boni Maroons might still be used as a source of plantation labour, moved in 1860 to recruit them. The Boni Maroons had until that year been placed under the tutelage of the Djuka, but were declared 'free' and urged to come and work in Surinam. This declaration met with little success. The Djuka refused to let the Boni leave. In any case the Boni themselves saw dealings with the French colonists as potentially much more rewarding, particularly since the abolition of slavery in 1848.

The failed attempts of the Surinam government to meddle in the lives of the Maroons, and to recruit them as plantation labour, soured relations between the Surinam authorities and the Maroons. As abolition of slavery approached in 1863, the government lost interest in the Maroons for many years to come, and turned their attention instead to rebuilding their economy by importing indentured labourers from abroad.

V

The Maroons had until the 1760s lived in a state of constant guerrilla warfare but managed nevertheless to build stable communities with an orderly structure based on their West African tribal experiences. They organised themselves into a number of separate groups along the upper courses of the Marowyne, Surinam and Saramacca rivers. Their societies were shaped by an amalgamation of various elements, as each group comprised slaves, or children of slaves, who had come from different parts of West Africa. Although historians can determine fairly accurately the tribal origins of the slaves brought from West Africa to Surinam, it is impossible to establish the tribal composition of Maroon groups. Some of the most salient features of their cultural patterns can, however, be traced to a region belonging linguistically to the West Sudanese languages. Five main groups may be distinguished: the Akan (the present-day Ghana), the Twi-Ewe (Togo), the Fon (Dahomey), the Yoruba (West Nigeria) and the Ibo group (Niger Delta).

The Surinam Maroons themselves have no written chronicle: their history has been passed down by word of mouth. Their oral tradition starts at the time of their struggle for freedom, in other words at the 'running-away time' (lonwé-ten). They know that certain of their customs, rituals and gods are of African origin, but not from which land or tribe they derive. The awareness however that Africa is the land of their forefathers has been kept alive. In the sphere of religion one can discern influences similar to those that existed in West African states: a Supreme Being, gods belonging to pantheons, special gods, ancestor worship, various forest and water gods, oracles, objects and beings invested with a magical function, priesthood, witchcraft.

The cultural pattern of the Maroons can be briefly described as follows. Everything connected with daily human existence – birth, disease, death; wealth and poverty; good and bad harvests – is closely related to the super-human world. To this world one can turn for advice. The Supreme Being, Nana Kediampon, has delegated his power to three pantheons that govern earth, air and water. Each pantheon has a chief god and a number of subsidiary gods, each of whom has a specific function. Next to the divine pantheon a second form of supernatural existence plays an important role: that of the ancestors. Through a priest they can intermediate with the gods on a person's behalf, but they can also play an independent part. Finally there are many other supernatural powers that usually have their 'abode' in trees, rivers, rocks or certain animals and who are also capable of influencing the fate of people. Happiness or misfortune is bound up with a knowledge of the wishes of these invisible and unpredictable powers. By consulting them, the priest can advise on what sacrifices to offer and what rules of conduct to follow, as well as explaining why one has failed, what has brought on the wrath of one of these powers, and how one can appease them again. The consultation is usually effected by 'conjuring up' the relevant power, that is to say, the priest – or his medium – goes into a trance with the aid of drum-beating and song, the god takes possession of him and 'speaks' through him. The priest interprets his words and passes them on to the interrogator. Another method of consultation is through an 'oracle'. This can be achieved in different ways, one of which is as follows. On a low plank a bundle is laid, made up of magical objects representing the essence of the oracle god. The plank is raised by two men, the 'bearers', and the ends are placed on their heads. Now the priest begins to ask the questions his 'patient' would like to have answered. The replies – in the form of nodding or shaking the head for yes or no, walking angrily or strutting about approvingly – are passed on by the oracle and expressed by the bearers. This form of consultation can also be used when someone has died. The body of the deceased is carried about on a plank and the priest enquires after the cause of death. Often this may be of supernatural or semi-supernatural nature. Instances of the former might include sinning against the divine laws, whilst examples of the latter would include death by 'black magic'. Many instances of misfortune, such as illness, death or crop failure are attributed to witchcraft. One may suspect a person of witchcraft, but not accuse him. Only after death, when the corpse is consulted by the priest, may the cause of death be attributed to witchcraft.

Despite the fact that the Maroon groups were originally composed of patrilineal and matrilineal groups, matrilineal structures have tended to dominate. Each group is sub-divided into a number of matrilineal, often exogamous, clans called 'lo'. The lo is composed of a number of matrilineages, the 'bére', whose size is determined by the number of relatives who regard themselves as sharing the same ancestress. In principle the members of a lo inhabit the same village. The Paramount Chief is usually chosen from one particular lo. Each lo has its own chief captain as well as captains and vice-captains or bassias. Every bére has a number of elders, who take decisions and attend meetings together with the village leaders. As a rule the election of successors takes place according to matrilineal principles.

Each village regulates the administration of everyday matters; family matters are resolved within the families concerned. The bond within the bére is strong and is shown in the general responsibility members show towards each other, and in their mutual solidarity against outsiders. The bére benefits from members' actions, but as a rule will also help to pay the fines, meet the obligations and contribute to the sacrifices imposed on one of its members.

In most cases a man has more than one wife; often the wives live in different villages along the river and with their own maternal relations. A man is allowed to have as many wives as he can support. He is expected, however, to provide each wife with a hut, a boat, domestic articles, and at regular intervals with a plot cleared in the jungle. The latter is necessary for the growing and harvesting of food crops, for which wives assume responsibility.

The administrative head of a Maroon group is the Paramount Chief, or Granman. He is assisted by a number of chief captains, each one being head of a lo; by captains or village leaders who have a number of assistant bassias; and by a group of notables who are elderly men and heads of matrilineages. Whenever religious considerations encroach on administrative matters, which is frequently the case, the priests also act as executives. The Granman is chosen from the lo and from the matrilineage of his predecessor. This also applies to captains.

The Granman's function is frequently, but not always, combined with that of High Priest. Candidates for the succession are usually trained in administrative as well as religious matters. The Granman is elected and installed by his tribe. The Surinam government officially sanctions the appointment and grants the Granman a salary. His other emoluments include a house at his residence, another in the city, an outboard motor for river transport and an official dress. The government is informed of the appointment of captains and other administrators, who also receive a salary.

For the exercise of their administrative function the notables gather in a 'krutu'. The nature and scope of the matters under discussion determine whether the meeting is held *en famille*, within the lo, in one village, in a number of villages, or at the Granman's residence. Appeals against the decisions of the krutu are possible, but only in the case of serious crimes such as murder or manslaughter is recourse had to the government in Paramaribo.

The Maroons have always satisfied their basic daily needs

by means of agriculture, hunting and fishing. What they manage to gather together in their way may be supplemented by supplies bought at small shops run by Creoles, Chinese or Maroons along the rivers or at Paramaribo. From these sources they were able to obtain salt, sugar and alcohol, particularly necessary when crop failures resulted in local food shortages. Today such demands are more readily satisfied as access to the coast has become easier since the advent of outboard motors and the construction of a number of small airfields.

The Maroons farm on land that has been cleared in the jungle. The men clear the land, felling the trees during the dry season in October and November. After the wood has been left to dry for some weeks it is burnt. Large trunks are left on the ground, branches are cleared away. The soil is not tilled until the short rainy season in December and January when the women do the planting. Various crops are planted together. The chief crop is cassava. Rice constitutes the second most important crop. Other crops include bananas and plantains, root-crops, maize, groundnuts, sugar cane, tobacco, pepper and gourds. Fruit trees are usually planted in and around the villages. The plot, planted with annuals and bi-annuals, yields all the year round, but has to be abandoned after two or three years as a result of soil exhaustion. Another reason for seeking fresh soil lies in the infestation of holdings by ants. The parasol ant (especially *atta sexdens*) attacks the crops, settles in the exploited area and infests adjacent plots. The exhaustion and infestation of holdings creates problems for Maroons for, notwithstanding the apparently immense region they have at their disposal, the area available to them for cultivation is limited. Transport problems prevent the growth of plots too far away from either dwelling places or rivers and creeks. Many Maroons are forced to pitch temporary camps at provision grounds far from their village. The choice of plots is restricted further by the method of land division: every village and every family is allocated a specific area.

Hunting and fishing are men's business. Although there are vast forests all around, the area where people hunt is confined within boundaries. Hunting is carried on with guns and hunting dogs, bought – ready trained – from Indians living further south. The unlimited shooting of game in a relatively limited region has led to a decrease in the stock of wild animals. Monkeys and leopards, wild boar, deer, rabbits, birds and reptiles are hunted. The jaguar, most snakes and the crocodile are taboo. Fishing is done with the help of traps, bow and arrow, rod and line as well as by stabbing fish with spears by lantern light or by means of poison. The last method is particularly harmful to the fish supply, since young fish are killed together with full-grown and spawning fish.

The evidence suggests that the Maroons have never been able to subsist purely on the produce of their own territory. As the supply of primary necessities is limited, they have always had to rely on their contact with the coastal area for supplementary supplies. As a result of such contacts the Maroon population, especially its male component, has remained mobile. Money for making supplementary purchases has always played a role in Maroon society. The Maroons have thus acquired a familiarity with money. Its role is small but not negligible. Payment for consultation with the oracle, village priests, funeral priests, obiamen or mediums, is made partly in trade goods such as liquor or cloth, partly in food and partly in money. If widows or spinsters require help to clear a provision ground, make a dug-out or build a hut, such assistance has to be paid for. If provision grounds yield more than is needed for one's own family, the surplus is sold. Fishermen and hunters also sell surpluses. There are no definite market-places, however; produce is sold locally to whoever wishes to buy.

As we have seen, the Maroons always kept in touch with the coastal area in order to earn money by trading, river transport and lumber-jacking. At the beginning of this century a minor but intensive goldrush occurred in the frontier area between French Guyana and Surinam. Many Maroons served as carriers of freight and labourers for the treasure hunters who had rushed to the area. This opportunity to earn money soon disappeared, however, as the yield of gold from the placers fell quickly. Up to World War II the traditional migration patterns of the Maroons remained intact as the men left the villages for varying periods in order to earn enough to buy provisions in the city before returning home and sharing them between their wives and relatives before setting out on their next journey.

Since 1945 this pattern has changed in some respects. Migrating has become much more intensive. Many more Maroons got involved in the money and labour economy of the coastal area. Although much of the work they undertook remained unskilled, possibilities for more skilled work grew. As a result of a comprehensive development plan for Surinam they began to find work in the construction of airfields, roads, in bauxite mining and the building of a hydroelectric dam. In spite of the time spent working alongside people other than their kinsmen, the Maroons do not seem to have attempted to integrate themselves into the multiracial coastal society. Integration through marrying a Creole girl is rare. And even if a Maroon does decide to settle at the coast he still keeps close ties with his kinsmen, stays in contact with his homestead, and retains habits based on Maroon religion and culture. Only recently have a small number of them received a western education. It must be said that the government and the people of the coastal area are reluctant to give the Maroons any special treatment or consideration. Housing conditions including the government's special guesthouses for Maroons are very poor indeed. They therefore prefer to rent cabins in the backyards of landlords who profit exceedingly from this arrangement. Conditions in these cabins are poor and rents are high, but the Maroons feel free to move and can choose with whom they want to share their tiny rooms.

Although the labour of Maroons is regarded highly they are treated no better and possibly worse than their co-workers. They are still considered as 'heathen', unkempt, boorish, uneducated 'bushnegroes'. There is, however, a good deal of romanticising about them: intellectual Creoles, looking for identity, find in their heroic history a source of pride. Moreover, the Creoles hold the Maroon magic in awe even though, or perhaps because, it resembles their own syncretised religious beliefs.

Growing Maroon migration to the coastal area in recent years has had consequences for Maroon village life, creating shortages of manpower for building houses and boats, for clearing agricultural plots and performing religious and political duties. The birthrate is falling and the structure of village society is threatened. This further encourages emigration. The coastal area which is already suffering from a high rate of unemployment has little to offer and more often than not the Maroons live in miserable conditions. Several plans to induce those Maroons who live in their own region to stay there and those who have migrated to return home have failed for various reasons. Only if the Maroons can be firmly convinced that their marginal society will really profit from a particular project – and it is not easy to convince them of the benefits of profound changes – will they be persuaded to take the risk of participating in it. Only then does any project have a chance of success. The Maroons are hardworking, intelligent, cooperative and inventive people if they believe in a cause and are given the correct tools.

VI

One of the reactions of blacks to their enslavement within the plantation systems of the Americas was to run away and to take to marronage. In Surinam during the era of slavery before 1863, five to ten percent of the slaves appear to have followed this course. Throughout their history the policy of the Maroons was relatively consistent. Initially they were concerned to protect their freedom and autonomy but as their numbers and military strength improved they gradually lost their fears of white reaction and suppression. Growing numbers and an associated desire for a more sedentary lifestyle led the Maroons after 1730 to seek for peace with the whites. The main aims of this policy were to protect the integrity of Maroon culture and to keep open their access to the coast for essential supplies. These objectives were largely secured by various treaties signed with the white authorities in Surinam during the century after 1760.

White policy towards the Maroons was largely dictated by the manpower needs of plantation production. Changes in these needs led white policy towards the Maroons to shift between attempts to exterminate them and, when these failed, to isolate them. Finally, as the abolition of slavery approached, efforts were made to recruit Maroons for plantation work. Self-interest disguised as morality never deceived the Maroons, however, and when their efforts to recruit Maroons as a free labour force for plantation work in the years immediately prior to the abolition of slavery in 1863 failed, the whites lost their long-standing interest in the Maroons and turned instead to the importation of indentured labour from Asia.

NOTES

1. Richard Price, *The Guiana Maroons* (Baltimore, 1976), p. 24.
2. Silvia W. de Groot, *From Isolation to Integration: the Surinam Maroons and their Colonial Rulers, 1845–1863* (The Hague, 1977), p. 11.
3. *Ibid.*, p. 12.
4. *Ibid.*, p. 15.
5. *Ibid.*, p. 28.
6. Richard Price, *Maroon Societies* (New York, 1973), p. 24.
7. de Groot, *Isolation to Integration, op. cit.*, p. 63.
8. *Ibid.*, p. 66.
9. Richard Price, *Saramacca Social Structure* (Puerto Rico, 1975), p. 32.

4

Emancipation by Law or War? Wilberforce and the 1816 Barbados Slave Rebellion

H. McD. BECKLES

Oh me good friend Mr Wilberforce make we free
God Almighty, thank ye! God Almighty thank ye!
God Almighty make we free!

Buckra in this country no make we free!
What negro to do? What negro to do?
Take force with force!
Take force with force![1]

About 8.00 p.m. on Easter Sunday, 14 April 1816, some of the slaves on the British island colony of Barbados in the West Indies made an attempt to secure their freedom by armed rebellion. The white community was shocked by the suddenness, as well as by the complex organisation, of the rebellion.[2] Barbados had not experienced any attempted slave uprising since the very minor aborted Bridgetown uprising in 1702, and the 1816 affair was the first time in the island's history that the slaves had succeeded in implementing an actual rebellion.[3] There were aborted uprisings in 1649, 1675, and 1692, but as the socially unstable frontier world of the seventeenth century receded Barbados appeared as one of the most stable slave societies in the British West Indies.

Evidence produced by the planters during their investigations into the rebellion suggested that most slaves held the opinion that Wilberforce and his fellow abolitionists were sympathetic, if not supportive, of their action to 'totally annihilate all property in the island with the lives of the white inhabitants',[4] thereby becoming 'masters instead of the slaves of the island'.[5] It is also suggested, furthermore, that Wilberforce's Parliamentary politics had created the context within which the slaves conceived their revolutionary solution to the issue of general emancipation – a popular theme of the day.[6] This paper is an attempt to identify the central features of the relationship between parliamentary reform and slave revolution. It is not intended therefore as an in-depth study of the mechanics of the rebellion but is concerned primarily with the slaves' reading of the politics of the day, both local and metropolitan, and with how they contributed to the debate concerning their freedom.

The uprising became known within the folk tradition as Bussa's Rebellion, after Bussa, an African-born slave and chief driver at Bayley, Plantation in the parish of St Philip where the revolt was initiated.[7] Captured, apparently, while leading his band of rebels against the St Philip militia and soldiers of the 1st West India (Black) Regiment, Bussa was accused of being a primary rebel leader, and was subsequently executed. Within three days the rebellion was squashed by a joint offensive of the local militia, the resident imperial troops and the left wing of the 1st West India Regiment.[8] The number of rebels killed in battle and executed during martial law totalled 'almost one thousand',[9] while only one white militiaman was killed and fewer than 50 were injured.[10] Martial law was proclaimed about 2.00a.m. on Monday, 17 April and was not lifted until 12 July. During this period close to 400 slaves were rounded up, tried and executed. In addition, some were tried and released unpunished, while others were publicly flogged and sent back to their estates. One hundred and twenty three were to be exiled to Honduras, but after much resistance from the Lieutenant-Governor of that colony were eventually sent to Sierra Leone.[11]

During the late eighteenth century Barbadian planters had developed a conception of their slaves as a rather 'non-violent' sort, prone more to running away, striking overseers or being sluggish on the job, than to armed rebellion.[12] Two weeks after the rebellion was put down, Colonel John Rycroft Best, assemblyman for Christ Church parish and commander of its militia, stated in a letter to his friend, Abel Dottin, absentee planter, that the white inhabitants were not psychologically prepared for such an occurrence as they 'never had any disturbances within the memory of the oldest inhabitant's grandfather'.[13] Some individuals, however, were not as complacent and felt that in terms of turmoil the island was more like a simmering volcano than an oasis in the West Indian desert. For example, Robert Haynes informed Thomas Lane shortly after the rebellion: 'I knew there was something brewing up in their minds, but never to the extent with which it burst forth'.[14]

The white backlash to the rebellion was extreme, and illustrative of a people unleashing their vengeance after an unexpected betrayal. In spite of President Spooner's proclamation of 16 April that it should be 'indispensable that the strictest scrutiny be observed in order to prevent persons, and particularly women and children from being implicated therein',[15] sections of the militia went on the rampage, burning slave houses, and executing blacks caught in transit – many of whom were returning to their homes having fled from the rebel bands. Robert Haynes expressed the notion of betrayal as follows:

> 'Tis impossible to restore immediately the confidence we had in our slaves. The night of the insurrection I would and did sleep with my chamber door open, and if I had possessed ten thousand pounds in my house I should not have had any more precautions, so well convinced I was of their attachment ...[16]

Blinded by a belief in the security of their rule, planters quickly dismissed any notion that the revolt was the result of their own mismanagement, economic incompetence or a lapse in their military strength. Their thoughts about the revolt were dominated by two basic ideas. The first was that it was rash and hopelessly conceived. The anonymous author of an account of the rebellion stated:

> what renders the insurrection the more extraordinary is that in no island or colony where slavery exists could such an attempt have been made with less hope of success than here. In an open country like this, almost level, without woods or fastnesses of any description, it was not possible they could make ahead for any length of time against a regular army which is constantly there and aided by a large white population to oppose them.[17]

Similarly, Governor Leith stated that the slaves in the 'wicked contest ... were without a shadow of hope that their efforts would have been successful'.[18] He thought, nonetheless, that he should threaten them in case they made another such attempt. He reminded them that he still possessed 'the most powerful means for the preservation of public tranquility', and urged them to 'save him from the painful task of using the ample powers at all times in his hands, to crush the refractory and punish the guilty'.[19]

The second planter idea about the revolt was that the slaves were among the best treated in the British West Indies, and had, therefore, no real grounds for such a violent demonstration. John Beckles, Speaker of the House of Assembly, admitted that the 'slave Laws wear a most sanguinary complexion and are a disgrace'[20] but added that the 'practice does not conform to [the] Laws ... and they are therefore in a great measure a dead letter'.[21] Furthermore, he argued, the slaves 'have comfortable houses, are well fed and clothed, have good care taken of them both in sickness and in health, and are not overworked'.[22] The Select Committee of the House of Assembly commissioned to enquire into the rebellion stated in its Report, published in January 1818, that the material-deprivation and extreme brutality theses of revolt did not apply in this instance. According to the Report,

> The year 1816 was remarkable for having yielded the most abundant returns with which Providence had ever rewarded the labours of the inhabitants of this island. The rich and extensive Parish of St Philip, in particular, is peculiarly qualified, from the nature of the soil, for the production of corn and other provisions; and the liberal allowance to the negroes, and abundant supplies in the granaries of the estates on which revolt occurred, evidently prove that the Origin of the Rebellion must be sought for in some other than in any local and peculiar cause'.[23]

Within the Report, however, there exists a thesis which it was not the intention of the commissioners to advance. By providing evidence to dispute the material-deprivation origins of the rebellion, they implied that the rebel slaves were acting, not against specific grievances, but against the entire system of slavery and white domination. Barbadian planters boasted about the ameliorations to their slave system since the mid-eighteenth century which were achieved without legislative action. They claimed that their slaves were given 'freedoms' which planters in other islands could not even dare to consider.[24] The general ability of slaves to travel the island at weekends in order to attend parties and to visit family and friends was advanced as proof of the long established mildness of slave relations in the society. So extensive were these perceived 'freedoms' that some whites identified them as the principal cause of the rebellion. The slaves, according to this view, had become accustomed to a relaxed regime, both in and out of the production process. Joseph Gittens, manager of Padmore Plantation in St Philip parish, told the investigative committee:

> Long before the insurrection, it appeared to me that the slaves were inclined to presume upon and abuse the great indulgences granted them by proprietor and overseers, such as, permitting them to have dances frequently on Saturdays and Sundays evenings, easing their burdens by the use of every species of machinery which they could effect ... all of which induced them to assume airs of importance, and put a value on themselves unknown amongst slaves of former periods.[25]

The causes of the revolt, according to the planters, originated in forces external to Barbadian slave society. The slaves were responding to the general politics of the period, characterised by the growing power of the abolitionist movement, the consolidation of the Haitian Revolution, and above all, the pressure being put to bear on the West Indian planters by the imperial government after 1815 in order to achieve general slave registration. These issues are looked at later in the essay, but first, a brief analysis of the socio-demographic context of the rebellion.[26]

The demographic profile of Barbados over the eighteenth century, when compared with that of other West Indian islands, presents considerable variation. The major differences are to be found in the size and density of the Barbadian population, differing race and sex ratios, a much higher percentage of creoles for both racial groups and greater class and status stratification, especially among the white population. As early as 1676, Barbados' population totalled 60,507 giving a density of 364 inhabitants per square mile – or one of the highest population densities in the world at that time. This pattern persisted and intensified during the eighteenth century. By 1816, the island had a density of 580 inhabitants per square mile. By contrast, Jamaica's density for 1713 was 14 persons per square mile and in 1814 was 75 persons per square mile. The high density of the Barbadian population meant that there were limited opportunities for movement on the part of the enslaved group, either as individuals or in groups. The control implied by this was heightened by the relatively large white population, which was well distributed throughout the island, as demonstrated in Tables I and II.

TABLE 1

Population of Barbados; 1715 and 1816/1817

Parish	Free-Coloureds	Black		White	
	1816	1712	1817	1715	1816
St John	100	3,937	5,469	837	1,246
St Joseph	89	2,450	3,466	969	1,124
Christ Church	82	6,979	9,915	1,913	1,618
St Michael	1,933	9,458	18,193	4,097	5,038
St Thomas	76	4,227	5,173	1,069	835
St George	94	5,508	6,762	1,108	945
St Andrew	178	3,666	3,394	925	630
St Lucy	35	2,918	5,466	1,248	1,058
St Philip	147	6,339	9,475	2,499	1,392
St Peter	240	3,784	6,230	1,447	1,379
St James	33	2,600	3,950	776	755
Totals	3,007	40,850	77,493	16,888	16,020
Percentage of total population		(70%)	(83%)	(30%)	(17%)

Sources: R.H. Schomburgk, *A History of Barbados* (London, 1971 edition), p. 82; 1715 Census of Barbados, Barbados Archives; P.R.O. CO 28/14; House of Commons Sessional Papers, 1831–32, vol. 20, pp. 519–20; Papers and Returns, 1823, pp. 34–36.

Because of the high proportion of whites in Barbadian society, effective monitoring and control of the black population was achieved more readily than elsewhere in the English-speaking Caribbean, and the 'garrison mentality' so common to West Indian whites was muted in Barbados; more paranoia was shown in the immediate pre-1816 period at the possibility of a French invasion than the likelihood of a slave revolt. Equally important was the fact that the sexes were evenly balanced for

TABLE 2

Ratio of Blacks to Whites: Barbados 1712–1817

	1712/15	1816/17
St John	4.7:1	4.3:1
St Joseph	2.5:1	3.0:1
Christ Church	3.7:1	6.0:1
St Michael	2.3:1	3.6:1
St Thomas	3.9:1	6.2:1
St George	4.9:1	7.1:1
St Andrew	4.0:1	5.3:1
St Lucy	2.3:1	5.1:1
St Philip	2.5:1	6.8:1
St Peter	2.6:1	4.5:1
St James	3.4:1	5.2:1
Totals	2.4:1	4.8:1

1712/15 Ratio of total blacks to whites – 2.42:1
1816/17 Ratio of total blacks to whites – 4.80:1

Sources: As Table 1

both racial groups, with a slight preponderance of women in both groups. As early as 1676, of the total slave population of 32,467, some 16,121 were females and 16,346 were males. Similarly, Handler and Lange have reported that 'islandwide figures indicated a distribution of 46 per cent males and 54 per cent females during the pre-emancipation decades of the nineteenth century'.[27] For the white population the 1715 census shows that 51.3 per cent were female and 48.7 per cent male and this ratio remained steady into the nineteenth century.

The impact of these sex ratios on the development of Barbadian society was striking. The family structures of both groups were enhanced, thus leading to greater social stability. But more important was the rapid growth of the Barbadian creole population. The first thorough census of the slave population, taken in 1817, shows that only seven per cent of the slaves were African-born. This is a remarkably low percentage and contrasts markedly with figures of 37 per cent African-born for Jamaica and 44 per cent for Trinidad.[28] The exact figures for the Barbadian slave population in 1817 were creoles born in other islands, 345; Barbadian-born creoles, 71,725; and African-born slaves 5,423.[29]

Another factor which operated as a device of socio-political control of the slave population was the presence of a large number of pro-slavery poor whites on the island. In excess of 50 per cent of the island's white population could be classified as poor white. The better placed of these possessed small units of land, on which they cultivated market gardening produce, and some had marketable artisan skills such as cobbling and tailoring. Others were employed as militia tenants on plantations. The role of the poor whites in Barbadian society was essentially that of a buffer group between the planter, merchant and professional white classes on the island and the enslaved population. It was the poor white group which was on most intimate terms with the slaves, frequently living in close proximity to them and in similar housing. Their relationship with the slaves was generally a very ambiguous one; they acted as receivers of stolen goods, on thc one hand, and on the other were employed by the authorities as slave catchers.[30]

The whites were confident that their military power was sufficient to ensure social stability. They had the comfort of knowing that permanently resident on the island were imperial troops stationed at the St Ann's Garrison. In addition, by 1816, there were just under 4,000 members of the island's militia. In 1812, a militia bill was passed which required all white and free coloured men between the ages of 16 and 60 years of age to enrol.[31] White Barbadians felt that in a flat and open country the movements of the militia would be swift, and that the slaves knew this. The ability of the militia to move quickly to various points on the island in response to any disorder would have certainly complicated plans for overt slave rebellion. The image that emerges therefore of Barbados in the early nineteenth century is one of tight control, arising from the island's physical landscape features and patterns of human settlement.

The rebellion, according to the Assembly's Report, had reduced the island to a 'period of anarchy', and 'in its ulterior consequences ... [gave] a rude shock to the whole system of colonisation in the West Indies'.[32] It commenced on two adjoining plantations, Bayley's and Wiltshire's, both owned by the Reverend Alexander Scott, located in the south-eastern parish of St Philip. It quickly spread throughout the southern and central parishes of Christ Church, St Thomas, St George and

St John. Small skirmishes also occurred in the northern parish of St Lucy but no violent clashes were recorded for the parishes of St Peter, St Andrew and St James. The news of the rebellion reached Bridgetown about 2.00 a.m. on Monday, 17 April. By 6.30 a.m. the various militia regiments were assembled, and together with the imperial troops, began to march into the parishes of St Philip and Christ Church – the heart of the revolt – at about 8.30 a.m. By this time, rebel groups were scattered throughout most parts of these parishes and were implementing a policy of property destruction; 'great houses', mills, barns and other buildings were burnt and looted, as planters rushed their wives and children into nearby forts for protection.[33]

The first major clash between the rebels and the militia took place about 10.00 a.m. at Lowther's Plantation in Christ Church. Here, the Christ Church batallion, led by Colonel John Rycroft Best, attacked the rebels, killing 30 before noon and forcing them to scatter in different directions. In the pursuit another ten were killed the following day.[34] Colonel Eversley, Commander of the St Philip parish militia, also killed and wounded several rebels, taking some 200 captive. Colonel Codd, Commander of the imperial troops, led his men against rebel bands at Sandford's Plantation and at The Thickett in St Philip's parish. He took many captives, some of whom were quickly tried and executed. The one white man who was shot dead in battle was named Brewster and was a private in the militia. He was caught in the cross-fire between rebels and the St Michael militia at Sandford Plantation. The defeat of the slaves at Lowther's in Christ Church, and then at Bayley's, Golden Grove, and The Thickett in St Philip's broke the spine of the revolt. By Tuesday night, 18 April, the slaves were virtually defeated, and the militia were in effective control of the southern parishes.[35]

The rebels, militarily ill-equipped to challenge the militia forces directly, resorted to arson as the most effective method of destroying or undermining the planters. The revolt was timed to coincide with the peak of the harvest season, and 20 per cent of the canes in the island were burnt.[36] In traditional agricultural societies, where the bulk of farmers' capital stock was tied up in, or maintained by the existing crop, arsonist tactics were effective in weakening their economic base, upon which their socio-political hegemony rested. Eliza Fenwick, Barbados school teacher, stated that the rebellion ruined many planters, many of whom could no longer pay their children's school fees, which resulted in her school suffering a 25 per cent loss of income.[37]

There is no evidence to suggest that the revolt had one central leader; each plantation involved had its rebel contingent, and the leaders of these groups met frequently to discuss strategy. Jackey, the head-driver at Simmons' Plantation, seemed to have been largely responsible for organising these various plantation groups. He held frequent meetings with the leaders from Gittens', Byde Hall, Nightengale, Congor Road, and Sunberry plantations and at the same time kept Bussa at Bayley's informed.[38] The frequency of these meetings increased in February and March, and the final session was held on Good Friday night at the River Plantation under the cover of a dance.[39]

At Bayley's Plantation, the leading rebels were Bussa (the driver), King Wiltshire (a carpenter), Dick Bailey (a mason), Johnny (the Standard Bearer), and Johnny Cooper (a cooper). At Simmons' Plantation, where much of the planning took place, the leading organisers were Jackey, John, and the admirer of the Haitian Revolution, Nanny Grigg. Much of the politicisation of this cellular planning was done by three free coloured men, Cain Davis, Roach and John Sarjeant. It seems to have been the general agreement that, if the rebellion was successful, Washington Francklyn, a free coloured man, was to be made Governor of Barbados, and was to reside at Pilgrims, the residence of the then Governor.[40]

These organisers of revolution were mostly elite slaves and free coloured men who had greater freedom of movement than most of the coloured population. They were clearly an elite in the slave community in every sense; their material living standards were superior to those of the field slaves; some were literate; and a few owned considerable property and had respected family relations. The four free coloured men, by throwing their support behind the slaves, had moved against their own social group, which was commended by the Assembly for its firm pro-planter stance during the Rebellion. Roach, Sarjeant, and Davis were either killed in battle or executed, while Francklyn was hanged after a court martial found him guilty, not of insurrection, but of inciting others to revolt.[41]

Colonel Best stated that the reason why so many rebels were executed in 1816 was that most of them appeared to have been leaders. In both the 1675 and the 1692 aborted rebellions, no one individual had emerged as the central leader. Cuffee was to be crowned king of Barbados in the 1692 revolutionary plans, and Francklyn made Governor in the 1816 plans, yet on neither of these occasions is there any evidence of these men being either planners of rebellion or military leaders of a rebel group.[42] In each of the three rebellions a number of individuals were identified as 'leaders', suggesting possibly a collective approach to 'revolutionary' leadership.

The Assembly's Report reflected the general opinions of the wider white community by locating the origins of the rebellion within the politics of the time, particularly the impact upon the slaves of propaganda emanating from Wilberforce and the African Institute. Wilberforce was accused by members of the Assembly of having agents and 'spies' in Barbados, who had informed the slave leaders that the process leading to their legal freedom had been obstructed after 1807 by the local planter class, and it was up to them to exert pressure from their end. It was during the debate over the Registry Bill of 1815 that white Barbadians launched their full attack upon the abolitionist movement.

Founded in 1807, the African Institute had among its patrons George Canning, William Wilberforce, Thomas Clarkson and Zachary Macaulay. Alarmed by the illegal importation of slaves into the English colonies after 1808, the Institute called for the total registration of all slaves in those colonies. Noting that the slave population of Trinidad had increased by 4,440 between 1810 and 1813, the result of large scale illegal slave trading, Wilberforce presented a Bill in the Commons in June 1815, calling for total slave registration.[43]

Barbados planters objected strongly to Wilberforce's proposal, arguing that it was merely another step in his programme of gradual slave emancipation. The registration issue was introduced into the Assembly by John Beckles, the Speaker of the House, on 14 November 1815. The ensuing debate was heated and abusive of the abolitionists' lobby in Whitehall. Wilberforce was identified as an ardent enemy of the West India interest, with a special disrespect for the Barbadian planter-class.

While the Assembly accused the African Institute of informing the slaves that registration was the first step in the process leading to full emancipation, the latter accused the former of making the connection during their unintelligent Assembly debates which were carried in local papers and read by the many literate slaves on the island. The Report of the Assembly stated that 'towards the latter end of 1815, a report became generally prevalent among the slaves of this island, that the benefits of freedom would probably be extended to them, through the interposition of the friends of the Blacks, in England ...'[44] Furthermore, the Report stated, the rebellion originated

> solely and entirely in consequence of the intelligence imparted to the slaves (which intelligence was obtained from the English News papers), that their freedom had been granted them in England ... that these reports first took their rise immediately after the information of the proposed establishment of Registries in the British Settlements in the West Indies ... and in the mistaken idea that the Registry Bill was actually their Manumission ...; these hopes were strengthened and kept alive by the promises held out, that a party in England, and particularly Mr Wilberforce ... were exerting themselves to ameliorate their condition, and ultimately effect their emancipation.[45]

An anonymous planter, referring to Wilberforce and other members of the African Institute as a 'dangerous crew', wrote a letter to the *Barbados Mercury and Bridgetown Gazette*, stating that they 'have pierced the inmost recesses of our island, inflicted deep and deadly wounds in the minds of the black population, and engendered the Hydra, Rebellion, which had well nigh deluged our fields with blood'.[46] *The Times* suggested that the Rebellion was due primarily to the 'impolite' and thoughtless interference of Wilberforce in the political business of the Barbadian planters. Furthermore, it suggested:

> the principal instigators of this insurrection, who are negroes of the worst dispositions, but superior understanding, and some of whom can read and write, availed themselves of this parliamentary interference, and the public anxiety it occasioned, to instill into the minds of the slaves generally a belief that they were already freed by the King and Parliament ...[47]

Evidence of Wilberforce's commitment to the gradual dismantling of the West Indian slave system was seen, according to the Assembly, in his association with the cause and interest of King Henry of Haiti. This angered white Barbadians, particularly John Beckles. During the debate over the Registry Bill in the House, Beckles stated, 'I must confess that I was one of the many who at one time had the highest opinion of Mr Wilberforce, and gave him the highest credit for the purity of his motives and intentions, but that is past'.[48] This is not surprising, since Beckles was favourable to the abolition of the slave trade, though not slavery. He stated on more than one occasion that Barbados would be much better off without that trade as it would injure the other competitive colonies, which unlike Barbados, were not overstocked with a self-reproductive slave force, thus giving Barbados the advantage on the London sugar market.

When Wilberforce chaired a meeting at Free Mason Hall, London, in early 1817, where he allegedly drank a toast to the health of 'King Henry of Haiti', Beckles read this as proof of his commitment to the proliferation of Black Republics in the Caribbean, and felt that he and his friends were a 'fanatical sect' to be 'kept a watchful eye over' by the British Government.[49] In view of the evidence that rebel slaves in Barbados made several references to the example set by the Haitian Revolution, that the local police arrested as a revolutionary emissary of King Henry a free coloured man, Loveloss Overton, trumpeter in the King's Dragoon Guards, who landed for a 24 hour stay in Barbados on 20 February 1817, and that rumours circulated in Barbados to the effect that Haitian soldiers were coming to assist the slaves, the content of Beckles' speech in the Assembly is critical for an understanding of how the planters perceived slave rebellions in the period.[50] Beckles asked the Assembly, in reference to the Free Mason Hall meeting,

> is it not astonishing that, in the very heart of London, in so public a meeting, any man, and especially a man holding a place under Government, should have been permitted, with impunity, to declare that King Henry of Hayti, was one of the most august sovereigns in the universe, and derived his title from a more legitimate source than the monarchs of Europe, having been raised to the throne from the abject condition of a slave ... and to predict that he was the glorious founder of a new dynasty, which would in no distant time subvert the relations of the western world ...?[51]

Wilberforce was not silent during these attacks. He frequently defended his firm commitment to anti-slavery, and the slaves knew this. He was, in addition, a tactical politician, and the cleverness of his campaign was not always fully grasped by either the planters or their slaves. In a letter to James Stephen in January 1817, he stated,

> as long ago as in 1781, the very first year of my being in parliament, and when I was only twenty-two years of age, I wrote ... expressing my hopes that sometime or another I might become the instrument of breaking, or at least easing the yoke of these poor creatures – the West Indian slaves.[52]

The slaves were informed, though not always correctly, about the content of Wilberforce's speeches, and no doubt linked his support of the Haitian Declaration of Independence in 1804 with a report which was published in a local newspaper the following year. The report stated:

> It now seems beyond all doubt that ... St Domingo ... that ill-fated country ... has again become the theatre of massacre and bloodshed, and the last remnants of French power almost completely overthrown.[53]

News of the Barbados rebellion reached Parliament during the debate concerning the tactics necessary to secure the Spanish abolition of the slave trade to the New World. Wilberforce considered the planters wholly responsible for the rebellion. It was their propaganda, he stated, which created the basis of information upon which the slaves acted. In a letter to Babington of 7 June 1816, he stated that from the earliest abolitionist efforts Barbadian planters kept clamouring that it

> is emancipation you mean, you mean to make our slaves free, we all the time denying it. At length, wonderful that not before – the slaves themselves begin to believe it, and to take measures for securing the privilege; in short the artillery they had loaded so high against us, burst among themselves, and they impute to us the loading and pointing of it.[54]

On his receipt of the content of Beckles' speech, Wilberforce wrote to Stephen: 'the Speaker of the House of Assembly at Barbados has made a very scurrilous speech and says he always thought you a dangerous man'.[55]

Such then was the nature of the debate being conducted in Barbados and London in relation to the Registry Bill and abolition, to which the slaves were privy by means of newspaper summaries and their own information networks. They understood, even if crudely, the political crisis confronting the planter class, the political significance of the Black Republic of Haiti, the power of Wilberforce and other abolitionists in Parliament, and more importantly, their own strength. The planter class was asserting its power through all its agencies, colonial and metropolitan; the abolitionists were directing pressure upon every quarter of the planters' world; the slaves meanwhile were analysing these developments, and began to make plans for the securing of their freedom by armed rebellion.

By January 1816, the leaders of the rebellion who, according to the Assembly, 'had gained an ascendency over their fellows by being enabled to read and write',[56] had obtained a reasonable amount of information concerning the political situation both in Barbados and the London West India community. This information was obtained from both local and British newspapers, which were read throughout the slave communities by the 'literate few'. For example, in the confessions of Robert, a slave rebel from Simmons' Plantation, it is stated that Nanny Grigg, a domestic slave on the plantation, frequently read British and local papers, and informed other slaves about developments in Haiti and in the metropolis. Her conclusion was that if freedom was to be obtained, they would have to 'fight for it, otherwise they would not get it, and the way they were to do, was to set fire, as that was the way they did it in Saint Domingo'.[57] Daniel, a slave from the River Plantation, where Bussa had met Jackey, Davis and Sarjeant, on Good Friday night, confessed that Davis had informed him and others that the British papers carried reports to the effect that 'Mr Wilberforce had sent out to have them all freed, but that the inhabitants of the island were against it ... and that they must fight for it'.[58]

Scholarly interpretations of the rebellion, nonetheless, have tended, with varying degrees of modifications, to accept most of the planter-elite views as presented in the Assembly's Report. Watson, whilst being critical of the planters' handling of the registration crisis, accepted the view that the origins of the rebellion lay within that crisis. He suggested that the planters' 'over reaction' to the Bill confirmed in the slaves' minds the view that it was of critical importance, thus making implicit the notion that registration was a 'prelude to emancipation'.[59] In addition, Watson suggested, the rebellion must be seen largely as the result of 'rising expectations unfulfilled'.[60]

There is, however, no independent evidence to support the Assembly's and Watson's thesis. Looked at closely, this thesis turns out to be largely part of the propaganda package which was used admirably by Barbadian whites against the metropolitan abolitionist lobby. The point which was made by the Assembly on this occasion was that slave unrest was primarily a result of uninformed metropolitan interference in local politics. In addition, the thesis denies the intellectual ability of slaves to comprehend effectively the political processes of the time, and suggests that the rebellion was an impulsive, if not primitive response on the part of the slaves to chronic psychological deflation. That is, having been led to believe that registration was really the political foreplay to emancipation, the slaves responded spontaneously with violence when they realised that this was not so.

Michael Craton's analysis of the rebellion is based on wider research and is presented in a more sophisticated manner. He refers to the organisational brilliance of the elite slaves, some of whom were literate and well-informed, who used the registration crisis of 1815–16 as a propaganda tool in order to mobilise the masses of slaves to revolt.[61] One can only deduce that by such political action, the slaves' intention was to focus metropolitan attention upon the colony, defeat the planters' assumption that the revolt could not be motivated by internal forces, and hopefully gain Parliamentary support for general emancipation. An element of this hypothesis is also to be found in the Assembly's Report, where it is stated that it was the few elite slaves who deliberately misinformed and misled the mass of the slave population. In assessing the impact of slave rebellion upon emancipation Craton approaches the issues with much caution. Looking at the Barbados, Demerara and Jamaica revolts of 1816, 1823, and 1831 respectively, he suggests that in themselves they did not gain the slaves their freedom, but what they illustrated was that West Indian slaves were no longer prepared to accept slave relations, and would not make efficient workers while slavery lasted. The implication was that the West

Indian slave system was after 1815 characterised by a matured political crisis, and that only extreme suppression could hold it intact.

Both the planters and their metropolitan critics denied the ability of the slaves to understand the changing nature of the West Indian experience, and to develop their own strategies based upon reasonably clear analyses of these changes. Yet, the Barbados rebellion was characterised by the mobilisation of most social force available to the slaves, both local and foreign. In terms of the social origins of participants it was probably the most complex of all British West Indian rebellions. Among the organisers were creole women, such as Nanny Grigg, skilled male creole slaves such as Jackey and John Barnes, African born skilled slaves such as Bussa and Numa, free coloured persons such as Sarjeant, Roach and Davis, an educated and propertied free coloured man, in the case of Washington Francklyn, and hundreds of 'unknown' slaves. The level of political mobilisation necessary to bring these people together in order to plan revolution could not be achieved by individuals, the generality of whom were 'wretchedly low in information and intellect'.[62] Since the seventeenth century, Barbados slaves had been organising revolutionary politics with a high level of sophistication. The abortive 1692 Barbados rebellion, for example, was skilfully organised by elite slaves, and involved as remote an element as a contingent of six Irishmen, illustrating their ability to perceive and exploit divisions within the white community in order to further their own political objectives.[63]

In spite of the planters' assertions, the rebellion was not particularly sudden. Since the beginning of the nineteenth century the slaves of Barbados had been unusually restless. Eliza Fenwick identified, in reference to domestic and skilled slaves, an embryonic management crisis between 1812 and 1815, the result of an open form of passive resistance and virtual non-cooperation.[64] The success of the abolition movement in 1807 had correctly informed the slaves that public opinion in Britain was growing increasingly critical of the West Indian planters and their slave systems. This, along with growing recognition of the Haitian Republic in respectable parts of British society, created a psychological profile amongst West Indian slaves in the second decade of the nineteenth century which was drastically different from that of the late eighteenth century.

The growth in the political confidence of Barbadian slaves in relation to planter authority after 1800 was reflected in the rapid increase in the number of slaves imprisoned and executed for individual acts of hostility towards whites and attempted marronage. Between January 1812 and April 1816, the names of over 300 slaves are listed in the *Barbados Mercury and Bridgetown Gazette* (hereafter *Gazette*) as captured runaways.[65] This figure is not the total number of runaways, since many were never reported. This evidence suggests that there was an upsurge of attempted marronage in the few years prior to 1816. The available data show that the number of runaway slaves during these four and a quarter years probably exceeded the total number for the entire eighteenth century. There is a predominance of males in the lists of runaways. Less than 25 per cent of the captives were female. What is particularly important is the large number of skilled and elite slaves adopting this method of resistance. These were the slaves upon whom the planters relied to manage and advance the plantation. They were also closer to 'freedom' as a social condition, and were better informed, largely because many of them were literate. These were the slaves who had more time and space to plan rebellion. The first two decades of the nineteenth century were characterised by their general restlessness and deep concern with the issue of general emancipation. Many were executed for running away. Large numbers were also sent to the Bridgetown cage to be locked away by the constables for refusing to work and for being hostile to managers and their owners.[66]

Advertisements for runaway slaves generally gave much detail. For example, an advertisement appeared in the *Gazette* of 13 January 1816 for Ben Stuart, a runaway mulatto carpenter, 'who looks very much like a white man with light straight hair and grey eyes'.[67] On 6 May 1815 the paper carried an advertisement for Joe, a runaway fisherman, described as popularly known in the parishes of St Thomas and Christ Church and in Bridgetown.[68] A week later, a remarkable advertisement appeared for a runaway twenty-three year old 'yellow skinn woman' named Molly, described as 'pleasing in countenance, dresses very tastily, and of course fashionably, known universally in Bridgetown and its vicinity'.[69] On 20 May 1815, an advertisement appeared for April, a runaway man who 'has a very English Tongue'.[70] For the first time since the late seventeenth century, emancipation by revolution was seen by the slave elite as a concrete possibility; this was a radical departure from the 'reformist' politics into which the slaves were forced in the eighteenth century. Political crises were now clearly visible in the West Indian slave system, and elite slaves were ready to exploit them.

The African Institute did not support the rebellion, and was as 'racist' in its views of the slaves as the planter–assemblymen. Neither did King Henry of Haiti express any specific concern for assisting the rebellion. The document of the African Institute on the rebellion, published in 1816, stated the following:

> If we suppose the generality of the slaves so wretchedly low in information and intellect, as not to perceive the insanity of such an enterprise, how can we believe that they should have acted on a speculation respecting the effects of the interference of the British Parliament with colonial legislation? If, on the other hand, we assume that they were misled by artful leaders, is it credible, that those leaders would have chosen such a time and place for such a project ...?[71]

In relation to the rebellion, and other forms of unrest in the West Indies, King Henry declared that: 'Since the first Declaration of our Independence, the maxim of the government which preceded mine, as well as my own, has been not to interfere with the internal affairs of our neighbours'.[72] By this he meant, of course, that his political ideology was 'revolution in one country' which was not to encourage slave rebellions in the neighbouring British, French and Spanish colonies. But from the point of view of the Barbados rebel leaders this policy was of little significance, since local political conditions seemed set for rebellion, and they were prepared to act.

Colonel Best had changed his views of the rebellion by September 1816, and became critical of the analysis presented in the Assembly's Report. According to Best, the slaves were neither misled by artful leaders, nor driven to rebellion through any misreading of the Registry Bill debate. They were acting on an informed view that they could defeat the whites at this particular juncture, and take effective control over their destinies and the government of the island. The registration crisis which was consuming the political energies of the planters, while at the same time hardening metropolitan views against them, together with the intensity of that year's Easter celebrations, merely provided the climate for the politics of rebellion. After interrogating slave rebels as late as August 1816 Best had accumulated data supportive of his changed analysis of the rebellion. He wrote, 'I once thought before, I am now convinced that they were not entirely if at all led away in the last business by delusion. They conceived themselves to be sufficiently numerous to become masters instead of slaves of the island, and that opinion influenced them into Acts of Rebellion'.[73]

The rebellion was characterised by four critical organisational shortcomings. Firstly, it was two days premature; the armed conflict with the militia was planned for Wednesday 17 April, not Monday 15 April.[74] Only the slaves in the southern parishes were able in parts to regroup and adjust to the sudden developments. The slaves in the north responded spasmodically, while those in the western and eastern parishes, St James, St Andrew and St Peter, were not involved in any violent clashes with the militia, though several of them were arrested, tried and executed for participating in rioting, looting and arson. The premature outbreak threw the rebels into disarray, and ensured chaos at the levels of strategy and logistics.

Secondly, the refusal of the 3,000 free people of colour to join the rebellion, in spite of the involvement of Roach, Sarjeant, Davis, and the apparent commitment of Francklyn, represented a significant loss to the slave struggle. During the Haitian Revolution, and the Fedon uprising in Grenada in 1795–96, the free coloured played critical roles in the organisation of popular anti-planter sentiments. In Barbados, the bulk of them threw their firm support behind the whites. On the whole, the slave rebels did not expect their loyalty to be otherwise. The Speaker of the House stated in January 1817 that this oppressed class [free coloureds] had always made 'their complaints ... in respectful language and in terms of moderation, and whenever opportunities have offered they manifested a determination to do their duty by the country, and a devotion to the interest of the whites'.[75] On this issue, Colonel Best noted that 'some have been of opinion, in the event, of rebellion, they would be the first involved, and would take the lead in opposition to the white inhabitants. I have invariably expressed my confidence in them, and never doubted ... they would be faithful to us'.[76] For their loyalty, the Assembly rewarded them with an extension of their civil rights.

The slaves had made similar analyses of the free coloured people's political commitments and were putting severe pressure on them before the rebellion was initiated. For example, Jacob Belgrave, the mulatto owner of the Ruby Plantation in St Philip, stated before the Assembly committee, that in December 1815, he was subject to much verbal abuse by slaves who were of the opinion that he was one of the many propertied men obstructing the progress toward constitutional emancipation. Also, that on Good Friday, 12 April 1816, on his way to town, he was abused by a black woman who made similar statements. Not surprisingly, during the rebellion, Belgrave was singled out for special treatment. His estate was attacked and extensively damaged; property destruction was estimated at £6,720, the third highest in the island out of a total of 184 damaged estates.[77]

Thirdly, the inability of the rebels to secure sufficient arms weakened their resistance to the militia. Rumours concerning the rebels' raid upon the St Philip's militia's arms storeroom have not been verified. The data show that in clashes with the armed forces, the rebels were generally armed with swords and cutlasses, as well as agricultural implements such as pitchforks. The militia were able to attack with confidence and efficiency, and dispersed rebel regiments whenever confrontations occurred. For example, during the battle at Lowther's Plantation on Monday morning, 15 April, Colonel Best, Commander of the Christ Church Militia, stated that his troops were

> too anxious, and began to fire while I was leading them close up, which it was my object to do before I gave word 'fire'. One negro was brandishing his sword which my soldiers could not witness without endeavouring to knock him over; others were armed with pitchforks, on seeing which the militia commenced firing on the irregular line the rebels had formed. They gave way immediately and we pursued and killed some.[78]

The rebel leaders were generally well armed, but the rank and file were usually unable to secure muskets. King William, the leader of the rebel band from Sunberry Plantation, was seen armed with a musket. So too was Toby, the leader of the band from Chapel Plantation, and a few others.[80]

Fourthly, the inability of the rebel leaders and organisers to secure, probably as a result of the premature uprising, the continuous support of the majority of the slaves allowed the militia to operate with great efficiency. Even in St Philip's parish where the rebels were in need of solid support commitment was scanty. At Lowther's Plantation in Christ Church parish the rebel leaders got full support from 'every negro belonging to the plantation'[80] but at the neighbouring Coverly Plantation the slaves watched passively as the Christ Church militia passed through the estate in pursuit of the fleeing Lowther rebels.[81] At Bayley's, Golden Grove and Wiltshire's, a good turn-out resulted in protracted fighting. It was during the battle at Golden Grove that two men from the West Indian regiment were shot dead. At Simmons' Plantation, the rebels, in spite of the presence of Jackey, got little support from the mass of slaves. These slaves had to be bullied and threatened before they assisted the rebels. It was only after King William, head of the Sunberry Plantation rebels, Little Sambo, head of The Adventure Plantation rebels, Charles, head of the Sandford Plantation rebels and Thomas, head of the Congor Road Plantation rebels arrived at Simmons' and ordered the slaves there at gunpoint to destroy all buildings, mills, barns, and to burn the canes, that these slaves got into the rebellion. Armed with guns, Toby and Charles threatened to shoot anyone who did not join the rebellion.[82] By this means, Simmons' estate was greatly damaged. However, when the militia arrived there, these slaves ran into their huts, and other places of shelter, and did not assist the rebels in combat. As a result of this disunity, the militia were able to defeat rebel contingents in every encounter.

In spite of these failings, however, and the widespread success of the militia, incalculable damage was done to white ruling class society. It is not enough to argue that since only one militiaman was killed in combat, and £175,000 of property destroyed, damage to the social order was minimal. Mrs Fenwick opens up a new avenue for investigation in her comment that 'many gentlemen lost their lives from the fatigues of the insurrection'.[83] Perhaps the greatest damage done was to the confidence and psychological well-being of the ruling class, in realising that their slaves were determined to overthrow them by violent revolution and to take control of the island. By their act of rebellion, the slaves of Barbados demonstrated that in spite of the abolitionist drive of Wilberforce and his colleagues, for which they were highly praised, they did not see reformist politics alone as sufficient to bring about their freedom. The rebellion was their contribution to the debate over slavery and freedom. Their intentions were clearly expressed. At that juncture revolution was their preferred instrument for the abolition of slavery.

NOTES

1. See Mathew 'Monk' Lewis, *Journal of a West Indian Proprietor, kept During a Residence in the Island of Jamaica* (London, 1834), p. 228. See also Michael Craton, 'The Passion to Exist: Slave Rebellions in the British West Indies 1650–1832', *Journal of Caribbean History*, 13 (1980), p. 12; Michael Craton, 'Proto-Peasant Revolts? The Late Slave Rebellions in the British West Indies, 1816–1832', *Past and Present*, 85 (1979), p. 119.
2. *The Report from a Select Committee of the House of Assembly Appointed to Inquire into the Origins, Causes, and Progress of the Late Insurrection – April 1816* (Barbados, 1818), p. A (hereinafter referred to as *The Report*).
3. See H. McD. Beckles, 'Rebels without Heroes: Slave Politics in Seventeenth Century Barbados', unpublished paper presented at the 14th Conference of Caribbean Historians, April 1982, and published in *The Journal of Caribbean History*, 18, no. 2 (1983). See also Jerome Handler, 'Slave Revolts and Conspiracies in Seventeenth-Century Barbados', *New West Indian Guide*, 52 (1982), p. 5.
4. P.R.O. Colonial Office series, CO 28/85, ff. 11–14, 25 April 1816, Colonel Codd to Governor James Leith.
5. New York Public Library (hereafter N.Y.P.L.), Mss. Division, 28 Sept. 1816, Colonel Best to Abel Rous.
6. *The Report*, pp. 12–13.
7. See three articles by a local historian, H. A. Vaughan, 'Joseph Pitt Washington Francklyn, 1782–1816', *The Democrat*, 18, 23 Dec. 1970, 8 Jan. 1971.
8. *The Report*, pp. 4–6. See also President Spooner's proclamation, 18 April 1816 in *Barbados Mercury and Bridgetown Gazette*.
9. Anon., 'An Account of the late Negro Insurrection which took place in the Island of Barbados on Easter Sunday, 14 April 1816', N.Y.P.L., Mss. Division.
10. 27 April 1816, Colonel John Rycroft Best to Abel Dottin, N.Y.P.L., Mss. Division; *The Report*, pp. 5–24.
11. See *The Report*, op. cit.; Claude Levy, 'Slavery and the Emancipation Movement in Barbados, 1650–1833', *Journal of Negro History*, 58 (1970), pp. 1–12. See also a series of articles on slavery in Barbados by Edward Stoute in *Barbados Daily News*, 4, 11, 18 Sept., 9, 30 Oct., 20, 27 Nov., 11 Dec. 1961.
12. H. McD. Beckles and K. Watson, 'Concessionary Politics: Slave Resistance in Eighteenth Century Barbados', unpublished paper; K. Watson, *The Civilised Island: Barbados. A Social History, 1750–1816* (Barbados, 1979), pp. 125–43.
13. 27 April 1816, Colonel Best and Abel Dottin, N.Y.P.L., Mss. Division.
14. 23 Sept. 1816, Robert Haynes to Thomas Lane. Newton Estate Papers, 523/781,

Senate House Library, London. See also Watson, *Civilised Island, op. cit.*, p. 132.

15. *Barbados Mercury and Bridgetown Gazette* (hereafter *Gazette*) 18 April 1816.
16. 23 Sept. 1816, Robert Haynes to Thomas Lane, Newton Estate papers, 523/781, Senate House Library, London.
17. Anon, 'An Account of the Insurrection', N.Y.P.L., Mss. Division.
18. Address to the slave population of the island of Barbados by Governor Leith, 23 April 1816, in *Gazette*, 26 April 1816.
19. *Ibid.*
20. Minutes of the House of Assembly of Barbados, 7 Jan. 1817, Barbados Archives. See also *Gazette*, 30 March 1816.
21. *Gazette*, 30 March 1816.
22. *Ibid.*
23. *The Report*, p. 15.
24. This subject is looked at in Beckles and Watson, 'Concessionary Politics', *op. cit.*
25. *The Report*, pp. 46–7.
26. Most of the following demographic data are from Beckles and Watson, 'Concessionary Politics', *op. cit.*, and Watson, *The Civilised Island, op. cit.*
27. J.S. Handler and F.W. Lange, *Plantation Slavery in Barbados: an Archaeological and Historical Investigation* (Cambridge, Mass., 1978), pp. 67–8.
28. *Ibid.*, pp. 67–71.
29. CO 28/72, Barbados Census, 1817.
30. See Jill Sheppard, *The Redlegs of Barbados: Their Origins and History* (N.Y., 1977); H. McD. Beckles, 'Land Distribution and Class Formation, 1630–1750: The Rise of a Wage Proletariat in Barbados', *Journal of the Barbados Museum and Historical Society*, 36 (1980), pp. 136–44.
31. R.H. Schomburgk, *A History of Barbados* (London, 1971 edition), p. 190.
32. *The Report*, pp. 3–4.
33. 27 April 1816, Colonel Best to Abel Rous, N.Y.P.L., Mss. Division.
34. House of Assembly minutes on the performance of Colonel Best in *Gazette*, 3 Sept. 1816; 27 April 1816, Colonel Best to Abel Dottin, N.Y.P.L., Mss. Division.
35. See a report by the Honourable John Spooner, President and Commander in Chief of the Island of Barbados, in *Gazette*, 30 April 1816.
36. *The Report*, pp. 3–4.
37. 26 Sept. 1816, Eliza Fenwick to Mary Hays, in A.F. Webb (ed.), *The Fate of the Fenwicks: Letters of Mary Hays, 1798–1828* (London, 1927), p. 179.
38. The confessions of Robert, in *The Report*, pp. 29–30.
39. *Ibid.*, p. 26, Evidence of Daniel, slave at the River Plantation.
40. Based on *The Report*. See also the letters of Colonel Best to Abel Dottin and Robert Haynes to Thomas Lane, N.Y.P.L., Mss. Division; *The Times*, 15 June 1816.
41. *The Report*, pp. 5, 15; Vaughan, 'Francklyn', *op. cit.*; Minutes of the Assembly, 15 Nov. 1816; Watson, *Civilised Island, op. cit.*, pp. 127–8.
42. See Beckles, 'Rebels without Heroes', *op. cit.*
43. G.L. Jordan, *An Examination of the Principles of the Slave Registry Bill* (London, 1816), pp. 10–14.
44. *The Report*, p. 6.
45. *Ibid.*, pp. 10, 12.
46. *Gazette*, 7 Sept. 1816.
47. 5 June 1816, On the Barbados Negro Insurrection.
48. Minutes of the Assembly, 7 Jan. 1817.
49. *Ibid.*

50. *Ibid.*
51. *Ibid.* See also *The Report*, pp. 5–15; Watson, *Civilised Island, op. cit.*, pp. 128–33.
52. R.I. and Samuel Wilberforce, *The Life of William Wilberforce*, 5 vols. (London, 1838), IV, p. 306.
53. *Gazette*, 9 April 1805; PRO CO 28/72, f. 91.
54. Wilberforce, *Life, op. cit.*, IV, p. 287.
55. *Ibid.*, IV, p. 305.
56. *The Report*, p. 6.
57. *Ibid.*, p. 29, evidence of Robert.
58. *Ibid.*, p. 26, evidence of Daniel.
59. Watson, *Civilised Island, op. cit.*, pp. 125–6.
60. *Ibid.*, p. 125.
61. Michael Craton, 'Slave Culture, Resistance and the Achievement of Emancipation in the British West Indies 1783–1838', in James Walvin (ed.), *Slavery and British Society 1776–1846* (London, 1982), pp. 101–6; Michael Craton, *Testing the Chains: Resistance to Slavery in the British West Indies* (Ithaca, 1982), pp. 254–67.
62. *Remarks on the Insurrection in Barbados, and The Bill for Registration of Slaves* (London, 1816), p. 7.
63. Beckles, 'Rebels without Heroes', *op. cit.*
64. Webb (ed.), *Fenwicks, op. cit.*, pp. 75–6, 163–4.
65. *Gazette*, 1 Jan. 1815 to April 1816.
66. Minutes of Assembly, 13 April 1811 and Minutes of Council, 9 April 1811, PRO CO 31/45.
67. *Gazette*, 13 Jan. 1816.
68. *Ibid.*, 6 May 1815.
69. *Ibid.*, 13 May 1815.
70. *Ibid.*, 20 May 1815.
71. *Remarks on the Insurrection, op. cit.*, p. 7.
72. Cited in David Nicholls, *From Dessalines to Duvalier: Race, Colour, and National Independence in Haiti* (Cambridge, 1979), p. 46.
73. 28 Sept. 1816, Colonel John Rycroft Best to Abel Dottin, N.Y.P.L., Mss. Division.
74. *Ibid.*
75. Minutes of the Assembly, 7 Jan. 1817.
76. *Ibid.*
77. For the Deposition of Jacob Belgrave, a free Mulatto, see *The Report*, pp. 38–9. For an account of the damage to Belgrave's estate, see *ibid.*, p. 59.
78. 27 April 1816, Colonel John Rycroft Best to Abel Dottin, N.Y.P.L., Mss. Division.
79. See the confession of Robert, *The Report*, pp. 29–30.
80. 27 April 1816, Colonel John Rycroft Best to Abel Dottin, N.Y.P.L., Mss. Division.
81. *Ibid.*
82. See the confession of Robert, *The Report*, pp. 29–30.
83. Webb (ed.), *Fenwicks, op. cit.*, p. 179.

5

Comments on the Papers by de Groot and Beckles

MARY TURNER

The study of slave rebellion has developed significantly in the last fifty years: from U.B. Phillips' categorisation of all resistance as slave 'crime' to Eugene Genovese's analysis which relates slave rebellions to the development of a world-wide revolutionary tradition. These papers also suggest, though in different ways, that we may be approaching the end of the current phase, slave political activity seen primarily in terms of rebellion.

Dr Silvia de Groot's admirable summation of her extensive, pioneer work on the Surinam Maroons, traces their history into the twentieth century, revealing their heroic struggle for survival as well as their cultural legacy, and the limitations of their political achievement. The Maroons created in the difficult conditions of the rain forests new social and political formations and managed to defend their way of life against persistent Dutch attack. They shaped, in part, the development of the plantation economy by dictating that Dutch resources, money and man-power had to be poured into their pursuit.

It is clear, however, that there was never a moment when the Maroons could have wiped out the plantation economy. Recruitment to the Maroon ranks cost the planters only 5 to 10 percent of their slave imports: 90 to 95 percent of the slaves stayed on the plantations. The plantation economy expanded and the Treaty signed in 1760 with two of the Maroon bands marks a stalemate, each side acknowledging the other's rights to exist.

The Maroons were not only unable to destroy the plantation economy, but were always, to a degree, dependent upon it. Given the extent of the backlands and their skills of survival the Maroons might have retreated far into the bush like the Maroons in Cuba and Brazil. But the 1760 treaty gave them the right to settle just two days, ten hours' journey from the plantations and they depended upon plantation contacts for guns, food and women. They did not therefore create an independent economic base from which to develop an autonomous society. What they created were encampments, large enough and permanent enough to evolve distinctive political and social mores, but with leaders whose world view was bounded by the need to keep the clan together and maintain their own authority within the clan, a purpose well served by the ethos of moral and military superiority over the whites and coastal blacks defined by Richard Price[1] and, arguably, by their command of the gifts sent by the Dutch. There was only one period, 1777–91 when, perhaps during the lifetime of a particular chief, the Maroon bands united, but even so the Dutch were able eventually to prise them apart.

The Maroons' dependency raises some interesting questions about their interaction with plantation slaves and their impact on plantation discipline and their role as traders. Theoretically the Maroons might have been transformed into a force to overthrow the plantation system if Surinam had generated in the eighteenth century a substantial plantation-based rebellion whose organisers could have won Maroon support. But, even in these circumstances, as experience of bandit chiefs with other revolutionary situations has demonstrated, the Maroons might have chosen to trade their skills as rain forest fighters to the Dutch as the power most likely to win.

As history in fact developed in Surinam the Maroons, having made themselves marginal to the plantation economy in the eighteenth century, have been fossilised into that condition. They had no need to become wage slaves after 1860 and subsequent economic development in Surinam has failed to reincorporate them. Their distinctive sense of themselves, their history and the resilience of their culture serve to demonstrate as much as disguise the limitations of free legal status as such.

The Barbadian slave rebellion of 1816 had features in

common with other Caribbean slave rebellions. It took place, as in Demerara in 1823 and Jamaica in 1831, when the political expectations of the slaves had been raised by controversy between the planters and the imperial government about slavery. It was organised on the plantations, as in Jamaica, by artisans, privileged workers and domestics. It effected considerable damage to property, but was comparatively easily suppressed because the rebels were not well organised and the whites had superior military power. The Barbadian whites, like the Jamaican whites, outraged and appalled that their most confidential slaves had led the rebellion, blamed 'outside intervention': Wilberforce and the African Institute in the Barbadian case, like the abolitionists and their missionary 'agents' in Jamaica, were cast in the role reserved for 'Reds' a century later.

The Barbadian rebellion, however, had a number of distinctive features. The leadership group included representatives of the small (3,000) free coloured population. It took place, allegedly, in prosperous times, and perhaps most significantly of all it took place in an island where the slaves, in distinct contrast to Demerara and Jamaica, had been unable to create a tradition of revolt. It was their first attempt at armed uprising since 1702. Barbadian planters, in fact, dreaded French invasion rather than slave unrest.

Dr Beckles convincingly attributes this stability to a comparatively high white population ratio of one white to 4.8 blacks, to the comparatively normal sex ratios for both groups which enhanced the possibility of some form of family life, and to the fact that almost 93 percent of the slave population was Barbadian born. One other factor might be considered here: the internal frontier was closed off in the seventeenth century, and from that moment rebellion could only aim at the elimination of the whites and the takeover of the means of production – a project that the number of whites and the size of the garrison made appear particularly formidable.

These circumstances focus particular interest on the basis for revolt. There seems no doubt that as the Assembly's Report claimed at the time, the controversy surrounding the proposed Registration laws played a part in stimulating the rebellion. Beckles stresses that the planters perceived Registration as another step in Wilberforce's 'programme of gradual slave emancipation' (p. 90), a commitment confirmed by his association with 'the cause and interest of King Henry of Haiti' (p. 92), although this commitment appears to have been better publicised in 1817 after the rebellion rather than before. The House of Assembly debates on Registration, however, and the overflow of verandah and dining room discussions alerted potential rebel leaders to the fact that the planters were under pressure from the anti-slavery group and, more importantly, from their own masters, the imperial government. As Michael Craton has conclusively demonstrated, perceived weakness in the planter class was a factor common to every British Caribbean slave rebellion.[2]

Beckles' primary concern is, however, that the use made of the Assembly's evidence both by contemporaries and historians essentially denies 'the ability of the slaves to understand the changing nature of the West Indian experience, and to develop their own strategies based upon reasonably clear analyses of these changes'. According to Watson, the slaves' responses were merely 'impulsive', whilst Craton sees them induced by delusions spread by well-informed elite slaves in pursuit of their own interests. The suggestion is that the Assembly's essentially racist analysis has not been purged of racist ambience by contemporary historians.

In that there is always a tendency for academics to underrate, misapprehend or effectually deny the intellectual capacities of working people, this historiographical aspect could be worth investigating. However, the African Institute, denounced here for being as racist as the planter Assemblymen (p. 98), perhaps deserves separate consideration. The *Remarks* quoted here (which were not published by the African Institute, although the Assembly's *Report* attributed the pamphlet to an agent acting on the Institute's behalf) asserted the abolitionists' basic position that the slaves, as men and brothers, had a right to rebel, and for the rest defended the abolitionists against the ready-made pro-planter propaganda package the insurrection provided.

Beckles sets out to redress the balance by emphasising organisation rather than spontaneity and knowledge rather than delusion. He also points to the fact that the leaders included Barbadian, African and women slaves working together with free coloured men. He argues, furthermore, that their knowledge encompassed Wilberforce's activities on their behalf and the revolutionary precedent of Haiti, and suggests that the slaves had matured in wisdom and self-consciousness over the previous decade, so that their rebellion was not sudden, but the culmination of an extended period of internal unrest.

The organisational element which is also detailed in Craton's work[3] is clearly established, and some of the rebels evidently knew about the Haitian revolution, a precedent which was, arguably, particularly important in an island with no indigenous rebel tradition. The fact of Christophe's conservative foreign policy had no place, Beckles points out, in the popular mind in which, possibly, rumours of the simultaneous struggles in South America (Bolivar proclaimed slave emancipation in Venezuela just weeks after the Barbadian rebellion) rekindled hope of creating a new Haiti.

The development of a new 'psychological profile', a new level of self-consciousness among the slaves, is unfortunately much less well founded or explored, and though such a perception could have led to more individual attempts to escape the system, the figures quoted by Beckles do not establish that this took place.

On reflection, Beckles' paper prompts one broader question: to what extent can our knowledge of slave rebellions, bounded as it is by limited sources, be usefully extended simply by re-interpretation of those sources? Though the field is as yet unevenly developed, the groundworks have been laid out and work could begin on placing chattel labour rebellions in the context of chattel labour relations: not just the heroic moments of action but the protracted daily struggles at the point of production. Walter Rodney's *History of the Guyanese Working People* contains many suggestive lines of enquiry to be pursued in relation to the slave plantations.[4] Are the patterns of leadership in strike situations adumbrated under slavery? Can the bargaining procedures of free labourers be traced back to the plantations? And what can be established about authority structures in the slave villages?

The history of chattel labour struggles needs, in short, to be shorn of rhetoric and tied down, as the history of wage-labour struggles has been, to what happens at the workplace. The progress that has been made in slavery studies to date has left the slaves where the abolitionists put them: as a special case, a special cause, people locked in a peculiar institution. Arguably at this juncture, it is necessary to break free from such modes of thinking and write about chattel labourers as a form of labour operating within a specific system of constraints – a system which differs from island to island and territory to territory. Chattel slavery and wage slavery are both aspects of the same system of oppression and the struggles for survival and the attempts to win power by the victims of both systems must have much in common.

NOTES

1. Richard Price, *The Guiana Maroons* (Baltimore, 1976), p. 21.
2. Michael Craton, *Testing the Chains: Resistance to Slavery in the British West Indies* (Ithaca, 1982).
3. Michael Craton, 'Slave Culture, Resistance and the Achievement of Emancipation in the British West Indies, 1783–1838', in James Walvin (ed.), *Slavery and British Society 1776–1846* (London, 1982), p. 105.
4. Walter Rodney, *History of the Guyanese Working People, 1881–1905* (London, 1981).

PART C

Connections Between the British and Continental Abolitionist Movements

6

Haiti and the Abolitionists: Opinion, Propaganda and International Politics in Britain and France, 1804–1838

DAVID GEGGUS

I

Amidst the ruins of once opulent Saint Domingue, the independence of Haiti was proclaimed on 1 January 1804. The wealthiest planter class in the Americas had been destroyed by its own, predominantly African, slaves, who in twelve years of desolating warfare had defeated every European army that had been sent against them, even that of the all-conquering Bonaparte. They now established a modern state apparatus, based on European models but displaying a passionate and defiant sense of racial identity. Even in the age of revolutions, contemporaries recognised the creation of Haiti as something extraordinary. The French planter Drouin de Bercy thought it a remarkable event, worthy of the contemplation of philosophers and statesmen, even though he himself wished to see it destroyed and its population massacred or deported.[1]

The colonial powers and American slaveholders viewed with deep disquiet the presence in the Caribbean of a victorious ex-slave army and the example it set to their own slaves. Never before had a slave society successfully overthrown its ruling class.[2] When even most abolitionists thought that West Indian slaves would need a long preparation for freedom, support in Europe for the rebel blacks was limited and ambivalent, and in Britain was chiefly a function of anti-French feelings and wartime strategy. Since only a few fringe figures were prepared to argue for the legitimacy of violent self-liberation, the abolitionists tended to be apologists for, rather than supporters of, the Haitian Revolution. In the two-year War of Independence (1802–3) Henry Brougham and the *Edinburgh Review* actually hoped the blacks would be defeated. On the other hand, the character of Toussaint Louverture elicited widespread praise, and his betrayal by the French evoked general sympathy. When independence came, it was largely welcomed in Britain as a defeat for France, and indeed was attributed by many to the help given to the insurgents by the Royal Navy. The blacks' resistance won them a qualified respect, but prejudice persisted and the massacre of French colonists that followed independence further alienated opinion, and was capitalised on by pro-slavery forces.[3]

Haiti became both a political issue in itself and a crucial test case for ideas about race and about the future of colonial slavery. Should the new state be recognised? What sort of a threat did it pose to the West Indian colonies? Was its trade worth engrossing? Could it maintain its independence? These were practical questions that had to be immediately confronted. In the war of words between the abolitionists and their opponents Haiti also acquired an exemplary or symbolic value, fuelling both sides of the anti-slavery debate. One can distinguish, therefore, two aspects of contemporary interest in Haiti, which concerned in part the specific and novel reality of a black power in the Caribbean, but also its implications for the future of Afro-America as well. Opinion and propaganda were thus closely interwoven. Writing on the Haitian Revolution had exhibited this dual nature ever since the great uprising of 1791, and this would continue at least until the 1830s, when Haiti ceased to be the only post-slavery society in the New World.

Although the British government showed no desire to recognise diplomatically the Haitian Republic, initially it was anxious to secure a commercial treaty with the new state, for security rather than economic reasons. Negotiations, however, were broken off in protest at the massacres of April 1804, and as fears of a Haitian invasion of the British West Indies rapidly subsided a formal treaty came to be thought unnecessary.[4] It was precisely such fears, however, that the evangelical James

Stephen tried to play on, when in a radical pamphlet published in the summer he advocated that Britain not merely recognise but also guarantee Haitian independence.[5] If the republic were isolated and bullied, he correctly surmised, it would build forts instead of sugar mills and become 'a nation of soldiers'. It therefore needed steering in a peaceful direction, and not towards France or the United States.

A lawyer who had made his fortune in the West Indies, Stephen was obsessed with the theme of guilt and divine vengeance, and this was neither the first nor the last time he would depict Haiti's 'sable heroes and patriots' as eager to emancipate the slaves of Britain's colonies. Though the pamphlet was enthusiastically reviewed by fellow evangelical Zachary Macaulay,[6] its assessment of the Haitian threat was not widely accepted, still less its advocacy of a Haitian alliance. Its boldest suggestion was that such a relationship with Haiti might serve as a model for an eventual decolonisation of the British West Indies, Britain one day handing over power to the blacks while preserving the commercial monopoly. For the time being, however, none of the major abolitionists, Stephen included, was willing to support even slave emancipation.

Stephen's views make an interesting contrast with those of his liberal, reforming colleague Henry Brougham, the abolitionists' new star recruit from Edinburgh. Like the pro-slavery lobby, Brougham argued that Haiti was bound for anarchy and stagnation, and would therefore pose no threat to its neighbours. Declaring that no slaves were yet ready for freedom, he criticised as absurd Stephen's distinction between the 'sable heroes' of Haiti and the 'dullness and stupidity' of the 'debased' slaves of the British colonies. The Haitian Revolution naturally caused men to reflect on the nature of power and subordination in slave societies. Stephen, the profoundly religious Tory, thought that white authority rested primarily on the slaves' irrational fears, 'fostered by ignorance and habit'. Somewhat like a belief in ghosts, this 'instinctive dread' was deeply ingrained, but once dispelled it vanished forever. The more secular Brougham believed that the slaves' obedience derived simply from a rational calculation of the costs of resistance. The question remains perplexing. Stephen evidently found it difficult to relate the dramatic transformation of Saint Domingue to the stability of

St. Kitts, where he had spent ten years. It was perhaps his experience of religious conversion that led him to see the problem as one of consciousness. Brougham, more free market-minded, thought in terms of stimulus and response.[7]

In spite of these differences, all the abolitionists agreed (or at least pretended) that Haitian independence placed the British West Indies in grave danger and brought new urgency to the abolition question. Though Brougham dismissed Haiti as a direct threat, he claimed that the example it set to other blacks increased a thousand-fold the risks of rebellion in the British Caribbean. It was thus more vital than ever to end the influx of resentful Africans into the region by abolishing the slave trade, and so compel planters to improve conditions. According to Wilberforce, the Haitian Revolution had demonstrated three things: that the blacks loved liberty and would pay a high price for it; that they were not an inferior race, but could 'conceive extensive designs', carrying them out with prudence and vigour; and that they had been taught 'but too intelligibly the fatal secret of their own strength'. The abolition question, he argued, now stood on completely new grounds. It had become what it always should have been, a political question.[8] After a lapse of eight years, the abolition committee re-assembled, and Brougham's *Concise Statement* was rushed out as a manifesto stressing the 'new motives to abolition derived from the state of St. Domingo'. Wilberforce introduced a bill for immediate abolition in the Commons, which was passed with large majorities in June. For technical reasons it was then withdrawn, but only when Pitt had hinted that the Cabinet would support the measure the following year 'as a new question, on the ground of the danger to the colonies'.[9]

The part played by Haiti in the anti-slavery movement's sudden resurgence in 1804 seems to have been entirely ignored in the scholarly literature. Yet its importance was apparently considerable.[10] Certainly it caused *The Times*, although pro-slavery and anti-Haiti, to espouse abruptly abolition at this time.[11] Apart from the apparent threat to the British West Indies, France's loss of her most important colony also must have lessened fears that, if the British withdrew from the slave trade, the French would step into their shoes. Haitian independence thus made abolition seem both more necessary and less problematical. It may also explain why the abolitionist cause slumped badly the following year, as the novelty of the 'Haitian threat', however perceived, wore off. Finally, it is noteworthy how since 1791 the emergence of Haiti encouraged abolitionist writers to adopt arguments based on self-interest, the tactic that would lead them to success in 1807.

As for events in France at this time, Napoleon's Caribbean campaign of 1802–3 signalled the end of the Revolution's hesitant flirtation with anti-slavery. Abolitionism, always an affair of small cliques in France,[12] now effectively ceased to exist. The attempt to reconquer Saint Domingue had been accompanied by a flood of literature concerning the colony, but it was largely the work of colonists who, with varying degrees of vituperation, blamed the black revolution on abolitionist influence. Then, as the Saint Domingue expedition came entirely to grief, a total ban was imposed on all works concerning the colonies.

The veteran abolitionist the Abbé Grégoire managed a few years later ingeniously to circumvent this ban with a work ostensibly devoted to the literary efforts of blacks writing in French and English. The book was mainly about African society, but in it Grégoire also took the opportunity to praise the Dominguans Toussaint Louverture and Jean Kina (who had led a revolt on Martinique) and to observe that, if Haiti was still politically unstable, this had also been true of France in the 1790s. The revolutions in both countries, he noted pointedly, had been corrupted by foreign intervention.[13] Censorship was subsequently lifted, enabling the colonists to reply. They attacked the atrocities committed by blacks and mulattoes in the Saint Domingue Revolution and, while recognising some of the abilities of Toussaint, criticised his hypocrisy and cruelty.[14] In 1812 censorship was reimposed and it continued to keep anti-slavery material out of the press until 1817.

II

The Treaty of Paris of 1814 left the restored Bourbon monarchy free to revive the French slave trade (though only for five years) and to attempt to reconquer its former colony of Saint Domingue. In France, both policies had widespread public support. Saint Domingue had been far more important to the French economy than all the British West Indies were to Britain. Several thousand refugee planters now lived in France, bitter, nostalgic and vengeful, and together with merchants and shipbuilders, they formed a powerful pro-slavery lobby. Martinique and Guadeloupe, long creolised, could provide but a tiny market for the revived slave trade; a reconquered Saint Domingue would create potentially limitless demand. As in 1802, there occurred a sudden spate of publications about Saint Domingue advocating restitution of French control. Many expected a war of extermination against the independent blacks and mulattoes, followed by a massive importation of slaves.[15]

The threat of repopulating Haiti with slaves meant that for the abolitionists the stakes were much, much higher than if it were merely a matter of reviving France's slave trade to other French and foreign colonies. On both sides of the Channel, abolitionists were immediately stung into action, in an effort to persuade the French government both to abandon the projected military expedition and to outlaw the slave trade. The British and French anti-slavery movements now came into much closer contact than ever before, renewing links broken since 1803. Notwithstanding the wide diversity of personalities involved, a fair degree of collaboration was achieved in a campaign of pamphleteering and direct political lobbying.

Zachary Macaulay and his brother became frequent visitors to Paris, and were joined in August 1814 by Thomas Clarkson. Their French counterparts introduced them to government ministers and the King, though to no avail, and Clarkson translated one of Henri Grégoire's works into English. As abolitionism in France had always been branded as an English plot, these links were not entirely to the advantage of the tiny group of French abolitionists, many of whom were in any case Protestant or foreign. On the other hand, since the French periodical press refused to print their articles, some had to rely on British subsidies to get them published separately as pamphlets. In the climate of post-war defeat and royalist reaction, both the proposed expedition against Haiti and the resumption of the slave trade took on the appearance of patriotic causes associated with national revival.[16] In August 1814 a special committee reported to the legislature recommending that a military expedition be sent to Haiti. The Chamber of Deputies decided to defer its decision but expressed general approval.

Despite the wide support for a re-conquest of Haiti, the case against it was overwhelming. It was set out succinctly in a shrewdly pragmatic pamphlet by the Swiss economist Sismondi. The Haitians, he argued, could never possibly be subdued without a genocidal war that would cost the lives of 50,000 French troops. It would be fruitless, furthermore, because France did not possess the capital and the French slave trade would not have the time to repopulate the country with the half million slaves that would be needed. The pamphlet, paid for by Wilberforce, sold few copies and, like French translations of works by Wilberforce and Clarkson, was largely ignored by the French press.[17] In his *Lettre à Talleyrand* (containing a preface by Mme de Staël), Wilberforce argued as did Sismondi that Haiti had made great material and moral progress since independence, which would render almost impossible any attempt to restore slavery there. Though the work was a little tactless, observed the *Edinburgh Review*, and poorly translated, it was said to have made some impact in Paris. When at the end of 1814 the French government abandoned the project for an expedition, it was to Wilberforce that Mme de Staël attributed the success.[18]

Henri Grégoire, on the other hand, ostracised as a republican and regicide, could not find a printer for his contribution to the debate until January 1815. Employing the classic device of role reversal, he asked his readers how they would feel if Haitians fitted out ships to enslave whites. He praised James Stephen's *History of Toussaint Louverture* (specially revised and re-issued for the campaign) and hoped it would rehabilitate the black leader's reputation. Grégoire also made the obligatory juxtaposition between the so-called savagery of the Haitian blacks and the atrocities the French had systematically committed against them – a perennial theme in literature. Finally, he noted how Napoleon had destroyed the army of his rival, Moreau, by sending it to Saint Domingue. The Bourbons, he implied, might now be happy to do the same with Napoleon's veterans.[19]

This was a telling point to make when the army was solidly anti-Bourbon, and Zachary Macaulay soon came to think that the army would never allow another Saint Domingue expedition to be mounted. Military men who had served there were saying that re-conquest was impossible, and commentators increasingly began to argue that France should negotiate for some sort of protectorate over the former colony, or even settle simply for an indemnity and commercial privileges.[20] For ten years, French governments were to engage in desultory negotiations, gradually scaling down their demands. The colonists, however, boosted by their links with the Ultra-Royalist party, never entirely gave up hope, and right up to 1824 they clamoured intermittently for a military intervention.[21]

A French re-conquest of Haiti, James Stephen observed, would 'keep the slave trade in business for a century', and not merely that of France. The growing Spanish slave trade to nearby Cuba, he claimed, was an incitement to the French to attack Haiti even after they had renounced their own slave trade. This continued threat forced the Haitians to maintain a large army which was a drag on Haitian development and might one day, Stephen suggested, be turned against the slave regime in Cuba. Anyway, the example set by the Haitians, together with the rate of slave imports into Cuba, would insure that before long the Spanish island was going to experience a huge revolt. Stephen thus resurrected the 'internal' and 'external' threat arguments of 1802–4, when it had previously been hoped that they would frighten the Spanish and Portuguese into abandoning their commerce in slaves.[22]

The Haitian question, therefore, considerably intensified the campaign for international abolition which led the British abolitionists into the field of diplomacy at the Congresses of Vienna (1815) and Aix la Chapelle (1818). Wilberforce, besides putting pressure on the Prime Minister and Foreign Secretary, found a willing collaborator in the Duke of Wellington, who was Britain's chief negotiator. In Paris, Wellington distributed copies of Sismondi's and Wilberforce's pamphlets to French legislators. Wilberforce got Stephen to send the Duke information on Haiti, while he himself wrote to the Tsar Alexander, deemed the most powerful voice in the Concert of Europe, to ask him to discourage the French from seeking to reconquer their former possession. At the Congress of Aix, Thomas Clarkson met the Tsar and showed him a letter from the King of Haiti to impress on him the latter's abilities.[23]

James Stephen had already dedicated to the Tsar the 1814 edition of his *History of Toussaint Louverture*, and from the Abbé Grégoire he was now collecting materials for a fuller biography or a history of the Haitian revolution. As repeatedly favourable references to him, even in pro-slavery journals, demonstrated, Toussaint was good propaganda material.[24] Stephen called him 'that illustrious and excellent man, the greatest hero of his age', and he suggested to Grégoire that

> his virtues were not more beneficient to his unfortunate countrymen while he lived than the memory of them may prove hereafter, by removing those cruel prejudices against the poor Africans as to their intellectual and moral character, by which their oppression has been excused and upheld ... This is a case in which accurate contemporary history may very powerfully serve the cause of humanity and justice.[25]

The fear that France would attempt to re-impose slavery in Haiti provided an issue that perfectly united abolitionist interest in the ex-slaves' well-being with their concern for their propaganda value in the broader anti-slavery struggle. By 1818, when France formally abandoned the slave trade and Spain became pledged to follow suit soon, the direct danger to Haiti was generally considered at an end. By that time, however, the abolitionists had been drawn into personal links with the Haitians, which were to endure about a decade.

III

The threat of a French invasion in 1814 threw both the black Kingdom of Haiti (the northern part of the former colony) and the mulatto-ruled Republic (the south and west) into a frenzy of defensive activity. While the mulatto president Pétion and his successor, Boyer, were willing to pay France an indemnity in return for recognition of their independence, the defiant King Christophe would offer only a resumption of commercial relations. Neither state, however, was prepared to compromise its sovereignty.

Christophe, a vigorous despot, launched a publicity campaign in Europe, publishing proclamations in British and French newspapers, and obliquely soliciting the aid of the abolitionists. In June 1814 his foreign secretary, the Comte de Limonade, wrote to Grégoire, expressing the King's admiration of *De la*

Littérature des Nègres and said he had ordered fifty copies for his senior officials. He sent with the letter a package of state papers, and commented on the kingdom's military strength and stable, paternal government.[26] However, these were not qualities that the aging republican cleric especially admired, and he refused to correspond directly with the King. Christophe thereupon contacted Wilberforce (excerpts of whose writings had appeared in Haitian newspapers under his predecessor, Dessalines) and in 1815 he wrote to Clarkson, similarly sending law codes and other state papers.

It thus came about that the British abolitionists became associated with the northern kingdom, while their French counterparts developed links with the republican south. As the two states were mortal enemies, these relations were of necessity mutually exclusive. The division was reinforced by a number of factors: the political preferences of the French (since the only French abolitionists concerned with Haiti, Grégoire and Lafayette, were republicans); the British preference for monarchy; the cultural leanings of the mulattoes, many of whose parents had been educated in France, whereas Christophe, who had been born in a British colony, had every reason to dislike the French and had pursued a pro-British policy; and the historical legacy of the War of the South, in which Britain had assisted Toussaint against the mulattoes. Stephen told Grégoire that he mistrusted Haiti's *anciens libres*, because of their former treachery towards the blacks, and he doubted the commitment of the mulattoes to status-conscious former slave owners in black emancipation. The Tory *Quarterly Review* voiced similar feelings, and suspected they might sell out to the French.[27] In general, French opinion tended to be much more hostile to Christophe than to his mulatto rivals, while in Britain the reverse was probably true. Even so, Wilberforce professed neutrality in the matter, while the liberal *Edinburgh Review* contrasted the cruel tyranny of Christophe with the virtuous, constitutional rule of Pétion.[28]

The help given to the Haitians by the abolitionists can be put into four categories: advice, particularly on political developments in Europe and on religious and educational matters; practical help, such as the supply of books, teachers and other specialists; favourable publicity to combat European prejudice;

and lastly, certain limited assistance in lobbying for the recognition of Haitian independence. In none of these fields were the abolitionists notably successful; the British, however, made somewhat more impact than the French. No leading abolitionist actually went to Haiti. That would have to wait until Victor Schoelcher's visit of 1841.

Wilberforce and Clarkson responded enthusiastically to the overtures from King Christophe. Until the King's overthrow and death in 1820, both men corresponded regularly with the monarch and his ministers, and it seems that James Stephen and Sir John Sinclair also wrote to him.[29] Clarkson, with characteristic energy, threw himself into writing voluminous letters offering advice with a bluntness that Christophe appears to have appreciated. Wilberforce also passed on political news affecting Haitian security, warned about adverse publicity in the European press and advocated the same schemes as did Clarkson. The reduction in the size of the army, the diversification of agriculture, the distribution of smallholdings and the education of women were prominent themes in their letters. Wilberforce, however, seems to have put more effort into behind-the-scenes activity, finding volunteers to work in Haiti. He took the task seriously, inviting candidates to stay with him a few days, so as to vet them. 'Never have I worked harder than at my Haytian letters', he told T.B. Macaulay in 1817.[30]

Wilberforce saw himself as 'sowing the seeds of Christian and moral improvement, and to be laying also the foundations of all kinds of social and domestic institutions, habits and manners'. He hoped the young Macaulay would live to see 'the new spectacle of a community of black men, of which the mass will be as well instructed as any nation upon earth'. He realised, however, that all would depend on Christophe living long enough, and apparently he prayed for him every day. If the experiment worked, he expected that Haitians would evangelise and 'civilise' all Afro-America. Three million souls were at stake. Christophe, for his part, wrote temptingly of how he would like to see his countrymen converted to Protestant Christianity, abandoning a Catholicism whose priests were corrupt and whose church defended slavery. He hoped, too, to see the English language one day replace French, being the best guarantee of his country's independence. Wilberforce responded by sending works on morality, Bibles in English and French, a manual of political economy and histories of the Jesuits and the Inquisition. Like his friend Sir Joseph Banks, he regretted that he himself was too old to go, and that Zachary Macaulay was too busy. He did persuade General C. Macaulay to agree to visit Haiti, though it was soon decided that this would embarrass the government, and the idea was dropped. Nevertheless, with the aid of the British and Foreign School Society, he and Clarkson seem to have sent out around a dozen teachers and missionaries, and apparently a mineralogist and naturalist as well. Zachary Macaulay sent details of new methods of cultivating and cleaning cotton, and Wilberforce made a present of two ploughs, for which he was afterwards obliged to recruit two ploughmen. In return, Christophe supplied abundant funds for these activities and also a large portrait of himself, dressed in the manner of George III, which was shown at the Royal Academy in 1818.[31]

The editors of the Clarkson – Christophe published correspondence put some stress on Clarkson's influence over the King. Certainly on one occasion Christophe delayed replying to French overtures before he knew the Englishman's opinion of them. However, in general it seems clear that Christophe followed Clarkson's advice only where it coincided with powerful influences closer to home – such as in the breaking up of large estates for the benefit of his soldiers, or in the lessening of tension with the mulatto south during the threat of French invasion. Griggs and Prator claim the latter development as an 'extraordinary' volte-face, but it amounted to little. Christophe merely expressed his willingness to ally with Boyer, while he continued to claim to speak for the 'one and indivisible Haitian people'. In the crucial matter of achieving recognition by France, Clarkson was never able to get the King to drop either his refusal to begin negotiations without prior recognition or his adamant rejection of France's claim for an indemnity.[32]

Christophe's ex-slave court, with its Duc de Marmelade and Comte de Limonade, was an obvious target for racist satire in both Britain and France. Colonial publicists mocked the 'gaudy prospect' or 'hideous fabric of "African sovereignty" in the West Indies', and concocted imaginative tales of a tyrannical Christophe shooting his foreign minister dead at the dinner table or throwing his son out the palace window for disturbing his sleep.[33] The abolitionists were not entirely sure what to believe themselves but did their best to combat such propaganda, some of which had originated in the rival Republic of Haiti. With the help of the black American Prince Sanders, whom they sent on missions to Haiti, the abolitionists published in London some of Christophe's state papers and also publicised his *Almanach Royal*. They were probably responsible for translating for *The Pamphleteer*, an extremely able riposte to Christophe's critics by his interior minister, the Baron de Vastey, and it is likely that the series of favourable eye-witness accounts of Haiti that appeared in *Blackwood's Magazine* had been passed on by them. James Stephen began collecting materials for a biography of Christophe and history of the Haitian Revolution, getting papers sent from Haiti.[34]

We also catch an interesting glimpse of Stephen in a pro-slavery pamphlet delivering 'a pompous and unmerited eulogium' on Christophe before 'a motley assemblage of white, black and tawney-coloured people, collected together at a tavern'. At the London Tavern in 1816 it appears that frequent toasts were drunk to the King of Haiti. One might as well praise any slave, the planters replied, whose 'cause was precisely the same – the emancipation of the slaves by the massacre of their masters'. Stephen and Macaulay had long argued that Haiti posed a threat to the British West Indies. The planters retorted that it was Stephen's public meetings that threatened to subvert the British colonies. Having become agents of 'these St Domingo Chieftains ... the great emancipators', the abolitionists were guilty of incitement to massacre.[35]

No matter how they might enthuse about Christophe's reforming zeal, his energy and moral vision, it was an uphill struggle for the abolitionists. Their efforts received a considerable setback in 1817, when the 'thumbscrew scandal' broke in the British press. A British merchant in Haiti, suspected of being an agent for the Republic, was tortured on Christophe's orders. The incident was played up by the pro-slavery lobby and raised in the House of Commons, to the abolitionists' embarrassment. Clarkson and Wilberforce warned Christophe about the damaging publicity, and added that instruments of torture no longer formed part of the apparatus of the modern state.[36]

The greatest setback, however, came with the overthrow of Christophe himself, and the incorporation of his kingdom into the economically languishing Republic. The uprising of 1820 provided an occasion to celebrate Christophe's cruelty (alias 'thirst for human blood') and the instability of the black state. Fearing for the safety of the royal family, Wilberforce wrote immediately and with a somewhat heavy hand to the new head of state. The eyes of the world were upon him, he said. Enemies of the blacks often claimed that their inferiority was demonstrated by their violence and cruelty. He hoped that the King's system of schools would be preserved.[37]

Wilberforce grieved that Christophe's reputation was now left to be picked over by the 'dogs and vultures' of journalism such as William Cobbett. Furthermore, with the incorporation of Christophe's kingdom into the mulatto-controlled Republic Haiti's prospects of developing into a prosperous, export-oriented showpiece for the anti-slavery movement rapidly vanished. President Boyer showed no desire to continue Christophe's correspondence. He replied frostily, when Clarkson wrote warning of French intentions, while the British missionaries who had been sent to Haiti came under increasing harassment.[38] Christophe's downfall was thus a double blow for the British abolitionists, effectively ending their direct links with Haiti and greatly undermining its propaganda value for the anti-slavery cause.

At the time of Henry Christophe's death, Clarkson had been making enquiries in Paris as to whether the French government would accept his mediation in negotiations for recognising Haiti's independence. Clarkson undertook the mission only at the urging of the King and discovered, as he expected, that there was no possibility of the King's conditions being accepted. This episode apart, the British abolitionists were able to contribute little towards ending Haiti's diplomatic isolation. Wilberforce told Christophe that recognition would first require combatting the many enemies of 'the African cause' to be found in Parliament and winning over the uncommitted majority of M.P.s who simply knew nothing about Haiti. In 1815, however, Macaulay's *Christian Observer* had called on the government to mediate between Haiti and France, as King Christophe wanted. Observing that the Haitians had shared Britain's struggle against Napoleon and 'nobly achieved their liberty', he argued that Britain should now play the same role as France had done in negotiating Britain's separation from her North American colonies.[39]

The abolitionists realised, however, that now that Britain and France were at peace such action was likely to be thought unacceptable meddling, prejudicial to Anglo-French relations and particularly to France's new experiment in constitutional monarchy. Hence not even a British consul was sent to Haiti until after France peremptorily recognised Haitian independence in 1825. This contrasted markedly with Britain's treatment of the *de facto* independent colonies of Spain. Moreover, even after the regularising of Franco-Haitian relations, Britain held back from according full recognition, doubtless to avoid antagonising its own West India planters. It was this ministerial deference to slave-owners that James Stephen lambasted in his *England Enslaved by her own Slave Colonies*. Because the British had failed to support him, President Boyer had been forced to purchase French recognition at the cost of a crippling indemnity and the replacing of British merchants' commercial privileges with most favoured nation status for the French. The British government had thus achieved the impossible – making France popular in Haiti.[40]

The French government's decision to recognise Haiti came entirely out of the blue, and like most of the achievements of French anti-slavery, seems to have owed little to direct abolitionist influence. It is perhaps best seen as a response to mounting pressure to revive French trade.[41] The abolitionists had assisted on two occasions in 1820–1 in the presentation of Haitian petitions to the Chamber of Deputies calling for the ending of slavery and the recognition of Haitian independence. However, the Haitian envoy's association with the Abbé Grégoire proved in the event a positive liability. Detested both by the government and by the Vatican, there was really nothing the revolutionary cleric could do to help. He remained, even so, much respected by the Haitians, including the northerners whom he had offended. Haitians in Paris frequently visited him, be they government envoys, poets trying to publish their poems, or victims of discrimination wanting help in writing a protest letter to a newspaper.[42] President Boyer offered him on two occasions a bishopric in Haiti, and also approached his collaborator the Abbé Guidicelly. However, the only French clerics to visit the country were those of an apostolic mission apparently intended to undermine Haitian sovereignty. As Grégoire himself was fairly poor, and received no funds from Boyer, he was unable to supply material assistance on the scale provided by the British.[43]

Like his British counterparts, Grégoire along with Lafayette interested himself in educational matters, sent out religious texts and offered political advice. His suggestion that Boyer give support to the Greek Independence movement and to international anti-slavery, and his praise of Boyer's annexation of Santo Domingo, contrasts noticeably with the caution recommended to Christophe by the British. It was also, however, in keeping with the wider political horizons of the Republic, which had already given substantial assistance to Simon Bolívar. Of more particular interest, Grégoire wrote a number of works especially for the Haitians. These reflected the same concern for family stability voiced by Wilberforce and also defended Roman Catholicism against the charge that it was indifferent to anti-slavery. To his credit, Grégoire also penned a defence of religious toleration when he learned that Protestant missionaries were being persecuted. Persecution and economic backwardness, he pointed out, could be used as pretexts for foreign intervention. Grégoire's disillusionment with Boyer's government came to a head in 1825 when, in order to settle the independence question, its envoys entirely ignored him while negotiating in Paris. The Haitians, he thought, had been too eager for French recognition. Boyer's introduction of a rigorous rural code and the closure of schools helped precipitate a formal and public breach between the two men at the end of 1826.[44]

Although France did not accord full recognition in 1825, Haitian independence ceased to be a public issue and interest in the country declined. Commercial contacts increased but the wave of French publications about Haiti came to an end in 1826.[45] It is true that Joseph Morénas's work on slavery and the slave trade that appeared in 1828 was dedicated to President Boyer, but it had almost nothing to say about Haiti apart from a few pages concerning French atrocities in Saint Domingue copied directly from Grégoire's *De la Littérature des Nègres*.[46]

French anti-slavery activity was dominated by the question of the slave trade, to which Haiti now had little relevance.

IV

In Britain, however, the campaign to abolish slavery which began in 1823 gave Haiti a central importance in the debate over the future of the British Caribbean. How would the slaves react if they all were freed? The Sierra Leone colony, some limited free labour experiments in Barbados and Cayenne, resettled black soldiers and 'liberated' Africans were all pointed to by the commentators as providing clues as to the nature of a post-slavery society. All agreed, however, that Haiti was the most important example, 'the great experiment'. An independent state, born of revolution and a long war, it did not really provide an adequate model for predicting how emancipation might affect the British colonies, and the abolitionists frequently pointed this out when it suited their case. Yet neither they nor their opponents, with few exceptions, could resist exploiting Haiti's propaganda value for all they thought it was worth. Controversy tended to centre on four topics – the danger or otherwise of emancipation, its demographic impact, blacks' abilities and, above all, the economic consequences of freeing the slaves.

In the European mind, Haiti was indissolubly linked with the 1791 slave revolt, whose garish images were reinforced by those of the massacres that followed independence. Fears that such a revolt would occur in the British colonies led a few colonists to accept that the indefinite continuation of slavery was not in their own best interests. It was on such fears that Thomas Fowell Buxton, opening the campaign in the House of Commons in 1823, hoped to play when he said that Haiti would always be a threat to the British West Indies as long as slavery lasted. Three years later, James Stephen repeated the point: Haiti was an 'enormous, ever-teeming barrack'.[47] The threat of a Haitian invasion, however, was never really taken seriously, especially after 1804. As for the danger of local insurrection, planter publicists invariably argued that it was not slavery but abolitionists that caused revolts. The Saint Domingue uprising was always blamed by them on the *Amis des Noirs*, and the Demerara rebellion of 1823 seemed to provide another case in point.[48]

This alleged association between anti-slavery and rebellion, emancipation and massacre, was one of the abolitionists' main obstacles. At the time of the 1804 massacres, Macaulay and others pointed to extenuating circumstances in the blacks' favour, but the bloodshed disillusioned even such enemies of slavery as Samuel Coleridge, who, concluding that 'degraded savages' could not cope with freedom, saw little future for the West Indies. William Cobbett remarked, 'The negroes are a bloody-minded race. They are made and marked for servitude ... it is the purpose which they were obviously intended for.'[49] The abolitionists' major attack on these assumptions came with Thomas Clarkson's *Thoughts* of 1823. Clarkson blamed the slave revolt of 1791 on the colonists and stressed that the revolt had preceded official emancipation, after which, he claimed, there was no evidence of any violence on the plantations. Clarkson's version of history proved vulnerable to his opponents' attacks, even though they were considerably more distorted. However, they could not gainsay his point that British emancipation was not likely to take place under the same chaotic circumstances.[50]

Though the product of violent emancipation, Haiti had become, the anti-slavery journals insisted, a land of law and order and a peaceful neighbour. Furthermore, if British West Indian slaves had not so far been inspired by its example to rebel, they were unlikely to do so when freed. The abolitionists appear to have got the best of this argument, and in the final campaign of 1833 the scaremongers had to pull out all the stops. 'Mangled bodies ... outrages of the most dreadful description' might not prove to be direct products of emancipation, one pamphleteer admitted, but they would follow from the economic ruin that emancipation would cause. The blacks would then 'return to their human sacrifices and the feast of the dead, as they have done in Haiti'.[51] Ever since the 1790s planter publicists had been describing the Haitians as 'relapsing into barbarism'. Christophe's rule was dismissed as an extravagant episode in alternating anarchy and tyranny. 'Soon ripe, soon rotten', predicted one writer in 1816. He expected white Americans, from the north or the south, to one day seize the country and drive the blacks into the mountains, where they would eventually die out. James MacQueen accepted that Toussaint had been a wise ruler, but depicted his countrymen as 'savages – lazy, ignorant, rude – more barbarous' than under slavery.[52]

The abolitionists replied, extolling the spread of education and Christian marriage under both Christophe and Boyer, though tending to stress in later years difficulties as well as achievements. In April 1819 a remarkable article in the normally pro-slavery *Quarterly Review* proclaimed that the development of Haiti 'affords one of the most interesting and instructive lessons ever offered to the contemplation of mankind'. 'After a fair experiment', it was now clear that blacks were not sub-human and that in Haiti they were making great progress, especially in literature and education. (The article was reviewing two Haitian works, as well as the pro-black histories of Barskett and Pamphile de Lacroix.) Europeans might be amused by the idea of a negro nobility, clergy and officer corps, 'appearing to our distant view like the dramatis personae of a mock tragedy'. Yet a closer look turned contempt to respect. Toussaint and Christophe were 'two wonderful men'. Even Dessalines received the reviewer's praise. The emancipation of the slaves was inevitable, he concluded, and British planters should speedily follow Haiti's lead in promoting religion, education and a transition to free labour. Echoing the *Annual Register* of fifteen years before, he envisioned Haitian ships soon sailing to Africa to spread freedom, Christianity and Western civilisation.[53]

By the time the abolitionists had decided to push for emancipation in 1823, the *Quarterly Review* had already abandoned this radical stance and its enthusiasm for Haiti. Christophe's overthrow and the Demerara rebellion were apparently contributory factors to the change. James Stephen, however, insisted that Haitian society was stable. The deaths of Christophe and Dessalines were due to military conspiracies, not revolutions. Haiti was still 'advancing in intelligence, respectability and wealth', the Anti-Slavery Society asserted in its 1825 report.[54] Attention was now shifting away from the heroic years of the Revolution to the condition of the contemporary Republic. Both sides were publishing eye-witness accounts of Haiti which suited their case. Apart from letters to the press, three full-length works appeared in the years 1827–30. The first, Harvey's *Sketches*, was critical but optimistic. Franklin's *Present State*, commissioned by the West India Committee, was explicitly propagandistic and warned the government against the folly of emancipation, while Mackenzie's *Notes* was similarly negative. Its author, Britain's first consul to Haiti, was the son of a West India planter and was much attacked in the anti-slavery press.[55]

Probably the most valuable argument that Haiti provided in favour of emancipation was the demographic one. The inability of the Caribbean slave populations to reproduce themselves was one of the strongest planks in the anti-slavery platform. It would be greatly reinforced, the abolitionists realised, if it could be shown that emancipation would cause an immediate reversion to positive growth rates. Stephen had predicted in 1804 that Haiti would demonstrate the 'super-fecundity of unoppressed human nature', and by 1815 anti-slavery writers were convinced that the Haitian population was increasing rapidly. The pro-slavery lobby, on the other hand, had predicted that Haiti's population would in fact decrease, racked by famine and internecine warfare. As late as 1824, James MacQueen reckoned it at only 400,000. All such estimates, however, were pure guesswork. The abolitionists were therefore delighted when Boyer published a census that year which put the total population at more than 900,000. Thereafter they were able to claim that the emancipated slaves had doubled their number in twenty years. Instead of pointing to Haiti's unusually favourable population structure, pro-slavery writers simply claimed that the census was inaccurate.[56]

The performance of the Haitian economy caused a similar though more complicated controversy, concerning not only gross output, but also the nature of labour relations in the Haitian countryside. It also divided the abolitionists in various ways. All believed in the superior efficiency of free labour, but they were less clear as to how well the laws of liberal economy would function in a tropical, post-slavery society. Zachary Macaulay simply declared in 1804 that the more freedom a slave had, the more he worked. This he asserted as a matter of universal agreement, and he therefore was certain that the 'infant negro republic' would not retrogress. Stephen, however, thought that Haiti's former slaves would work less industriously, but that the decline in productivity would be offset by a rapidly rising population. Brougham, on the other hand, was at first entirely pessimistic. As Africans lacked a tradition of wage labour and ex-slaves shunned work, he thought Haiti was bound for economic stagnation. Emancipation in the British West Indies could not be considered for several generations and would require a long transition period – an opinion he publicly had to recant in the House of Commons twenty years later.[57]

Clarkson would seem to have shared Macaulay's views. His 1823 *Thoughts* presented a glowing picture of the plantation economy under Toussaint Louverture, and since independence, he noted, Haitians were reportedly working 'with as fair a character as free labourers anywhere else'. He did not stress the matter, however. The abolitionists were perhaps unlucky that no trade figures were published during the reign of Christophe, when the export economy was probably at its strongest. Wilberforce, it is interesting to note, avoided using Haiti for propaganda purposes. In 1817, he advised, 'it is better to keep Hayti in the back ground, till it is better able to stand on its own legs'. He observed in his 1823 pamphlet that virtue and prosperity usually went hand in hand, but he conspicuously omitted any mention of Haiti when listing examples of industriousness and population growth among former slaves. More strikingly, Adam Hodgson did the same in a work devoted to proving the economic benefits of abolishing slavery, a work which Wilberforce admired.[58]

When Haitian trade figures were published in the following year, they were seized on by the anti-slavery lobby. They were quoted approvingly in Parliament and in the Abolition Society's second report. No wonder, commented the *Edinburgh Review*, that the 'wily Frank' wanted to regain possession of 'this most prosperous and interesting state'. The statistics, it was claimed, testified to the existence of a competent administrative machine as well as a thriving economy.[59] On this occasion the abolitionists played into the hands of their opponents, who pointed out various inconsistencies in the figures (such as between stated value and volume, and between shipping and export statistics). Comparisons with British and U.S. Customs reports further increased the impression that the figures were exaggerated. Even if they were not, they revealed what the planters had long been predicting – a massive decline in trade since 1789, an increasing foreign debt, and almost total disappearance of sugar cultivation. James Stephen continued to refer to Haitian trade as 'a commerce of vast importance', but this was clearly not an argument that the abolitionists were going to win.[60]

Even with the stimulus of profit-sharing, Haitians evidently did not wish to provide the gang labour needed to grow sugar. With considerable eloquence, the Anti-Slavery Society struck out at the planters' obsession with sugar, and R. W. Horton, the Under-Secretary for the colonies, accepted much of their argument. Haitians, he agreed, might be well-fed and contented, and become increasingly prosperous without exporting sugar. But this did not mean, he said, that emancipation would not harm British sugar planters. Compensation would therefore be necessary.[61] The British government showed close interest in the Haitian experiment. Consul Mackenzie was instructed in 1826 to provide detailed information on Toussaint's agricultural regulations, and to compare Christophe's and Pétion's policies. Parliament also had printed Major Moody's hostile report on free black labour (which deduced from the Haitian constitution that black and white could never live together in equality), and in 1829 Mackenzie's very critical dispatches.[62]

It is not easy to say exactly how the abolitionists had envisaged the organisation of a post-slavery economy. Haiti itself did not provide a clear model. Whereas Christophe had striven to keep the plantations alive with a system of forced labour, Pétion had allowed peasant smallholdings to develop, while Boyer in 1826 abruptly tried to revert to Christophe's system. As already seen, Wilberforce and Clarkson favoured the division of large plantations and their replacement, not with subsistence farming, but with a mixed system of landowners, tenants and wage-labourers producing for the market, as in Britain. On the other hand, they also appear to have admired Toussaint and Christophe's regime of coerced plantation labour. Sir Joseph Banks said Christophe's rural code ought to be written in letters of gold. This use of forced labour was naturally claimed by the planters as further evidence that blacks had to be compelled to work beyond the minimum necessary for subsistence. James Stephen himself had observed that under Boyer's rule many Haitians were working only half an hour per day. This was embarrassing for his colleagues who were claiming that freed slaves were more productive than slaves.[63]

Boyer's rural code of 1826 instantly became a subject of hot dispute. After a bogus copy, sent from Jamaica, had appeared in the British press, several editions were published in 1827, one by order of Parliament. According to the pro-slavery edition, the code proved the 'utter hopelessness' of trying to get blacks to work regularly without compulsion, and would dispel the 'total ignorance of the rest of the world as to what has been happening in the interior of Haiti'. The *Anti-Slavery Monthly Reporter* accepted that the code was not ideal, but insisted with some exaggeration that Haitians were no more coerced than were Englishmen by the laws of contract and vagrancy. W.W. Harvey did admit that the code infringed personal liberty but thought it otherwise good, while T.S. Winn claimed that it was entirely compatible with the freedom of labour. T.B. Macaulay, however, roundly condemned forced labour, and suggested that coercion, not freedom, might be the cause of Haiti's low productivity. If coercive laws were enforced there, it merely showed that the nation's leaders were misguided, not that it was necessary to coerce black labour.[64]

Macaulay's article, in the *Edinburgh Review*, was a showy tour de force, a mixture of superficially brilliant debating points and perceptive analysis. Haitian agriculture, he argued, was blighted by the need to maintain a large army and by fear of invasion, which discouraged investment; government taxation policy had destroyed the incentive to export coffee, while it was perfectly reasonable to abandon sugar, when its world price was so low. Haitians were working irregularly, indeed less than before (though he tried to fudge this point), but simply because their standard of living was now much higher than when they were slaves. They still behaved in an economically rational way, and could be tempted by the market to increase their output and their material prosperity. Today's luxuries were tomorrow's necessities. This was paring down to nothing the economic arguments that Haiti could furnish in favour of emancipation. Macaulay's article reflected a growing disillusionment with Haiti and desire to see it as the product of peculiar circumstances, not really relevant to the British case – a point that was accepted by some pro-slavery writers.[65]

Despite Macaulay's commitment to free-labour ideology, most anti-slavery leaders, according to David Eltis, wished to accompany emancipation in the British West Indies with coercive labour laws, so as to preserve the plantation system. Committed to the idea that emancipation would be both just and profitable, they were prepared to curtail the freedom being offered the slaves in the interests of the European consumer. To what extent it was the abolitionists' observations of Haiti that caused them to modify their laissez-faire principles is a subject needing further investigation. In any event, T.F. Buxton, who strongly favoured coercive measures, recommended Boyer's rural code to the House of Lords committee on emancipation in 1832. The previous year he had spoken in the Commons of Haiti's 'vice and misery'. The Haitian example was thus increasingly seen by the abolitionists in a negative light. When Edward Stanley introduced the motion for ending slavery in May 1833 he told Members of Parliament that the 'St Domingo' case was both irrelevant and inconclusive, adding that anyway the Cubans had proved that free labour would cultivate sugar.[66]

For the British abolitionists, Haiti now began to fade from view. James Stephen's long-projected history never appeared. Zachary Macaulay went on gathering material for a book, but it was in Paris that he published it in 1835 as the French campaign for emancipation was getting underway.[67] However, the French abolitionists were to show far less interest in their former colony than had their British counterparts. Antoine Métral had published two works on Saint Domingue, in 1818 and 1825, yet his *Les Esclaves* of 1836 avoided the subject. Agénor de Gasparin, writing in 1838, could make only modest claims on Haiti's behalf. In 1833, Victor Schoelcher found little to praise but argued that it was still too early to judge the new state. A decade later, however, he was quite disenchanted with Haiti, or more particularly with its mulatto elite. It is interesting that, insofar as Schoelcher and his colleagues saw emancipation as economically profitable, it was to be through the immigration of European labour into the Caribbean. Much more than the British, they insisted on emancipation simply as a question of justice.[68] Such differences, as Eltis and Engerman suggest, might reflect profound differences of motivation.[69] However, they might also derive from changing perceptions of Haiti, which in the 1830s could no longer be put forward as a desirable economic model (nor as a threat to the distant French islands).

In 1838, the black populace of the British colonies achieved 'full freedom' and the governments of France and Great Britain accorded full recognition to the Republic of Haiti. Haiti thus ceased to be a political issue at the same time as it lost its propaganda value as the sole post-slavery society in the Caribbean.

NOTES

1. Drouin de Bercy, *De Saint Domingue* (Paris, 1814), p. 7.
2. Eugene Genovese argues in *From Rebellion to Revolution* (Baton Rouge, 1979), p. 88, that Haiti was intended to be a modern state able to play an autonomous role in world affairs, and that this was why it was feared, not because of the defeat of whites and the creation of the black state, which had happened before. However, I do not think that the example Genovese cites, that of Palmares in Brazil, was a significant precedent. Moreover, few of Haiti's enemies thought it was capable of either economic development or political power. The Haitian revolution's most potent message was simply that slaves could successfully supplant their masters.
3. David Geggus, 'British Opinion and the Emergence of Haiti, 1791–1805', in James Walvin (ed.) *Slavery and British Society 1776–1846* (London, 1982), pp. 123–49.
4. *Ibid.*, pp. 144, 146.
5. James Stephen, *The Opportunity* (London, 1804).
6. *Christian Observer* (1804), pp. 418–21.
7. Geggus, 'Opinion', in Walvin (ed.), *Slavery, op. cit.*, pp. 138–9, 146–7.
8. Henry Brougham, *A Concise Statement of the Question Regarding the Abolition of the Slave Trade* (London, 1804); *Edinburgh Review* (hereafter *ER*), vol. 4, pp. 476–86, vol. 5, p. 238.
9. R. I. and Samuel Wilberforce, *Life of William Wilberforce*, 5 vols. (London, 1838), III, pp. 180–1.
10. Cf. C. C. Southey, *Life and Correspondence of Robert Southey*, 6 vols. (London, 1850), II, pp. 203–4. Moreover, it was the Haitian Revolution that first interested Henry Brougham in the West Indies; see C. W. New, *Life of Henry Brougham* (Oxford, 1961), pp. 13–14.
11. *The Times*, 27 and 28 Jan., 31 May 1804.
12. See the papers by Serge Daget and Seymour Drescher in Christine Bolt and Seymour Drescher (eds.), *Anti-Slavery, Religion and Reform* (Folkestone, 1980).
13. Henri Grégoire, *De La Littérature des Nègres* (Paris, 1808), pp. 161–2.
14. F. R. de Tussac, *Cri des Colons* (Paris, 1810), pp. 236–40.
15. Drouin de Bercy, *De Saint-Domingue, op. cit.*; Antoine Dalmas, *Histoire de la Révolution de Saint-Domingue* (Paris, 1814).

16. Wilberforce, *Life, op. cit.*, IV, pp. 209–12; Lt. Col. John Gurwood, *Dispatches of the Duke of Wellington*, 13 vols. (London, 1838), XII, pp. 114–16, 142.
17. J.C. de Sismondi, *De l'Intérêt de la France* (Paris, 1814); R.I. and Samuel Wilberforce, *Correspondence of William Wilberforce*, 2 vols. (London, 1840), II, p. 301; [Henri Grégoire], *De La Traite et de l'Esclavage* (Paris, 1815), p. 27.
18. William Wilberforce, *Lettre à Monseigneur le Prince de Talleyrand* (London, 1814); Southampton University, Wellington Papers, bundle 425, letters of Wilberforce and Macaulay, 18 and 20 Oct. 1814; *ER*, no. 24, pp. 66–138; Wilberforce, *Life, op. cit.*, IV, pp. 215–16.
19. [Grégoire], *De la Traite, op. cit.*, pp. 9–10, 18, 43, 45; R. Necheles, *The Abbé Gregoire* (Westport, 1971), p. 200.
20. C. Malenfant, *Des Colonies* (Paris, 1814); Leborgne de Boigne, *Nouveau Système de Colonisation* (Paris, 1817); F. J. P. Lacroix, *Mémoires*, 2 vols. (Paris, 1819); Charles-Malo, *Histoire d'Haiti* (Paris, 1819 and 1825).
21. Viscountess Knutsford, *Life and Letters of Zachary Macaulay* (London, 1900), p. 409; Necheles, *Grégoire, op. cit.*, p. 221.
22. James Stephen, *An Inquiry into the Right and Duty of Compelling Spain to Relinquish her Slave Trade* (London, 1816), pp. 89–91; *Christian Observer* (1815), p. 850.
23. Wilberforce, *Life, op. cit.*, IV, pp. 209–12; Gurwood, *Dispatches, op. cit.* XII, pp. 142, 145; E. L. Griggs and C. H. Prator (eds.), *Henry Christophe, Thomas Clarkson. A Correspondence* (Berkeley, 1952), pp. 60, 72, 122.
24. *Quarterly Review* (hereafter *QR*), vol. 6, p. 536; 13, p. 491; 16, p. 240; 19, p. 148.
25. Papiers Grégoire, Ms. 6339, Bibliothèque de l'Arsénal, Paris, letter of 7 Sept. 1815.
26. Papiers Grégoire, f. 44. The package was brought from London and delivered to Grégoire by General C. Macaulay; see Southampton University, Wellington Papers, bundle 425, undated letter.
27. Papiers Grégoire, ff. 53–59; *QR*, vol. no. 21, pp. 456–7.
28. Placide-Justin, *Histoire Politique* (Paris, 1826), pp. 486–7; Wilberforce, *Correspondence, op. cit.*, I, pp. 363–5; *ER*, 24, pp. 124–9. Cf. *Gentleman's Magazine* (June 1818), pp. 564–5, (May 1821), p. 460.
29. *Blackwood's Edinburgh Magazine* (November 1818), p. 132.
30. Wilberforce, *Life, op. cit.*, IV, p. 357; Griggs and Prator (eds.), *Christophe op. cit.*; Wilberforce, *Correspondence, op. cit.*, I, pp. 366–86, 387–91.
31. Wilberforce, *Life, op. cit.*, IV, pp. 352–61; Wilberforce, *Correspondence, op. cit.*, I, pp. 353–91; Griggs and Prator (eds.), *Christophe, op. cit.*, pp. 62–3; Joseph Marryat, *More Thoughts Still on the State of the West India Colonies* (London, 1818), p. 32.
32. Griggs and Prator (eds.), *Christophe, op. cit.*, pp. 67–70, 126–7, 155, 177, 195.
33. 'Colonist', *The Edinburgh Review and the West Indies* (London, 1816), pp. 200–10; Wilberforce, *Correspondence, op. cit.*, I, pp. 363–5; *Blackwood's Edinburgh Magazine* (Dec. 1821), p. 551.
34. Prince Sanders, *Haytian Papers* (London 1816); *The Pamphleteer*, vol. 13, no. 25, pp. 165–240; *Blackwood's Edinburgh Magazine* (Nov. 1818), pp. 130–5, (June 1821), pp. 267–8, (Dec. 1821), pp. 545–552; Wilberforce, *Correspondence, op. cit.*, I, p. 387.
35. Marryat, *Thoughts, op. cit.*, pp. 37–40; 'Colonist', *Edinburgh Review, op. cit.*, pp. 200–10.
36. Griggs and Prator (eds.), *Christophe, op. cit.*, pp. 106, 223–5; *Gentleman's Magazine* (April 1817), p. 358; Wilberforce, *Correspondence, op. cit.*, I, p. 369.
37. *Gentleman's Magazine* (April 1821), p. 366, (May 1821), p. 460; Wilberforce, *Correspondence, op. cit.*, I, pp. 391–5.

38. Wilberforce, *Life, op. cit.*, V, p. 108; Griggs and Prator (eds.), *Christophe op. cit.*, pp. 78, 224–5; Necheles, *Grégoire, op. cit.*, pp. 382–3.
39. Griggs and Prator (eds.), *Christophe, op. cit.*, pp. 71–73; *Christian Observer* (1815), p. 850; Wilberforce, *Correspondence, op. cit.*, I, pp. 382–3.
40. James Stephen, *England Enslaved by her own Slave Colonies*, 2nd edition (London, 1826), pp. 17–24.
41. See Charles-Malo, *Histoire, op. cit.*, p. 427.
42. Necheles, *Grégoire, op. cit.*, pp. 240–1; Griggs and Prator (eds.), *Christophe, op. cit.*, pp. 179–80; Papiers Grégoire, ff. 61–67, 77–86, 105–6.
43. Bolt and Drescher (eds.), *Anti-Slavery, op. cit.*, p. 70; Papiers Grégoire, ff. 98–103; Necheles, *Grégoire, op. cit.*, pp. 232–6.
44. Necheles, *Grégoire, op. cit.*, pp. 243–5, 323–9.
45. Cf. David Geggus, 'Unexploited Sources for the History of the Haitian Revolution', *Latin American Research Review*, 18, no. 1 (1983), fn. 27. As for purely literary works, Victor Hugo's *Bug Jargal* of 1819 was reprinted in 1826, and the anonymous and undated epic, *L'Haitiade* may have appeared as late as 1827 or 1828. However, Charles de Rémusat's *L'Habitation de Saint-Domingue, ou l'Insurrection*, written in 1824, never found a publisher.
46. [Joseph Morénas], *Précis Historique ... de l'Esclavage Colonial* (Paris, 1828), pp. 61–5.
47. William Dickson, *Mitigation of Slavery* (London, 1814), p. ix; *Substance of the Debate in the House of Commons on the 15th May 1823* (London, 1823), p. 9; Stephen, *England Enslaved, op. cit.*, p. 24.
48. James MacQueen, *The West India Colonies* (London, 1824), pp. 183–94; 'Britannicus', *A Reply ... on Thomas Clarkson's Treatise* (London, 1824), pp. 3–18; Marryat, *More Thoughts, op. cit.*, pp. 26–40; Alexander Barclay, *A Practical View of the Recent State of Slavery in the West Indies*, 2nd edition (London, 1827), pp. 145–6.
49. Geggus, 'British Opinion', in Walvin (ed.), *Slavery, op. cit.*, pp. 144–5.
50. Thomas Clarkson, *Thoughts on ... the Condition of Slaves* (London, 1823), pp. 19–29.
51. *ER*, 39, pp. 126–7; 41, pp. 497–507; *Anti-Slavery Monthly Reporter* (hereafter *ASMR*) (1825), pp. 25–8; Anthony Brough, *The Importance of the British Colonies in the West Indies* (London, 1833), pp. 21–2.
52. 'Colonist', *Edinburgh Review, op. cit.*, pp. 200–10; MacQueen, *West India Colonies, op. cit.*, pp. 190–4.
53. *QR*, 21, pp. 430–60.
54. *QR*, 29, p. 481; 30, pp. 560–87; Stephen, *England Enslaved, op. cit.*, p. 16; *Second Report of the Committee of the Society for the Mitigation and Gradual Abolition of Slavery* (London, 1825), pp. 38–40.
55. W. W. Harvey, *Sketches of Hayti* (London, 1827; reprinted Frank Cass, 1972); James Franklin, *The Present State of Hayti* (London, 1828; reprinted Frank Cass, 1972); Charles Mackenzie, *Notes on Hayti* (London, 1830; reprinted Frank Cass, 1972); *ASMR* (1829), pp. 147–62, (1830), pp. 207–8.
56. Stephen, *Opportunity, op. cit.*, pp. 18–21; *ER*, 24, pp. 110–30, 41, pp. 497–507, 42, pp. 495–6; Marryat, *More Thoughts, op. cit.*, p. 27; *ASMR* (1829), pp. 147–62.
57. *Christian Observer* (1804), pp. 309, 418–21; Stephen, *Opportunity, op. cit.*, pp. 18–21; H.P. Brougham, *An Inquiry into the Colonial Policies of the European Powers*, 2 vols. (Edinburgh, 1803), II, pp. 120–1, 141–84; Anon., *Opinions of Henry Brougham Esq* (London, 1826), pp. 19–25.
58. Clarkson, *Thoughts, op. cit.*, pp. 19–49; Wilberforce, *Life, op. cit.*, IV, pp. 358–61; William Wilberforce, *An Appeal to the Religion ... of the*

Inhabitants of the British Empire (np, 1823), pp. 8, 49; Adam Hodgson, *Letter to M. J-B. Say* (Liverpool, 1823).

59. *ER*, 41, pp. 497–507, 42, pp. 495–6; *Second Report, op. cit.*, p. 40.
60. *QR*, 30, pp. 560–87; Barclay, *Practical View, op. cit.*, p. vi; Stephen, *England Enslaved, op. cit.*, p. 24.
61. [R. W. Horton], *The West India Question Practically Considered* (London, 1826), pp. 53–9. Anon., *Letter to R. W. Horton* (London, 1826), did not controvert this.
62. David Nicholls, *From Dessalines to Duvalier: Race, Colour and National Independence in Haiti* (Cambridge, 1979), p. 62; *ER*, 45, pp. 387–9.
63. Griggs and Prator (eds.), *Christophe, op. cit.*, p. 45; *QR*, 30, pp. 572–82.
64. *The Rural Code of Hayti ... with a Prefatory Letter* (London, 1827), p. v; *ASMR* (1827), pp. 309–10, 324–5, 329–66; Harvey, *Sketches, op. cit.*, p. xiii; T. S. Winn, *Supplement to a Speedy End to Slavery* (London, 1827), p. 16; *ER*, 45, pp. 387–416.
65. 'A West India Proprietor', *Opinions and Remarks on Slavery* (London, 1829), pp. 23–4.
66. David Eltis, 'Abolitionist Perceptions of Society after Slavery', in Walvin (ed.), *Slavery, op. cit.*, pp. 201–5; Charles Buxton, *Memoirs of Sir Thomas Fowell Buxton* (London, 1855), p. 221; *ASMR* (1833), p. 104.
67. Buxton Papers, letters of Sept. and Oct. 1835, Rhodes House, Oxford; Zachary Macaulay, *Haiti ou Renseignements Authentiques sur l'Abolition de l'Esclavage* (Paris, 1835).
68. Agénor de Gasparin, *Esclavage et Traite* (Paris, 1838), pp. 23–5, 102; Victor Schoelcher, *Colonies Étrangères et Haiti* (Paris, 1843), pp. 267, 281.
69. See David Eltis and S. L. Engerman, 'Economic Aspects of the Abolition Debate', in Bolt and Drescher (eds.), *Anti-Slavery, op. cit.*, p. 288.

7

The Abolition of the Slave Trade by France: The Decisive Years 1826–1831*

SERGE DAGET

Between January 1826 and November 1831, France virtually put an end to two centuries of participation in the slave trade. This turnabout had been prepared for three-quarters of a century by abolitionist thinking, revolutionary reality and the action of militants of the *Société des Amis des Noirs*.[1] As early as 1814, at the same time as the economist Simonde de Sismondi, Madame de Staël had played a part in re-establishing abolitionist ideas by supporting and circulating the writings of William Wilberforce. After the death of the latter, the Abbé Grégoire, his disciples Morénas and Guidicelly, and from quite a different direction, the Duke de Broglie and a few others reformulated the humanitarian doctrine. However, from the beginning of this paper it must be stressed that the authentic French abolitionists were so strongly influenced by the works, the deeds and the successes of their British counterparts that a certain section of French opinion went as far as to accuse them of being in the pay of Britain. This accusation was not correct but was thought up by French pro-slavery reactionaries. But by repetition it stuck to the abolitionists like a trade mark.[2]

The turnabout had the effect of doing more than had been expected, for it led to the first *Entente Cordiale*, or at least to what has been called an 'idyll'. In this process we shall see how the different factors in a complex conjuncture came together and we shall seek to measure the relative importance of French attitudes and British influence. We shall also consider factors foreign to the question itself, asking whether these were not perhaps the most significant. A long time in preparation, the abolition of the slave trade by France did not come about by pure chance. Did it come about by design or by accident? Why and how far were these years decisive?

Although the affairs of Saint Domingue had been settled diplomatically in 1825, the men of the Restoration had not forgotten earlier disasters which they blamed on the abolitionists. The impact of abolitionists' ideas on public opinion was weak. The conviction that the colonies of Martinique, Guadeloupe, Guyana and Réunion were short of labour kept alive a state of mind favourable to the slave trade. These psychological and economic factors partially explain why from June 1814 to December 1825 there were 472 voyages by French ships suspected of trading in blacks in African waters. They are only a partial explanation, however, because on investigation, it is clear that French slave traders did not supply the French Antilles in the main but preferred to land their black cargoes in foreign colonies, preferably Cuba. Among the suspected ships, 131 were new, often entering the slave trade as soon as they left the shipyard. The demand for technical and commercial goods associated with the preparations made in the metropolis for slave voyages required the investment of capital. It also created jobs and guaranteed wages at a time when work was scarce among workers and sailors. The slave trade could thus claim to be an instrument of economic activity and social peace. Between 1814 and 1825 French shipowners resumed the slave trade on approximately the same scale as at the end of the eighteenth century.

Despite this, the slave trade was prohibited. The Restoration government paid lip-service to the international abolition of the trade, whilst reserving its freedom of action. In 1818 French legislation made the trade illegal and at once military steps were taken to enforce the law: patrols by warships charged with the repression of the slave trade were instituted. But the law and the patrols were scarcely operational before 1822. The trade continued despite various administrative steps intended to prevent it. It was carried on despite continuous dissuasive attempts made by the British. The latter were expressed diplomatically through Foreign Office channels. Militarily, they took the form of the Royal Navy and its repression of the slave trade in the Atlantic and around Madagascar and the Mascareignes. But the French saw such activities in juridical terms, describing them as a violation of international maritime law, a claim that the British Admiralty did not contest. The contradiction between the stupidity of French measures on the one hand and the pressure and actions of the British on the other led, as Yvan Debbasch has so well expressed it, to the offices of the Ministry of the Navy in Paris being 'haunted' by continued French participation in the slave trade.[3]

The Foreign Office continuously denounced French participation in the slave trade. The Restoration government complained about the lack of proof; the evidence was not verified, was unverifiable, or at any rate was exaggerated. The government wanted tangible proof. It was a French subject, the brother of Madame de Staël, who produced it. Auguste de Staël, who was a member of the *Société de la Morale Chrétienne*, a humanitarian organisation formed at the end of 1821, was sent to Nantes on a mission of enquiry, adopting the Clarksonian method of on-the-spot observation. In Nantes, Staël was able to buy slave-irons freely. In Paris, through the medium of members of the *Société*, such as the Count d'Argout, de Broglie, and above all, Philippe d'Orléans, this material passed up the abolitionist network as far as the royal entourage. This enabled the royal family to see *de visu* and actually to handle evidence of the reality of the slave trade which owed little to British propaganda or diplomacy and everything to the French traders. It expressed its horror.

By this simple means the possibilities of delays based upon the rejection of allegations made in London were brought to an end. Above all, credibility was given to the 'revelations' which Staël and the abolitionist organisation added to this concrete demonstration. They announced that 80 vessels were being prepared to go in search of blacks on the African coast.[4] This figure was probably blown up for the needs of the cause. All the same, it has been established that in 1824 and 1825 46 and 50 slavers respectively left Nantes, from a total of 71 and 76 for all French ports.

Following this, thanks to the enquiries of consul-general Clayton and vice-consul Macintosh – a technique some ten years old – the Foreign Office received reliable information which was sent at once to Granville, the ambassador in Paris. He scrupulously passed this on to Baron de Damas, Minister of Foreign Affairs.[5] A triple current of information thus converged on the French authorities: triple, because France itself was not without knowledge of the activities of its slave traders, which it repressed militarily and judicially. But the information that came from Britain was considered to be in bad faith.

The shock tactic of the *Société de la Morale Chrétienne* was the culmination of a period in which several factors favourable to abolition showed themselves. In several French ports petitions were presented, crowned on 13 February 1826 by that from '130 inhabitants of Paris, heads of the leading commercial houses and other notables, who called in the name of public morality' for the ending of the outfitting of slave traders in France.[6] To those collective petitions were added individual petitions of absolute sincerity, for their authors were not official abolitionists dependent upon a position of opposition to the government in power.[7]

Another important event had effects throughout the metropolis. On 14 January 1826 the *Cour de Cassation* (Supreme Court of Appeal), the highest judicial authority in France, handed down a judgement which for the first time rigorously defined the nature of the slave trade: '[it] does not consist only in trade which takes place on the coast of Africa, but in the part of this trade which takes the form of a series of preparatory acts which constitute it, organize it and ensure its success ...'.[8] Henceforth, French jurisprudence admitted that slave traders could be prevented from carrying on their preparations in France itself.

It is possible that this judicial decision had repercussions on the coast of Africa and in the Antilles. For the sailors of French patrols established to repress the trade its effects were as much military as psychological. Until 1823 their official instructions, full of severe recommendations, were contradicted in practice by the indecision of the colonial and metropolitan authorities, and by the judgements pronounced on the slave traders which were seized. The naval patrols seemed to be nothing more than schools of despair. But in August 1823, a general mobilisation order of the war fleet against slave traders of French nationality changed the course of things. Under the command of *Capitaine de vaisseau*, La Treyte, the new patrol became really effective, the brig, *Le Dragon*, commanded by Esprit Lachelier, particularly distinguishing itself. The increased support of public opinion, the metropolitan judiciary and the new men in command of the men-of-war may have encouraged the belief that the patrol of 1826, commanded by Massieu de Clairval (descendant of an eighteenth-century slave trader from St Malo) would rival that of the British patrol. After several years' discussion, a decision in 1825 gave a decisive impulse to French repressive action; following British practice, France offered its sailors on the coast of Africa a reward of 100 francs for each black 'recaptured' on board ships which were seized. Henceforth, for a certain time, repression of the trade on the coast took the form of a competition between two rival navies, each spurred on by the other, both harnessed to the same task.

In Nantes itself, the intervention of the *Société de la Morale Chrétienne* and the decision of the *Cour de Cassation* produced three benefits. Firstly, several forges which made irons were forced to close.[9] Secondly, the commissioner of the Navy, Clemansin Dumaine, and probably his superior, the commissioner resident Fourcroy de Guillerville, were severely reprimanded by the minister, Chabrol de Crouzol.[10] Finally, a special autonomous ministerial commission was set up with the task of putting an end to the Nantes slave trade. These developments were not, of course, of equal importance.

The ministerial commission for Nantes was supervised by the *capitaine de frégate*, Esprit Lachelier, former commander of the brig, *Le Dragon*. He had inflicted damage on slave traders on the African coast during 1824.[11] He was quite ready to do likewise in the home of the slave trade in 1826. This was perhaps less from humanitarian sentiment than, quite simply, from bitter feelings. Placed above the top local administrative officials of the Navy and invested with real powers, Lachelier was not always precise in distinguishing intuition from legitimate doubt and the latter from guilt. There was also the fact that a 'foreigner' could not feel himself at ease in the slave-trading *maquis* of Nantes. Nevertheless, even if Lachelier committed some notable errors, he was able to prevent the sailing of three slave traders, and had them found guilty according to the judgement handed down by the *Cour de Cassation* at the beginning of the year. From 16 May 1826, his zeal was tempered by a ministerial note which revoked the commission's autonomy and granted it the right to bring a vessel before the courts only after authorisation from the minister. The Nantais had influence in the right places in Paris. In principle, the authority of the Lachelier commission did not extend beyond the limits of Nantes. But as Table 1 below shows, it is possible that its real effect extended beyond the slave-trading capital for quite some time.

TABLE 1

French slave traders from 1826 to 1831

	French	from Nantes	Others
1826	44	25	19
1827	34	13	21
1828	25	6	19
1829	28	10	18
1830	33	21	12
1831	13	3	10
	177	78	99 (a)

(a) Saint-Malo, La Rochelle, Bordeaux, Bayonne, Marseilles, Guadeloupe, Martinique, Saint-Thomas des Antilles, and 42 unknown, of whom an uncertain number were surely from Nantes. Recall that in 1825 the total number of French slave traders amounted to 76 of which 50 were from Nantes.

Previous decisions had not obtained this result. In his time, ambassador Stuart had suggested to the French government the need to publish in the *Moniteur Universel* the sentences passed for slave-trading activity, counting on the discreditable character of such publicity. This principle which was not included in the law of 1818 tended, however, to become the rule in 1825; ambassador Granville sent to London press cuttings which included names.[12] In 1826, the *Moniteur Universel*, copied by the *Annales Maritimes et Coloniales*, published the official list of the sentences passed by the metropolitan and colonial courts for contravention of the law; 65 captains and vessels were named, but not a single ship-owner – a difference which smacked of class justice.[13] The extent to which this dominant state of mind was implanted was, equally significantly, reflected by the reticence of the local magistrates in applying the decisions of the *Cour de Cassation*. In two trials of slave traders sent before the royal courts of Paris and Rennes during 1826 the decisions of the supreme court were not upheld and the slave traders were released. It is difficult to decide whether it was to extend a helping hand to the government or the application of a brake by the magistrates themselves on their own initiative which accounted for this attitude.

In order to prevent any further delay, the minister of the Navy took advantage of this situation to modify the French legislation, though not without contradictions and difficulties. In June 1826, the Count de Chabrol was still defending the first French abolitionist law, using the traditional arguments produced by each of his colleagues since May 1818. Despite its mediocre results, the law was good and adequate. By 26 December 1826 the ministerial turnabout was complete. Circumstances had shown that the law of 1818 was bad. Chabrol expounded before the Chamber of Peers the main lines of a new law. There was some astonishment from the Peers and from the Deputies who suspected that it embodied the ideas of Canning, since he had spent several days in Paris in October. In reply Chabrol referred to the lack of understanding of the courts and national honour. The new law proposed the degrading penalty of banishment for any individual who contributed to the preparation or the carrying on of the slave trade; monetary fines equivalent to the value of the ship and its cargo; and various terms of imprisonment for the members of the crews of slave ships and a ban on their service in the Navy.

In contrast to the small amount of discussion raised by the law of 1818, the 1827 law gave rise to important debates in both chambers. Eight speakers took part in the Peers and twelve in the Deputies; their speeches took up 223 printed pages in the *Annales Maritimes et Coloniales*, amounting to about 75,000 words. It was a courteous debate without too many insults, but it was not in any sense a rearguard action on the part of the anti-abolitionists. The Peers had been worked on by the up-and-coming young politician, the Duke de Broglie, one of the founders of the *Société de la Morale Chrétienne* and recognised by Wilberforce as an authentic spokesman for the cause. Among the Deputies, the best representative of the abolitionists, the celebrated Benjamin Constant, was still somewhat suspect to his colleagues. It was a debate in which the opponents of the new text made use of three principal time-honoured arguments of the late eighteenth century anti-abolitionists. First, the slave trade was necessary for trade, for the colonies and for the Royal Navy. This argument seemed to be so evident and so commonplace in the view of the speakers that they did not consider it necessary to comment on it or to support it with figures. Second, the slave trade was necessary for the welfare of the Africans themselves. Abolition would condemn to over-population a continent capable of giving up each year 150,000 individuals. Over-population would lead the barbarous chiefs to kill off those inhabitants they could no longer sell.[14] At least the slave trade enabled the blacks to learn in the colonies what liberty was like. Third, abolition was not a French national decision. Victorious Britain in 1814 and 1815 had dictated it in such a way that its many aspects converged on one real objective: to bring about the ruin of France, by suppressing French colonial production, which would be impossible without black labour, and by making useless the mercantile marine and the navy which would follow from the suppression of the activities of merchant vessels, with all the dire social consequences which would follow. Ever since the Congress of Vienna this standard caricature of British Machiavellianism had not varied one iota among most of the spokesmen for this particular French mentalité.

In support of these old assertions, the Duc de Fitz-James appealed to history and events to confirm his arguments.[15] History showed that Wilberforce himself had encountered the opposition of the shipowners of Liverpool and the planters of Jamaica for twenty years, but France had not waited twenty years to take genuine measures in favour of the blacks. The Duke used the authority of his friendship with the late General MacCarthy to pass judgement on the experiment of Sierra Leone. Repression produced labour and troops for the British colonies, consequences which raised a question mark over the aim and the success of Wilberforce.[16] The events included the recent statement by Canning, which was 'a great insult to France'. Fitz-James accepted the denials and the corrections made by the British, as the French government had done. Nevertheless, proclaiming himself a supporter of peace, he pronounced against wallowing in pacifism.[17] A few years previously, under the ministries of Portal and Clermont-Tonnerre, certain Frenchmen had already passed quickly from resistance to the abolition of the slave trade imposed by Great Britain to the idea of a possible war (of revenge?) against Britain.[18]

If there was nothing new in the arguments of the anti-abolitionists, there was nothing new either from the supporters of humanitarianism who had exhausted the possibilities of regenerating their doctrine since the end of the eighteenth century. There remained for them the denunciation of the illegal activities of the traders in blacks; they did it with fine persistence, relying heavily upon information obtained from London, whether through the official channel of the reports to the African Institute, or privately from publications in French supplied mainly by the Quakers.[19] It seems unlikely that they obtained any information from the Ministry of the Navy, where very large amounts of information much too compromising for the sincerity of official statements and policies were kept for internal use. They had also to denounce the arguments of the enemies of abolition which itself was no small matter.

Broglie, a visionary and a prophet, proclaimed the unfailing alignment of France with Britain as much on the question of rights of search as on that of slavery. Hyde de Neuville, a future Navy Minister, used his oratorical talents to remind deputies of his past as an ambassador in Washington and to protect his reputation during the following months. Bergevin, the man of every ministry, was able to sustain the paradox of supporting the pro-slavery motion of the Count de Vaublanc, the appointed representative of the colonies, asserting that only Spanish entrepreneurs had carried on the slave trade from Bordeaux, and that it had disappeared from that port a long time ago – a specious point. On 14 March 1827 de Geres produced the fourth history of the slave trade and rendered fervent homage to Wilberforce for the way in which he had been able to stir up the House of Commons. That said, the orator threw doubts on the purity of the intentions of the honourable members, and, more generally, of Britain as a whole.[20]

Finally, the good of the cause made it necessary to moderate some contributions, whose form was not always able to conceal the content. The majority of parliamentarians formally recognised the officially criminal character of the slave trade and announced this as some prodigious discovery of the intellect. Punishment of offenders, however, was not to exceed reasonable limits. Here was *the* transformation, a product of manicheism, of the notions of the just and the unjust, of the good and the bad. For example, solitary confinement, demanded by Benjamin Constant, was in excess of the common level of understanding of the penalty to be applied. By contrast, banishment, an ignominious penalty, offered many guarantees. The mover of the bill, de Martignac, explained at length to his colleagues that it would be impracticable, because of the absence of specific conventions with foreign countries.[21] The spirit of the bill was more important than its substance. In reality, the discussion enabled a good number of participants to work off part of their anger against Britain. Approved by the Chamber of Peers, the text was voted without amendment by the Deputies.

On 8 May 1827 the minister gave orders to the French ports on the measures to be taken to implement the law of 25 April 1827.[22] They were rather strange instructions. They insisted on the criminal character of the penalties to be applied but used this as an argument to absolve the maritime administration almost entirely from the many obligations imposed upon it by circulars issued since 1818. Henceforth, the law would aid justice but not take precedence over it; sailors who were 'almost always illiterate' would be informed about the penalties and their immunity if they became informers. These instructions thus helped in a way those administrators who, despite the hundreds of recommendations issued after the law of 1818, had never willingly assumed the role of inquisitor which had been imposed upon them, whether at the time of departure or arrival of vessels. The ministry had brought to an end an out-dated cycle.

With the beginning of changes in public feeling, reinforced repression on the African coast, carrying out of repression on the national soil, and the passing of a new law, it was true that in sixteen months more had been done than in the dozen previous years. Table 1 shows the effects on slaving voyages. One wonders if they were entirely the result of official measures against the slave trade.

In Nantes, the dual success of the ministerial commission and of the new law were clearly apparent. It was only after two years of experimentation with the effects of the text of 1827 that the Nantais returned without too much prudence to their accustomed rhythm of fitting out ships for the slave trade. They were the only ones in France to do so, with the exception of the Antillais. The new law was not simply a piece of paper. Repression took place, much less in the metropolis however than at sea or in the Antilles. Simply from the statistical point of view, between the years 1827 and 1831 the slave traders of French nationality captured at sea by French warships were more numerous than the seizures by the British patrols. The French patrols were strengthened in means and effectiveness. The British extended a strategy which had previously existed only in outline; although ships seized in waters under British influence were condemned first of all at Sierra Leone, those slave traders recognised as French were taken, after their condemnation and the freeing of the blacks, to Gorée and handed over to French justice.[23] Table 2 compares the results of the two repressive forces.

TABLE 2

French slave traders captured 1826–1831

	French captures	British captures	Total captures	Total slavers
1826	4	5	9	44
1827	11	2	13	34
1828	6	5	11	25
1829	8	6	14	28
1830	4	2	6	33
1831	2	1	3	13
	35 (a)	21 (b)	56	177

(a) of which 19 on the west coast of Africa, 10 in the Americas, 5 at Bourbon, 1 unknown.
(b) of which 18 on the west coast of Africa.

The success of the repression by the French was not without its bizarre aspects. Among the 21 vessels seized by the British 13 reported on the number of blacks freed; 18 of the 35 vessels seized by the French produced similar reports. According to these reports, the number of blacks freed totalled 2,494 and

2,660 respectively. Half of the 13 British reports related to captures made in the proximity of Sierra Leone and Old Calabar. The French offered little explanation of the regional origin of captures, referring vaguely in nine cases including 1028 blacks to 'the African coast'. These figures confirm, first, the extreme discretion of French sailors concerning their captures, and second, the perceptible difference between the average number of blacks found on board the ships captured by the British and the French: 192 individuals per vessel in the British case; only 148 or even 114 in the French. This difference certainly does not affirm that the French patrols chose to stop and capture by preference the less loaded vessels. In theory, the accountants of the Treasury or of the *Caisse des prises* should have clarified any uncertainty about the accuracy of this information through their payment of the bounty to the capturers, but this information is incomplete, in both Britain and France.[24]

Although figures on re-captures are inaccurate, they were at least food for thought for the entrepreneurs engaged in the trade. More and more subject to repression by law and naval patrols, the trade became an all too risky speculation. 'Speculation' is a rather euphemistic term, for it was infused with a moral content as the speculator plunged Africa into fear, poverty and death. The abolitionists alone gave the term its full economic meaning. However, a series of indices leads one to think that once the slave trade had become illegal returns on the whole were no better than a very prudent speculation. The large ships of the eighteenth century were no longer employed in the illegal traffic: the average size of illegal French slavers was 142 tons. This well-established fact implied a deliberate limitation of the need for capital investment, trade goods, and crews; the latter numbered 25 to 35 on average. It also limited the possibility of loading slaves on the coast; rarely did ships carry more than 200 blacks, a reflection of limited loading time on the coast. Of 71 loadings which can be checked, 62 lasted from one to six months. Cargoes of slaves were certainly smaller in number, but the slave-trading entrepreneur obtained two advantages: a coastal trip or a call of shorter duration offered less opportunity for capture by warships and a smaller cargo was theoretically less liable to eventual 'wastage'. Another indication of the greater risks is provided by the fact that the French ship-owners preferred to deliver to those slave-owners who were good payers: the Cubans and the Danish colonists of Saint-Thomas.[25] Once illegal, the trade conformed more than ever to what Thomas Clarkson had called it: 'a lottery'.[26] The search for alternative opportunities was a realistic decision on the part of the ship-owners: to keep their distance from and restrict a traffic which had become economically dubious and socially dangerous. This was the attitude of the capitalist speculator, moving from one activity to another, if the first proved unsafe or did not give sufficient guarantees. For slave traders, other activities such as 'legitimate' trade with other parts of the African coast offered better opportunities by 1827. These suggestions, which reflect the influence of business conditions, can be verified in two ways from figures of French output and trade.

Proponents of advanced economic models argued twenty years ago that the 'industrial revolution' began in France around 1820. Historians have now revised this idea, but even today it is difficult to assess the impact of this improbable industrial revolution on the final abolition of the slave trade. However, it is clear that in the case of Nantes, the technological exhibition of 1826 drew some ship-owners away from the traditional pre-occupations. It cannot be said that they abandoned maritime activities, but they did turn to other forms of investment, especially ashore. Their capital or that which they brought together, was less attracted by speculations which were more hazardous than they had ever been.[27]

A complementary explanation is even better founded. It is to be based on the figures of trading activity. In 1827 the foreign trade of France amounted to 1168 million gold francs. It thus reached for the first time in 40 years the level attained before the Revolution. Trade by land amounted to 357 million francs; trade by sea to 811 million. Exports by land and sea were 602 million francs and were about 10 per cent more than imports, which stood at 566 million. Exports by land were 157 million francs, but those by sea were three times as great at 445 million. Until 1831, despite a crisis and a fall of about 10 per cent during the Revolution of 1830, the level of exports remained stable. In 1833 commerce by sea alone exceeded 1,000 million francs.[28]

Between 1787 and 1789, at the height of the slave trade,

French ship-owners employed 99, 109 and 131 ships each year respectively in the trade.[29] While it is not possible to calculate exactly the relative proportion of the trade in blacks to the total foreign trade of France at this time, a minimum estimate of about 20 per cent is reasonable. In other words, of the 1,000 million francs of French maritime trade on the eve of the Revolution about 200 million consisted of that arising from the trade in blacks. This was obviously considerable. In 1827, the ship-owners did not have to make elaborate calculations to realise that a reduction of trade in blacks of more than two-thirds compared to 1788 and by four-fifths compared to 1789 had not prevented foreign trade from making a very good recovery. In other words factors other than the slave trade accounted for the flourishing state of maritime trade. This occurred without the slave trade and without ship-owners assuming the ever more costly risks which participation in it was henceforth likely to produce. At the very least, this forced ship-owners to abandon the old view that the slave trade was an essential guarantee of general prosperity. As a result it stood condemned, probably even in the short run, by its own practitioners.

Such observations tend to call into question the importance to be attached to the activities of the abolitionists, British pressure and the repression of the slave traders. Moral and physical factors were not the key elements in the decisive years, but subsidiary factors. The problem is not to assess the relative importance of the forces responsible for ending the trade but to seek the conditions which brought about a new conjuncture. One cannot be sure that moral and physical factors, economic agents, speculation, or changes of trade or output were exclusively determinant. Other factors, although lying on the extreme periphery of our concerns, are relevant to the solution of a problem which required international collaboration. For example, the Anglo-French economic treaty of 1826 indicated that the two leading powers in the world felt the need 'to establish commercial relations ... on a footing of complete reciprocity'.[30] There was at the same time a need for co-operation and for the definition of the zones of interest and influence. The purpose of the treaty was to reduce the difficulties encountered in maritime trade, and it made allowance for special conditions to the advantage of the colonial interests of both parties. On the political level, one cannot overlook instances of Anglo-French co-operation (or agreement not to interfere) from the time of the joint expedition in Greece to the giving of a free hand to the French in Algiers. Navarino was obviously not a crusade against the Barbary pirates who had been denounced as slave traders since the London conferences of 1816. The link with the abolition of the slave trade is that the *Société de Morale Chrétienne* had for humanitarian reasons also formed a committee of support for the Greeks. Navarino was above all a case of collaboration within the framework of a certain kind of super-nationality which was based upon support for the right to board.

Such developments could not be without consequence for a matter which had dragged on too long. Doubtless the supporters of slavery remained unshakable. Louis Dejean still rose up against the calumnies to which the colonists were generally subject, suggesting also that those speakers who were blinded by the humanitarian appearance of Britain lost sight of its real aim which was 'to take over world trade'.[31] The abolitionists were less negative. A former colonist from Martinique, a proprietor of a château and a *rentier*, Louis Vitalis, looked forward to the rooting out of smuggling. It was generally thought of as wrong, he said, and it was false that abolition would lead to the ruin of the colonies, false that Britain wanted to wipe out trade, and intolerable to evade the law. A conscious or unconscious Fourierist, he suggested the exploitation of human passions, and had noticed in the field that the negroes possessed at least one, love. They should therefore be offered 18,000 negresses and be required to produce '6,000 children per year'.[32] The changes were more striking to advanced reformers. Thus for Auguste Billiard, making a considerable leap, the new law was not bad in itself, but committed some errors of appreciation. For example, regarding acclimatised slaves, the real producers, it was not a good thing 'to teach them that it was a crime to bring new companions into slavery with them'.[33] With one exception his solutions were commonplace. He proposed to keep a register of slaves to compensate the colonists (there was rarely any thought of compensating the slaves), and to import 2,000 to 3,000 child-bearing young negresses, thereby adopting the principle of pardoning the immorality and existence of the trade. The real novelty lay in the recommendation of the solution almost unanimously rejected by the French since 1814. The rarity of such a viewpoint leads us to quote it in full:

> For the repression of the offence of slave-trading,[34] there is one means of reconciling honour and humanity. A patrol is necessary on the African coast; it can consist of combined French and British forces. A reciprocal right of search will do no harm in these waters, where commercial operations and European establishments are far from having the same importance as on the opposite coast.[35] Common interest makes such a right necessary. By agreement with each other, a smaller number of vessels will be employed. As for the captured vessels, this will be the object of a special convention the main points of which it should not be difficult to define. Agreement will be reached on the forces which each one will contribute. Everywhere else but on the African coast a reciprocal right of search cannot be permitted, unless it be around the territories of the various colonies.[36]

Another factor contributing to the change in attitude after 1826 was the fact that the movements of opinion spread outside the limits of the metropolis, affecting equally the slave-holding colonies or the consular representatives in the Americas. From Martinique, Renouard, Marquis de Sainte-Croix, was not satisfied with addressing to the Deputies a petition calling for respect for the rights of slaves.[37] He reinforced it not only by denouncing the slave ships which delivered blacks but by listing the names of the purchasers and the houses which received them.[38] The consuls at Bahia, at Santiago de Cuba, at Pernambouc, and even at Saint-Thomas, the Danish colony, informed the Ministry of the Navy about the continuation of the trade and gave details of French participation.[39] In Bourbon (Réunion), the Crown prosecutor informed the Governor that the courts were ready to apply the law rigorously. One of the most important colonists on the island, Charles Desbassyns, whose family had ties with the former minister Villèle, argued positively for the necessity of bringing the trade to an end.[40]

Even more important than these theoretical positions were those taken up by those entrusted with enforcement of repression at sea. In the Antilles, the Rear-Admiral Dupotet, while 'despairing' of ever being able to end the trade, considered that there should be no hesitation in arresting on land those blacks who had been disembarked.[41] On the African coast, Captain Massieu de Clairval studied the strategy of the slavers, captured ships, and took up a radical position by advocating that they should be burned purely and simply.[42] His successor, Villaret de Joyeuse, as a result of the problems caused by the capture of the slave trader *La Coquette*, alias *Venus*, which had been taken first by the British and picked up later by the frigate *L'Aurore*, expressed a military opinion which might have been inspired by the civilian Auguste Billiard. He suggested that Britain and France should grant each other rights of search:

> For this it is sufficient that [the Governments] order their war vessels to arrest all slave traders without distinction and bring them to justice before the power whose flag they were flying at the time of their seizure. This measure, which does not compromise the dignity of any nation, will be the most effective blow at the trade, and it will be easy to carry out because Spain, Portugal, Brazil and Holland recognise the competence of the tribunal established in Sierra-Leone.[43]

In all this it is strange that the original abolitionists should have played such a small part and appeared so disappointed. Certainly, their contribution was evident but it did less to strengthen the general movement and invest itself with glory than to evoke and settle personal scores. The purely literary abolitionists after 1826 were embittered by misunderstanding of their position or by the attacks from which they had suffered. The Abbé Grégoire, the old teacher of philanthropy, turned towards misanthropy, arguing that

> times have greatly changed. The persecuted of every kind, like the children of Africa, are sure to find defenders today in the Paris bar[44] and in those of the departments [but there is]no pension to be earned in defending the slaves.[45]

Joseph-Elzéar Morénas was one of his followers. His book is probably not a strictly personal product.[46] Setting himself up as the spokesman of French abolitionism, the author probably received aid from his old master with whom he was already collaborating in 1820, as well as from Thomas Clarkson whom he knew from the same period,[47] and from whom the fundamental ideas contained in his work – that the slave trade is bad policy, immoral, inhuman and barbarous – were taken.[48] Morénas' book was badly constructed but had some originality in its attempt to use statistics. It would be bold, however, to suggest that they are satisfactory. They are accurate, imitating the method of Clarkson and making use of recent figures obtained by British parliamentary publications. By 'proving' that between 1814 and 1827 the number of blacks taken from Africa could have reached '700,000 and perhaps as many as a million',[49] Morénas and his inspirers indulged themselves in the luxury of going against the stream of general opinion: denouncing the lack of conscience of the fine speakers of the Chambers, whom they regarded as legislators incapable of resorting to draconian measures to annihilate the slave trade, they demanded the abrogation of the abolitionist texts in order to insist upon the full application of the codes protecting Africans and 'which could defend them'.[50] The disappointed old innovators seem to have gambled on a return to the past in order to better advance things.

In different ways one notices the more or less specific appearance of the shift from informal involvement in abolitionism to a formal agreement on it. The solution depended upon the political authorities in Paris. The Count de Martignac, the mover of the law of 1827, became president of the council for a year. He appointed to the Ministry of the Navy, Hyde de Neuville, formerly ambassador in Washington and then in Lisbon.[51] He had filled abolitionists in the Chamber with enthusiasm with an 'improvised' speech on the importance and the value of the new law. During the short liberal interlude of Martignac, the principal service which Hyde de Neuville rendered to a cause in which he was personally involved was to inform public opinion, and perhaps even form it in a pedagogic and political sense.

In a general instruction to all the services dependent upon his department, whether in France and the colonies, or the consuls and agents in foreign countries, he presented the law of 1827 as being not only the duty but also 'the formal wish of the country'. The result of the vote, 220 in favour out of 264, enabled him to support this opinion. The authorities were expected to conduct themselves with 'severity'; without negligence, or indulgence, or consideration for private or local interests.[52] What was novel was not the firmness of tone which was characteristic of Neuville, but his publication in the press of various facts concerning French slave-trading activities, a development that his successors could not go back on. This was important, for we know that illegal activity, which tended to decline after the promulgation of the law, began to increase, if somewhat timidly, under the ministry of Polignac, when Haussez held the naval portfolio.

Henceforth, as the official organ, devoting two or three pages to daily news, the *Moniteur Universel* systematically published the sentences passed in cases against slave traders. Certainly, the character of this paper limited its daily subscription to 1,400 but it reached an appreciably larger readership. Newspapers with much bigger subscriptions, *Le Constitutionnel* with 15,000, *Le Journal des Débats* with 8,500, *Le Courrier Français* with 3,600, *Le Journal du Commerce* with 1,500 and the *Gazette des Tribunaux*, which together reached perhaps 150,000 readers in all, pursued the hunt for information about slave trading. Among the readers was the ambassador of Great Britain who, no less systematically, reported back to London.[53]

Martignac's successor, Prince de Polignac, became at first Minister of Foreign Affairs. From 1823 to 1829, as ambassador in London, he had to settle various matters concerning the slave trade: the blockade of Gallinas by the Royal Navy at the time of the offensive of Governor Turner,[54] the settlement of the reward for the capture of the slaver *Le Succès*, and the negotiations relating to the pension or the indemnity which the British government had promised to pay to the widow Baron, wife of the captain of the slave-ship, *La Caroline*, who was killed aboard his ship by the lieutenant of a British patrol vessel. Polignac had constantly to reply to repeated British denunciations, which was as good as an education in abolitionist matters.[55] In other words, as with public opinion, ministers could no longer settle for a wait-and-see attitude, although that does not mean that they were very active in suppressing slaving. There was also the fact that internal questions concerning notably the press and the Algerian problem occupied the attention of the government until its downfall in the July Revolution. Why, then, refer to these men who might have succeeded but were bogged down in the tracks of their predecessors? It was because it marked the end of fifteen years of delays.

Newcomers to the movement, the abolitionists amongst the former parliamentarians of the Restoration sought what was unquestionable and efficacious. They invested in a policy of rapid change, but limited their objectives to the national plane. Membership of a supernational agreement was not yet realised. To achieve this last step, a further year would be necessary.

Louis Philippe's Minister of the Navy after 17 November 1830, the Count d'Argout, had been fed on the abolitionist doctrine of the *Société de la Morale Chrétienne* ever since its foundation. Four months in power was sufficient for him to prepare and submit to the Chambers a new law on the slave trade and to have it voted on. It was not innovative but it was draconian. The law of 4 March 1831, promulgated on 6 March, gave strength and rigour to a text which had been under examination by the offices of the Ministry of the Navy seventeen years earlier, had been approved by the interim minister Ferrand at that time and had been read out to the council in the presence of his successor, Beugnot, on 12 January 1815.[56] What was interesting was the desire to get rid of a burdensome matter. The Chamber of Peers gave the new legislation massive support, with only one blank vote and six votes against out of 107. Lecouteulx de Cantelou raised some problems for form's sake. Among the Deputies, representatives of local interests and other shades of opinion could not conceal a similar level of support: 190 votes in favour overwhelmed 37 opposing ones. Among the latter, Cabanon still defended the spirit of 1815 with its refusal to innovate, and its emphasis on the inopportune nature of the projected measure, British Machiavellianism, and the pragmatic justification of the trade. 'Neither divine nor human laws prohibit the introduction of blacks' wherever they are needed, he argued. In the provinces, at Le Havre, for example, a journalist as notable as Edouard Corbière[57] accused d'Argout of excessive philanthropy and challenged him never to bring it about that 'a slave trader was regarded as an assassin'.[58] The Chamber of Commerce of Marseilles was less aggressive, calling for an amendment in favour of investors. The penalties for the fitting out of voyages or engagement in the trade were heavy. At their mildest they included imprisonment; at their worst they concurred with British law in inflicting hard labour on the ship-owner, the supercargo, or the captain of a slave-trading vessel, who were condemned as well to heavy fines. These were blows to the body and to capital. A very dissuasive law, it still admitted that the trade would take place, for it envisaged a kind of legal status for blacks seized on board a slave trader: their liberty was guaranteed by law, but they were required to serve for a limited period for the public authorities in the colonies. It was thus a decisive text against the slave trade and a text satisfactory to Britain, but it did not go beyond that in its respect for Great Britain. It said not a word about slavery itself, a question which the British had been discussing for eight years already and to which they gave their answer two years later.

From 8 April 1831, the new Minister of the Navy, de Rigny, circulated orders to the port and colonial authorities requesting them to inform the maritime population without delay of the grave risks that would be run thereafter by any slave trader of French nationality. On 29 August, using the new technique of lithography, every French authority in the world was sent 240 copies of a circular applying the law.[59] Indirectly, this prepared the maritime and diplomatic world for the definitive acceptance of the change.

On 30 August 1831 the General Count Sebastiani de la Porta, Minister of Foreign Affairs, analysed, as a number of his predecessors had done, the questions of piracy and rights of search. However, he went back on the position he had held a year before when he had held the naval portfolio. What had been inconceivable yesterday was thinkable today, probably because Britain appeared to think differently by tolerating diplomatically the July regime and in not opposing the Algerian adventure. The inconceivable of yesterday? Collaboration with the cabinet in London. The thinkable? Reciprocal rights of search for the navy of any merchant ships suspected of being slave traders. The main reservations concerned the attitude taken up in practice by the commanders of the French repressive patrols. The higher ranks, the old ones, had certainly not yet digested Trafalgar. But for the young ones – Villaret de Joyeuse (as we have seen) and Bouet-Willaumez (as we have said elsewhere)[60] – the Spanish War, Navarino, Algeria, and some rebuilding of the French war fleet and the officer corps acted as an assurance that they would not be eaten up by the British sea-lions.[61] For his part, Palmerston relaxed the recommendations relating to rights of search which Granville transmitted to Paris. The controllers of the ports of the Ministry of the Navy drew up a proposed convention regarding reciprocal rights of search. It was signed by the two countries on 30 November 1831. A matter which had dragged on for seventeen years had thus been settled in three months.[62] In March 1833, Talleyrand, the ambassador in London and the Duke de Broglie, Minister of Foreign Affairs, signed an additional protocol of which they were the principal sponsors. The French slave trade practically disappeared: it seems very likely that there were less than six ships engaged in it between 1831 and 1838.

The historian cannot reject the anti-abolitionist point of view which suggests that the long preparation for the last eighteen decisive months of French abolition was no greater than the time taken by Granville Sharp, Thomas Clarkson, William Wilberforce, and Charles Fox between 1787 and 1807 to impose first of all on the British nation, and then in the crucial years 1806–1807 on the Western World, the abolition of the slave trade. In France, most of the conditions for the realisation of abolition were appreciably different. It appears, however, that it took less than a quarter of a century or the space of a generation or less – the time taken indeed for the formidable revolutionary and Napoleonic upheaval – for France to join the very limited circle of complete abolitionists. But the conditions of abolition in France were not the same as in Britain. While the latter made a choice in which economic interest perhaps outweighed moral considerations, France accepted an obligation in which political interest without any doubt superseded the humanitarian interest. Formally, French abolitionism presented to the world an anti-slave trade law which was at the same time juridically unquestionable and technically effective. The whole thing became identified with a contract tying the petitioner to the initiator. It was achieved though not without some last minute finishing touches.

The crystallisation was accomplished. The second and third of the French abolitionist laws carrying degrading penalties indicated that the French government was sensitive to a diplomatic scandal whose menace was more and more serious. Its method of escape was precisely to demonstrate its will through legislation which although unpopular (for it was a response to incessant British pressure) was at least harsh. It showed also that it had decided to gamble on the fear of social stigma attached to slave traders. It scarcely appreciated the economic lassitude created by repressive measures which slowly raised costs. A 'speculator' only plays as long as the lottery offers a chance of winning. Furthermore, changes in circumstances apparently having no connection with 'the great affair' intervened to facilitate its achievement. The improvement in the balance of trade; the diffuse but real appearance of new advances in technology which called into question older, outdated economic practices; the renewal of the belief of the military men in their own potentialities; all were determining factors in these decisive years. By contrast, the lack of rethinking by abolitionists and the weak nature of humanitarian demands, neither of which bore witness to the strength of conviction in the compelling universal morality of their cause invoked by the original abolitionists, does not support the proposition that philanthropy towards the blacks played a preponderant role in the overturn of centuries-old habits. Coming in the midst of the period of literary romanticism, the decisive years were ones of pragmatism, not of faith.

NOTES

* The editor wishes to thank his colleague, Tom Kemp, for his work in translating this paper from French.

1. Doctor M. Chatillon has begun a long-term study of the *Société des Amis des Noirs*, from the original documents of the society. See François Thesée, 'Autour de la Société des Amis des Noirs: Clarkson, Mirabeau et l'abolition de la traite (août 1789–mars 1790)', *Présence Africaine*, 125 (1983), pp. 3–82.
2. In recent years several authors have taken up the abolitionist question from the French side, sometimes in a comparative way. See especially D. B. Davis, *Slavery in the Age of Revolution* (Cornell, 1975) and Seymour Drescher, 'Two Variants of Anti-Slavery: Religious Organization and Social Mobilization in Britain and France, 1780–1870', in Christine Bolt and Seymour Drescher (eds.), *Anti-Slavery, Religion and Reform* (Folkestone, 1980), pp. 43–63. See also my own work in 'L'Abolition de la Traite des Noirs en France de 1814 à 1831', *Cahiers d'Etudes Africaines*, 11 (1971), pp. 14–58; 'Les Mots Esclave, Nègre, Noir et les Jugements de Valeur sur la Traite Négrière dans la Littérature Abolitionniste Française de 1770 à 1845', *Revue Française d'Histoire d'Outre-Mer*, 60 (1973), pp. 511–48; and 'A model of the French abolitionist movement and its variants', in Bolt & Drescher (eds.), *Anti-Slavery, op. cit.*, pp. 64–80.
3. Yvan Debbasch, 'Poésie et Traite. L'Opinion Française sur le Commerce Négrier au Début du XIXe Siècle', *Revue Française d'Histoire d'Outre-Mer*, 48 (1961), pp. 311–52.

4. Archives Nationales, Section d'Outre-Mer, Paris (hereafter ANSOM), dossiers Généralités 191/1475, 25 Dec. 1825, Morale Chrétienne to Minister of the Navy, letter of Auguste de Staël. The cover note was signed by Guizot-Ternaux, Remusat, Wurst, de Guizard, Kerartry, Coquerel and Mahul who made up the abolitionist committee of the society. The letter itself was counter-signed by Remusat.
5. Archive Ministère des Affaires Etrangères, Paris (hereafter Aff.étr.). Afriques 26, Traite des Noirs, 1823–1830, Granville to Damas.
6. Archives Nationales, Chambres des Pairs, CC iv, b, 437/119, n. 44. The original is in ANSOM, Gén. 191/1475, with 142 signatures.
7. ANSOM, Gén. 191/1475 and 457/97, from 12, 15, 17 Feb., 1 March 1826.
8. Cour de Cassation, Receuil Sirey, 1825–1827, p. 258, act of 14 Jan. 1826 against Mr Blais. The sentence was delivered by President Portallis. The reporter was Chantereine; the summing up was made by the attorney-general de Vatimesnil.
9. The fact cannot easily be checked. However, in the *Etrennes de Nantes* for the years 1825 and 1826 one can verify that in the latter year a steel manufacturer was no longer listed and that all the naval forges had disappeared from the list of names. In 1825 the big cotton manufacturer Fabre, Petit-Pierre and Co., still advertised goods 'for the slave trade'; it no longer did so in 1826. Cf. Etrennes de Nantes 1825, pp. 176, 178 and 1826, p. 172.
10. ANSOM, Gén. 154/1288, instructions à Nantes. These authorities had been implicated by Auguste de Staël.
11. Lachelier seized at least five slavers, including *L'Hippolyte*, captain Blais. This affair was behind the decision of the *Cour de Cassation* in 1826. On Lachelier, see the opinion of Louis Lacroix, *Les Derniers Négriers* (Paris, 1967), who detested the *capitaine de frégate* because of his repressive activities at Nantes as well as on the African coast. On this point see my 'France, Suppression of the Illegal Trade, and England, 1817–1850' in David Eltis and James Walvin (eds.), *The Abolition of the Atlantic Slave Trade* (Madison, Wisc., 1981), pp. 193–221.
12. There are numerous examples in P.R.O., Foreign Office, 84/59, 84/72, 84/83, 84/94. Périer, the British consul at Brest, gave notice of the arrival of slave traders escorted by warships.
13. *Annales Maritimes et Coloniales* (hereafter *Ann.Mar.Col.*), 11 (1826), part 2, pp. 460–7. The list provides the name of the ship and the captain, the juridical nature of the judgement and its date. It begins in August 1818 and ends in September 1826.
14. *Ibid.*, 12 (1827), Part 2, pp. 549–773. See the speech of the Count de Courtivron, pp. 701–10, notably p. 707, the note on the blackmail used by the 'Ashantées' for the continuation of the trade.
15. *Ibid.*, pp. 608–20, Chambres de Pairs, 23 Jan. 1827, Duke de Fitz-James.
16. *Ibid.*, pp. 614–17.
17. *Ibid.*
18. ANSOM, Gén. 191/1471 and 1474, the commission of Baron de la Mardelle, ordered by the minister in 1823, which produced a lucid report. The case of war had already been raised in 1818, but the event was then considered to be 'improbable'. The idea was taken up again as a working hypothesis in a conversation which de Portal had with Louis XVIII, cf. *Mémoires* of Baron Portal, in 1819. It is remarkable that in a number of diplomatic fields, a military solution regarding Britain was always raised in the end; see, for example, H. Contamine, *Diplomatie et Diplomates sous la Restauration* (Paris, 1970).
19. From 1821 the African Institute in London published reports in French, notably *Etat Actuel de la Traite des Noirs*, which formed the annual report presented

to the Directors on 8 March 1821. These reports assumed great importance on the French market for information about the slave trade with the formation of the *Société de la Morale Chrétienne*. In 1822, a *Résumé du discours* ... of Wilberforce given on 22 June in the House of Commons as well as his letter of 1814 to the Tsar Alexander were published in French. Also published in French by the publisher Schultz of London were the letters of Forster, a Quaker who, in 1823 and 1824, exposed the slave trade in general and the French part in it in particular. In 1826 the collection entitled *Faits Relatifs à La Traite des Noirs*, published by Crapelet, the usual bookseller of the *Morale Chrétienne*, included for example the letter from de Staël, the latest known information about the French, and the subsequently well-known plan of the slave-ship *La Vigilante*, lithographed by Last.

20. *Ann.Mar.Col.*, 12 (1827), part 2, pp. 743–52, especially 749.
21. Notably before his presentation to the Peers. At the time of the presentation and the final report to the Deputies, after two months in office, the tone had changed perceptibly, a sign that minds had evolved.
22. *Service Historique de la Marine*, Cherbourg, 3 P3/113, to the commissaire for the Navy, in charge of the service, Dunkirk. With copies to the divisions requiring strict conformity with the orders.
23. Some French slave traders operated with false papers and under a false flag, almost always Dutch. If captured, they were dealt with by the mixed Anglo-Dutch commission. The bounty for the capturers led British commanders to report as Dutch or Spanish slave traders which were assuredly French. This was especially the case with Owen, commanding the *Eden*, and Gordon, commanding the *Atholl*. Cf. their problems with *Le Jules, La Jeune-Eugénie*, Sierra-Leone Duplicate Despatches, 1828–1829, vol. 6.
24. In the Admiralty records in the P.R.O. and in Archives Nationales, Marine, EE, caisse des prises, signs exist that some officers charged with repression did not receive the bounties to which the law entitled them; was this a sign of abolitionist morality? On the other hand, claims were made for bounties that the administration had not paid for several years.
25. Our view differs from the thesis of David Eltis who assumed that all those vessels which did not disembark their slaves in the foreign Antilles must have done so in the French Antilles. The demography of these islands contradicts such an hypothesis.
26. Thomas Clarkson, *An Essay on the Impolicy of the African Slave Trade* London, 1788), p. 21.
27. One finds mention of these exhibitions in the *Etrennes de Nantes*, cited earlier. See also Ange Guépin and C.E. Bonamy, *Nantes au XIXe Siècle* (Nantes, 1835). Societies were formed, notably an horticultural society. A celebrated ship-owner, a 'little' slave trader of the period, Heantjens, successfully founded a model farm in the Nantes region, with a 'gardener', Rieffel.
28. *Tableau Décennal du Commerce de la France, 1827–1836* (Paris, 1838), Vol. 1, part 1, p. xi.
29. Jean Mettas, *Répertoire des Expéditions Négrières Françaises au XVIIIe Siècle*, vol. I (ed. Serge Daget), vol. II (eds. Serge and Michèle Daget) for Société Française d'Histoire d'Outre Mer (Paris, 1978 and 1984 respectively). In diminishing order of 'importance' the ports are: Nantes, Bordeaux, Le Havre, La Rochelle, Honfleur, Marseilles, Saint-Malo, Rochefort, Lorient, Dunkirk and Ile de France.
30. *Notices Statistiques sur les Colonies Françaises* ... (Paris, 1837), II, *Commerce*, pp. 107–9. J.C.P. Rougier, *La Liberté Commerciale, les Douanes et les Traités de Commerce* (Paris, 1878), p. 398, on the growth of exports from France to

Britain. Cf. *Tableau Décennal du Commerce ... 1827–1836, op. cit.*, vol. I, part I, p. 13; Britain was France's best customer until 1830 and then second after the United States.
31. ANSOM, Gén. 191/1475, Dejean petition.
32. ANSOM, Gén. 191/1475, 1 Sept. 1829, Vitalis petition.
33. Auguste Billiard, *Abolition de la Traite et de l'Esclavage dans les Colonies Françaises* (Paris, 1827).
34. Billiard did not use the official term of crime.
35. The American Atlantic coast.
36. Billiard, *op. cit.*, pp. 81–3.
37. Marquis F. Renouard de Sainte-Croix, *Pétition à la Chambre des Députés sur le Régime Intérieur des Esclaves aux Antilles Françaises, avec la Demande d'une Autorité Spéciale et Protectrice, Chargée de Surveiller l'Exécution des Lois et des Ordonnances en Vigueur, Concernant la Nourriture, les Travaux et Traitements des Nègres Esclaves* (Saint-Germain, 1829).
38. ANSOM, Gén. 191/1475, petition of Sainte-Croix, 9 March 1830.
39. ANSOM, Gén. 166/1342, 154/1285, July and August 1828.
40. ANSOM, Gén. 154/1289, Bourbon, May 1829.
41. ANSOM, Gén. 154/1287, Fort-Royal, on the *Jeanne d'Arc*, to the minister, 15 March 1829.
42. *Ibid.*, 8 May 1827, external station to the minister.
43. The affair of *La Coquette* is well documented, cf. Archives Nationales du Sénégal, 1 B 26, f. 7; P.R.O., F.O. 315/58, n. 17; Public Archives, Sierra Leone, *Service Historique de la Marine*, liquidations, FF2/117 (1832). Villaret's report is contained in ANSOM, 166/1340, Sierra Leone, 29 Jan. 1829.
44. An allusion to Isambert.
45. Abbé Grégoire, *De la Noblesse de la Peau, ou du Préjugé des Blancs contre la Couleur des Africains et Celle de Leurs Descendants Noirs ou Sang-mêlés* (Paris, 1826), pp. 60–1 especially.
46. *Précis Historique de la Traite des Noirs et de l'Esclavage Colonial* (Paris, 1828). There is a good reprint by Slatkine Reprints, Geneva, 1978. An enquiry to the original publishing firm of Firmin-Didot produced no information about the distribution of this work.
47. G. Debien, 'J. E. Morénas à Saint-Louis en 1818–1819', *Bulletin de l'Institut Français d'Afrique Noire*, série B, 30 (1968), no. 2, pp. 691–727. On the relations between Morénas and Clarkson, see my 'J. E. Morénas à Paris. L'Action Abolitionniste, 1819–1821', *Ibid.*, série B, 31 (1969), no. 3, pp. 875–85.
48. Clarkson, *Impolicy of the African Slave Trade*, *op. cit.*, Morénas, *Précis Historique, op. cit.*, pp. 363–72.
49. Morénas, *op. cit.*, chapter XXV, pp. 194–203.
50. *Ibid.*, p. 420. The question of the participation of Grégoire and Morénas in the *Société de la Morale Chrétienne* has not been resolved. In his book, Morénas leads one to understand that he had heard the report given by Auguste de Staël, *ibid.*, p. 372.
51. An anecdote found in the memoirs of John Quincy Adams shows Hyde de Neuville, in 1821, in the name of France, threatening to go to war with the United States if the problems raised by the seizure of French slavers by the American navy were not quickly settled.
52. Cf. for example, the notification to Benoît Chassériau, the French agent on the Danish island of Saint-Thomas, through the intermediary of the Governor of Guadeloupe, Paris, 22 April 1828, Bibliothèque Municipale de La Rochelle, Papiers Chassériau, mss. 2482–2484.

53. The reference to the subscriptions in *Journal de Nantes, Le Breton,* Thursday, 2 Dec. 1830, no. 240, col. A. See P.R.O., F.O. 84/94, f. 219, the cutting from the *Courrier Français* of 4 June 1829, which reported that seven slave-ships had landed their blacks in Martinique. The names of the ships, the number of blacks and the names of the houses are given.
54. P.R.O., F.O. 84/59, 6 Feb., 11 Sept., 10 Nov. 1826, Granville to Damas and Polignac to Canning. In September the ambassador declared himself 'astonished' at not having received information regarding this blockade which constituted a 'unique precedent' and would permit Britain to have exclusive control of trade. Nevertheless, Polignac's note still remained confidential, showing a desire not to make matters worse. The British government supplied the official information in November.
55. The Foreign Office did not necessarily go through the French ambassador, but through its ambassadors in Paris, Stuart, then Granville, and then Stuart again who had now become a Lord. The procedure for passing information was more rapid, and it was better distributed among the different ministries in Paris: a veritable campaign of a psychological nature.
56. See my thesis, *La France et l'Abolition de la Traite des Noirs de 1814 à 1831* in Archives et Documents, micro-édition, Sciences Humaines, no. 82 03 15, Institut d'Ethnologie (Paris [1969], 1982), pp. 37–8.
57. In 1832 he published a novel called *Le Négrier* which made him famous. In the preface to the reprint published in Paris around 1950 in *Editions Littéraires de France*, Pierre MacOrlan recalls that Corbière lived in a British prison-ship from 1812 to 1813.
58. ANSOM, Gén. 155/1292, open letter to the minister, *Journal du Havre*, 17 Dec. 1830. In the same box is a letter from the Chamber of Marseilles dated 24 Dec. 1830.
59. ANSOM, Gén. 155/1293 to the ports, consuls and representatives of France in forcign countries.
60. In Eltis and Walvin (eds.), *Abolition of Atlantic Slave Trade, op. cit.*, pp. 193–217, especially 200.
61. There are two sources, one manuscript, the other printed. The figures provided do not agree, but both indicate a marked recovery. See Archives Nationales, Marine, CC 1/777, mss., Cabinet du ministre, Espèces des bâtiments de l'Etat from 1687 until December 1862; between 1822 (when the Portal plan came into force) and 31 December 1831 the total number of ships of all categories afloat went from 238 to 275, including 13 steamers. The number under construction rose from 32 to 77. The printed source indicates that 298 vessels were afloat at the end of 1833 and 66 were in dockyards. For the same year, the manuscript document gives 273 and 77 respectively. The officer corps went from 1,188 to 1,563 between 1822 and the end of 1831.
62. Aff. étr., Afrique 27, Traite des Noirs, 1831–1836, f. 94, 30 Aug. 1831. See also f. 99 et seq.

8

Emancipation in British Guyana and its Influence on Dutch Policy Regarding Surinam**

J.P. SIWPERSAD

Before 1833 the abolition of slavery in their West Indies colonies was never seriously considered by Dutch governments. The British Emancipation Act of 1833 changed this, however. Thereafter the question was asked, both within government circles and elsewhere, whether the Netherlands should follow the British example and abolish slavery, particularly in Surinam, economically the most important Dutch colony in the West Indies. During the years 1833–1840 the idea of emancipation was not very popular in The Hague, but by 1841 the abolition principle had been accepted by the government. With regard to Surinam three emancipation plans were the subject of official correspondence during the period 1833–1840. Between 1841 and 1860 further official and unofficial plans were put forward, some of which were seriously discussed; six Bills were considered during this period. Finally the Dutch Parliament passed a Bill in 1862, emancipating slaves in the Dutch Caribbean colonies. On 1 July 1863, 34,000 slaves were free in Surinam, and another 10,000 on the islands in the Caribbean. The total operation cost the Dutch Treasury about 14 million guilders.

** This paper is mainly a summary of several chapters of my dissertation: 'De Nederlandse regering en de afschaffing van de Surinaamse slavernij' (Groningen, 1979). An earlier version of this paper has appeared in Dutch as 'Emancipatie in Brits Guyana en het Beleid Inzake Suriname', in *OSO, Tijdschrift Voor Surinamse Taalkunde Letterkunde en Geschiedenis*, 2, no. 1 (May 1983), pp. 25–33.

The object of this paper is twofold: first, to show in what ways British abolition initiated a process of gradual acceptance of the emancipation principle in Dutch government circles, particularly with regard to Surinam; and second, to indicate how British slave emancipation in Guyana in particular influenced the Dutch authorities in their approach to the problem of Surinam abolition.

I

In the eighteenth century slave-owners in Surinam were repeatedly faced with the problem of marronage and other forms of resistance among the black masses. Thousands of slaves escaped to the forests, from which they undertook raids and attacks on the plantations. Thus they indirectly brought the colony as a whole to the brink of ruin.

Compared with the eighteenth century, the nineteenth century was a relatively calm period for the masters. The escape-route to the forests was for the most part blocked for potential new runaways by peace treaties with the Maroons in 1760, 1762 and 1767, and also by a ring of defence posts around the built-up areas of the colony. The presence of Maroons and their raids were thenceforth seen as mainly troublesome and damaging to the plantations in their immediate vicinity. Forest patrols were regularly sent out to catch them, to drive them further into the woods or to destroy their allotments and camps.

This is not to say that Surinam was completely free of tension and conflict between masters and slaves in the nineteenth century. Refusals to work and other forms of passive resistance continued. But an investigation of a number of plantation and regional archives indicates that such resistance was not the order of the day. In any case these forms of resistance did not present any real danger to the colonists. Individual violence against whites was a rare phenomenon in the nineteenth century. Nor was collective violence in the form of rebellions a chronic or permanent trait of Surinam society at this time; there were in fact no major or general uprisings. However, there are examples of plantation-based conspiracies or revolts. For the first six decades of the nineteenth century seven notable conspiracies or rebellions occurred, most of which were quickly discovered and suppressed. These took place in Nickerie in 1820 and 1831, in Coronie in 1836 and 1854, in Commewijne in 1857, and in Para in 1852 at Berg en Dal and in September 1862 at Rac à Rac.

Our inquiry into the levels of rebelliousness in the nineteenth century supports the conclusion that in particular open resistance against the established order was not a matter of course, but depended on essentially local circumstances. The absence of forms of resistance which were dangerous for the established order as a whole (such as chronic marronage or mass uprisings) was one of the factors that contributed to the relative calmness with which the Dutch government was able to study and deal with the abolition problem, and also partly explains why the Netherlands was one of the last European countries to abolish slavery in its colonies.

There was, however, one expression of resistance which caused considerable anxiety to the Dutch authorities: the desertion of slaves to free British Guyana, mainly from the border districts of Nickerie and Coronie after 1833. During the period 1837–1841 the number of reported escape attempts became alarming, but most in fact failed owing to the alertness of the planters and the authorities. In retrospect the number of successful attempts was lower than might have been expected. Evidence available suggests that during the period 1833–1863 some 400–450 slaves succeeded in reaching the British colony from Surinam, the equivalent of only one per cent of Surinam's slave population in 1862. At the time, however, every attempt at escape caused considerable consternation: it was a new phenomenon and the British colonists were suspected of secretly stirring up strife among the slaves in Surinam in order to obtain additional labourers. Furthermore, attempts at desertion came to be viewed with greater suspicion after it was learned that the abortive rebellions in Nickerie in 1831 and Coronie in 1836 were associated with efforts at desertion.

As with the escapes to the forests, desertions to British Guyana were kept reasonably under control by the authorities. But in contrast to marronage, escapes of Surinam slaves to her neighbour had a more pronounced impact on the Dutch government's attitude to emancipation as will appear below.

Anxious about the influence of a free British Guyana on the

feelings of the slaves in Surinam, W.H. Lans, a high official in Surinam, submitted a plan for the emancipation of the slaves in the colony as early as 1833. Partly on the advice of Governor-General E.L. Van Heeckeren (1832–1838) the government of The Hague was very cool towards Lans' proposals. Van Heeckeren thought the moment premature for considering abolition. Unlike Lans he judged that imminent emancipation in British Guyana would not have 'immediate effects' upon Surinam and argued that Lans' proposals would mean the end of Surinam as an agricultural colony. In addition Van Heeckeren judged that Lans' plan was 'completely impracticable' because the means of financing it was unsound. Similar considerations led the government to reject proposals for emancipation submitted in 1833 by W.H. Travers, an 'ex-consul of the Netherlands in the Bay of Honduras'.

All this took place before the actual emancipation of the slaves in Britain's colonies. Once this became a fact in 1834, Van Heeckeren gradually became inclined towards emancipation in the Dutch territories, particularly as unrest and desertion increased. Thanks to military guarding of the mouth of the Corantine river and limited shipping connections between Surinam and British Guyana, Van Heeckeren succeeded in preventing mass desertions: between 1 January 1833 and 1 January 1837 only ten slaves managed to reach the British border district of Berbice. Still, developments worried the governor. In 1836 there was a conspiracy led by the slave Colin. This conspiracy 'intending solely the murder of all the whitemen [of Coronie] and then to escape to the colonies of Berbice and Demerary' was discovered and suppressed. On 19 August 1837 Van Heeckeren wrote to the Minister for Colonial Affairs at The Hague, Johannes van den Bosch, that desertions to the British colonies – which had been the subject of repeated correspondence with the home country – had lately acquired 'a threatening character'. He pointed out that four slaves from Paramaribo, the heart of the colony 'from where the crossing ... with such small boats is not easy, and even perilous', had managed to reach the British banks. Van Heeckeren's difficulties were made worse by the attitude of the British Guyanese authorities, who refused to expel the refugees. In consequence of such developments Van Heeckeren reported to The Hague that without emancipation he was pessimistic about the future of the colony. In February 1837 he advised the immigration of free Africans, as a means towards 'gradual preparation for emancipation'. A month later he urged the need for emancipation as a consequence of attempts made by several Britons to buy slaves in the Netherlands Antilles in order to take them to the British colonies as free labourers. According to Van Heeckeren, the government of British Guyana, 'inspired by unbridled fervour to enlarge the labouring class', had passed laws that had encouraged such purchases and threatened surely 'all the slave colonies in the West Indies with certain ruin'. Despite such forecasts, van den Bosch rejected abolitionist arguments from Surinam. Pointing to free Haiti and numerous Maroon communities, whose existence had failed to cause major uprisings among the slaves, he rejected abolition in the Dutch territories as premature, unnecessary and disastrous for colonial agriculture.

Close investigation reveals that emancipation did not accord well with plans that van den Bosch himself had already developed for the Dutch colonies. Those plans amounted to the expansion and revitalisation of large-scale agriculture in Surinam by new capital investments, improvements in machinery, and the increase of the existing labour force by better treatment of the slaves. Van den Bosch judged that improvement of the material condition of the slaves and appointment of a strong man in succession to Van Heeckeren offered a sufficient guarantee for peace, prosperity and security in Surinam.

The death of Van Heeckeren in 1838 gave van den Bosch an early opportunity to pursue his ideas. Van Heeckeren's successor was an extremely competent Vice-Admiral, J.C. Rijk. On his arrival in the colony in 1839 Rijk took extensive security measures. An advocate of 'summary justice', because he believed this impressed 'uncivilised' people, he authorised the planters in the threatened border-districts to punish deserters on the spot. No major revolts occurred during Rijk's administration from 1839 to 1842, but he still did not feel much at ease, as appears from his letters to the Minister for Colonial Affairs. These letters are particularly interesting and deserve close examination. Asked for his opinion about an emancipation proposal submitted by a private individual, Rijk wrote on 20

June 1840 that 'the proximity of the English possessions is already dangerous for us'. Should slavery be abolished in French Guyana as well, he argued, the position of Surinam would become 'very critical'. For this reason Rijk considered emancipation desirable, though not without a thorough preparation of the slaves. On 26 July in the same year Rijk wrote that the disposition of the slaves was 'continuously good'. Seven slaves had tried to escape from Coronie to British Guyana, but the government had been able to frustrate this attempt as well as an earlier one. He indicated, however, that despite the quiet state of the colony, he remained anxious about the future: as the British possessions declined 'as a consequence of precipitate emancipation', their envy of foreign colonies that stuck to the 'old system' increased. 'Their abolitionists travel around everywhere, in order to proselytize; feelings are running high', he added. Recognising the consequences that were likely to flow from this, Rijk was of the opinion that the subject of abolition should 'most certainly' be brought to the attention of the minister. A year later, on 26 July 1841, Rijk again wrote that the situation in the colony was quiet 'as far as external evidence is concerned'. But noting that two negroes from Coronie had escaped to the neighbouring colony and eight slaves from the Saramacca had also managed to reach the British banks, he added that the tendency among the slaves to take to their heels as soon as they got the chance was exacerbated by the meddling of 'dangerous neighbours', who did not shrink from any means to encourage emancipation and would not hesitate to cause an uprising in the colony if they could do so.

In early August 1841 Rijk was again alarmed by news from Coronie that a conspiracy of 21 negroes to escape to British Guyana had been discovered. Referring to this, Rijk wrote on 6 August 1841 to the Minister that the ferment among the slave population 'was becoming more and more conspicuous in a most distressing way'. This particular conspiracy had been frustrated but, he noted, 'fermentation is becoming apparent everywhere'. The situation in Coronie especially was a source of 'great anxiety', because the district was so remote from the capital that it was impossible to offer aid quickly to the handful of white men there. Rijk remarked that he considered the state of the colony to be 'very alarming'; the calm still generally prevailing could not be 'relied upon too much', for once the impulse to desertion had been aroused, it naturally resulted in 'fatal imitation'. Seeking to quell this, Rijk argued that he would prefer to bar all English ships from Surinam 'for nothing guarantees us that they will not bring many agents here to stir up our slave population'. His distrust of the British was nourished by the tone of some British Guyanese newspapers in connection with the escape of the eight slaves from the Saramacca referred to above. The most unfriendly tone was struck by the *Guyana Times* on 16 July 1841. The newspaper welcomed the eight fugitives as heroes and proposed a toast to the 'speedy depopulation of all Slave Countries, by emigration to British Guyana'. These remarks led to a protest from The Hague on 12 November 1841 to the British Government. But this had no significant effect because Lord Aberdeen, the British Prime Minister, refused to criticise the colonial press.

British Guyana continued to tease Surinam. In 1841, the authorities in British Guyana submitted a curious proposal to the Dutch offering to buy the 6,000–7,000 Maroons in Surinam and to ship them to British Guyana. Officials in The Hague viewed this offer with great misgivings. It was seen basically as an attempt to provoke rebellion, confirming an earlier remark made by Rijk that 'they try everything that may disturb the peace among our slaves; it is a *Guerre à Mort* which England seems to afflict upon our system'. There is much to validate Rijk's judgment and to indicate that the British planters were bent on recruiting labourers from Surinam or 'kidnapping', as he once called it. The beginning of mass immigration of indentured labour into British Guyana led to some reduction in complaints about British trouble-making. But free British Guyana continued to be troublesome to the authorities in Surinam. This is revealed by an incident in May 1853 and the ensuing reaction of the Governor. Three soldiers guarding against desertions on a schooner on the coast of Coronie were suddenly attacked by 'a band of negro slaves', and forced by them to take them to Berbice. In writing about this in a 'strictly private' letter, the Governor of Surinam claimed that the 'demonstrated desire for freedom' of the Coronie negroes 'had been so unmistakably proved that we may be prepared that they eschew no perils, or will not leave untried any attempts to attain that goal'. He further noted:

> Our position is ... anything but favourable; on the contrary – and why gloss over the fact? – the situation is very precarious. Positioned between the English and the French colonies, where everything is free, it cannot but be that our slaves must be inspired by the desire to attain that condition also; the more so because our western neighbours do not scruple to use any means or machinations in order to arouse and incite that desire for freedom among our blacks.

In his pessimism the Governor intimated that the situation was 'truly' becoming more and more 'untenable' every day and that it would 'eventually result in emancipation anyway, either voluntary or forced'.

As has already been said, mass desertion from Surinam into British Guyana did not occur. Severe punishments must have discouraged many potential deserters from undertaking the risky crossing. Military and geographical barriers to desertion were also formidable. With regard to military barriers the authorities in Surinam were assisted by groups of Indians that collaborated with the white community. Won over by periodical share-outs of food and gifts and encouraged by considerable premiums for every fugitive caught, the Indians revealed themselves as fanatical and extremely successful negro-hunters, ready day and night to assist soldiers and armed civilians in pursuing runaway slaves.

Official reports from Surinam such as those from Governor Rijk and his successors about the dangers threatening the colony helped to convert the authorities in The Hague to the idea of abolition. In this they were assisted by the appointment of J. C. Baud as Minister of Colonial Affairs in 1840 in succession to van den Bosch. Baud, who was more sympathetic to abolition than his predecessor, continued in this office until 1848. Whilst British Guyana undoubtedly played a significant role in converting the Dutch authorities, other factors also affected the situation, including the arousal of public opinion, visits to the Netherlands by British abolitionists and French initiatives on abolition. Of great importance in the period after 1843 for the growing popularity of the idea of emancipation was the government's conviction that, economically, slavery had become an anachronism and that without emancipation Surinam would certainly be lost as an agricultural colony as a consequence of the steady decline in the number of slaves. It is beyond the scope of this paper to examine in detail all the factors that contributed to the acceptance of the idea of emancipation by the Dutch authorities. We have highlighted the significance of British Guyana largely because it was in consequence of incendiary articles in some British Guyanese newspapers that the Dutch government officially acknowledged for the first time the desirability of emancipation.

This occurred in the Memorandum from The Hague to London of 12 November 1841, referred to earlier. That progress was being made by abolitionism before this public announcement in The Hague appears from a Memorandum dated 18 August 1841 and drafted by J. B. Elias, a high-ranking official at the Ministry for Colonial Affairs in 1841, and Governor of Surinam from 1842 to 1845. Elias pointed out to Baud, Minister for Colonial Affairs, that the emancipation in British Guyana must have made a deep impression on the slaves in Surinam. He added that it might be expected that among them the desire for freedom had been 'strongly' aroused and that to leave this desire unsatisfied would sooner or later result in attempts to attain freedom by violence. It was possible, Elias argued, to suppress uprisings, but in the event that this became impossible 'Surinam would be lost for the Netherlands'. In the margin of this Memorandum, Baud noted: 'It is very often that I have revolved in my mind the subject of this Memorandum. Both as a man and a Christian, I wish nothing but the emancipation of the negro-slaves ...' Some weeks later, at the annual opening of the States-General the King hinted in guarded terms at the necessity of abolition because of the opposition between free British Guyana and slave-owning Surinam. At the beginning of 1842 prominent Christians and Liberals, urged and inspired by British Quakers, presented two petitions to the government. These, the first petitions of their kind against slavery, elicited from Baud, speaking on behalf of the government, the response that the government supported abolition in principle. With this repeated and now public acceptance of the principle of emancipation a new episode started in the history of the abolition of slavery.

II

The Dutch authorities' approach to abolition was shaped by their assessment of the results of emancipation in the colonies of other nations. They attached particular importance, as we shall see, to the behaviour of freed slaves in British Guyana, and reports to the Dutch authorities from this colony had a considerable influence on their policy with regard to Surinam. It is necessary, therefore, to review briefly reports from British Guyana to the Dutch from 1833 onwards.

In February 1834 Governor Van Heeckeren advised The Hague 'to allow some time to observe the consequences in the British colonies and to take advantage first of the experience of some years'. Similarly in March 1839 Minister van den Bosch wrote to the King that emancipation in Surinam should not be considered 'as long as it has not appeared elsewhere that with the free negroes the soil can be cultivated in a sufficient way'.

The first reports affirmed the stereotyped picture that the whites had of the negroes. As early as 1833 ex-consul Travers had portrayed the negro as an 'indolent creature, to whom 'dolce far niente' was greatest bliss', and in a ministerial report of 1833 it was said that free negroes 'were not to be induced to any work however easy'. 'It is pure fantasy to suppose that the negro will work if this is left to his free choice', Van Heeckeren wrote in 1838. For this reason the Governor wanted to educate them for freedom before actual emancipation took place.

Developments in British Guyana were followed especially closely. It was not until after the Apprenticeship ended in 1838 that the reports about the colony really started to appear. C. W. Ellents Hofstede, a Dutchman living in Demerara, 'desiring to be useful to his home country and to save its colonies from ruinous consequences', warned The Hague in 1838 not to follow the British example of total emancipation. Following certain reforms in Surinam, he argued, the government should give the slaves the status of *glebae adscripti* in order to prevent them from wandering from plantation to plantation as they were permitted to do in the British colony. In this way, it was thought, the freemen would be prevented from shirking plantation labour by refusing to hire themselves out as labourers. Hofstede reinforced his pessimistic story by sending an official report in

1838 about the behaviour of the freed slaves in British Guyana to The Hague. The report contains numerous comments about labour conditions on various plantations. At Gelderland Plantation, for instance, it was reported that 'not more than two thirds of the able people work', whilst at Broer's Lust Plantation workers were said to be 'making only half days labour'.

Such reductions in labour supplies were broadly reflected in trends in the total production of staple crops in British Guyana after emancipation. A Dutch report in 1841 pointed out, for instance, that sugar output had been over 87 million pounds in 1833, but had fallen to around 60 million pounds by 1838. During the same period coffee output had declined from some 2,600,000 pounds to less than 600,000 pounds. Reports about the unsatisfactory behaviour of former slaves and the decline of agriculture in British Guyana continued to circulate in Surinam and the Netherlands as late as the 1850s. In 1851, for example, at a time when the British colony was beginning to recover its former level of production as a result of the immigration of indentured labour, Minister Pahud at The Hague drew the attention of the Dutch Parliament to the phantom of British Guyana in urging members to proceed with great caution. Only recently, he argued, he had received reports which pointed to the disastrous consequences of British emancipation: 'Those consequences are so awful that they are really beyond imagination. In British Guyana they are distressed that the free negroes nowadays are nothing but half-savages'. He supported his argument by quoting extensively from the British Guyana newspaper the *Royal Gazette* of 7 August 1851 in which the negroes were generally portrayed as indolent, lazy, happy-go-lucky savages. On the coast of Essequebo district, it was reported, only a fourth of the population worked as plantation labourers: 'the other three fourths sit down, go fishing, hunting and stealing, both from the plantation and from each other'. Having also described similar reports about the situation in French Guyana, Pahud asked, 'Here too in the Netherlands there is talk of emancipation of the slaves, but I ask you, Gentlemen, who would dare to declare emancipation of persons so unprepared for and so unsuited to freedom as our slaves when confronted with such examples?'

Of course such arguments, and the reports upon which they

were founded, were ideologically coloured and biassed; only the interests of the planters were considered and not those of the freed slaves. But modern studies such as that of Michael Moohr have revealed a substantial decline of plantation agriculture in British Guyana after 1838. Recovery came about gradually, however, and as Engerman's study below indicates (p. 238), production levels of sugar in British Guyana returned to their pre-emancipation days during the late 1850s. The long depression in sugar production in British Guyana after 1833 served, nevertheless, as a powerful obstacle to slave emancipation in the neighbouring Dutch colony, despite the commitment in principle to abolition by the Dutch government in 1841. Formal emancipation in fact was not achieved until 1863.

Reports about the behaviour of former slaves in British Guyana were instrumental in delaying the actual abolition of slavery in the Dutch Caribbean until this date. By indicating that abolition was almost certain to harm plantation agriculture, particularly in Surinam, and thereby reduce the revenues of the Dutch Treasury at a time when it was already struggling with substantial budget deficits, the reports from British Guyana were viewed with some alarm by successive governments at The Hague. As a result they adopted the principle that unrestricted and complete abolition was impracticable unless the slaves themselves covered the costs of their freedom by agreeing to remain on the plantations or hiring themselves as regular labourers to the plantation owners. Such ideas determined the content of almost all of the abortive bills about abolition put forward by the Dutch authorities before 1858.

After 1858, the Dutch authorities became more sympathetic towards abolition and within five years slaves in all the Dutch Caribbean possessions were unconditionally set free. This was due essentially to two factors. First, in 1858 the government recognised for the first time the possibility of using imported indentured immigrants as plantation labour in place of former slaves, and was induced therefore by parliamentary pressure to abandon the principle of making the slaves pay for their own emancipation. Second, there occurred a substantial improvement in the budgetary position of the Dutch Treasury during the 1850s and 1860s, largely as a consequence of increased revenues from the trade in Java sugar. Revenue from sugar imports from Java doubled between 1851 and 1870 to an average of some 24 million guilders a year during the late 1860s. In 1863, therefore, abolition of slavery in Surinam and the other Dutch possessions in the Caribbean was made possible by state revenues derived from free sugar from the East.

PART D

Caribbean Adjustments to Slave Emancipation

9

Was British Emancipation a Success? The Abolitionist Perspective

W. A. GREEN

I

A week before the Emancipation Act received the royal assent, Thomas Fowell Buxton wrote to Thomas Clarkson: 'It is a mighty experiment at best; but we must trust that it will answer to the full ...' Answering to the full, in Buxton's view, meant 'pulling away the cornerstone of slavery throughout the world'.[1] For him, as for most people involved with the slavery problem, the success or failure of emancipation was a complex issue. Considering its many dimensions, *did the free labour experiment succeed?* Few historians have asked that question – fewer still have tried to answer it. It must not be confused with the much simpler question: was emancipation morally right? The most vitriolic pro-slavery spokesmen of the 1820s willingly conceded that point.[2] Retrospective judgment on the degree to which British emancipation succeeded must depend on the extent to which it fulfilled the goals of its proponents and served the general welfare in societies affected by it.[3] Within the British community, three groups strongly advocated emancipation: the permanent staff of the Colonial Office, the anti-slavery party, and the slaves themselves. This paper assesses the results of emancipation in terms of the hopes and expectations of the abolitionists.

British anti-slavery combined several overlapping but complementary strains of thought. A Painite tradition, dating from the 1790s, emphasised the fundamental rights of man.

Exponents of popular political economy challenged slavery because it failed to meet their standards of utility. Both views merged with and were enveloped by humanitarian evangelicalism which, for thirty years, dominated the movement.[4] Abolitionists took their cause to the people, creating a national anti-slavery crusade. Despite resentment expressed by English 'wage slaves' that the employing classes were blinkered and hypocritical in their special solicitousness for colonial slaves,[5] the 'Saints' achieved their legislative victory by virtue of deep-lying public support at all levels of British society.[6] Continuing support of this kind was needed if abolitionists were to pursue further humanitarian objectives in the former slave colonies. After emancipation, however, strains of anti-slavery thought which had combined in triumph during 1833 exhibited increasing incompatibility. By 1850 the movement had become deeply fragmented and politically ineffectual, victimised by its own standards of conduct and the misleading nature of its propaganda.

The standards of conduct in question were fundamental to evangelicalism. Wilberforce confided in his diary in October 1787 that God had set before him two great objects, suppression of the slave trade and the reformation of manners.[7] Like other evangelicals, he was not aggrieved by social hierarchy or pervasive poverty, conditions 'ordained by God',[8] but he lamented poverty in the human soul and set out to redeem society through the moral regeneration of its individual members. Brutality appalled evangelicals. They attacked duelling, cruel sports, the abuse of pauper children and chimney sweeps, flogging, and capital punishment as well as the trading and owning of slaves.[9] Their creed was more a way of life than a theology, though it called its converts to an intense personal encounter with God. Above all, evangelicals were serious: seriousness was a sign of conversion; abstemiousness, hard work, and self denial were hallmarks of the evangelical life.[10] Censorious of indecency, evangelicals plunged headlong into the affairs of this world invading the slums of darkest London[11] and the forests of darkest Africa, bearing the torch of Christian salvation while admonishing all whose rules of conduct did not meet the standards of respectability demanded by born-again Christians.

G.M. Young opened his *Victorian England: Portrait of an*

Age with an assessment of evangelicalism, calling it 'the strongest binding force' in the nation.[12] Similarly, Elie Halévy considered it 'the moral cement of English society', attributing to evangelicals the reform of a loose-living, free thinking upper class.[13] Writing of British approaches to India, Eric Stokes declared evangelicalism 'the moral agency responsible for Victorian 'respectability', the power which tamed and disciplined the anarchic individualism of the Industrial Revolution'.[14] In India, southern and western Africa, and the West Indies, hundreds of evangelicals, representatives of metropolitan missionary societies, built their chapels and set about transforming alien cultures – some primitive, others infinitely complex – in their own God-fearing, sober, and eminently European image. The zeal of missionary endeavour paralleled the rise of anti-slavery.[15] Both expressed absolute certainty of conviction; both peaked in the 1830s; and both required positive responses from the oppressed and benighted objects of their philanthropy in order to sustain the intense level of their own commitments as well as the credibility of their endeavours among fellow Englishmen.

Where evangelicalism intersected with the reforming currents of utilitarianism, each influenced the other, and together they established standards of conduct calculated to enhance individual self-reliance and respectability. Thrift, sobriety, industry, and the intelligent exercise of 'moral restraint' were deemed essential personal qualities for success in this world and salvation in the next.

II

Did the reformers have a vision for the slave colonies after emancipation, or were their mental and physical energies entirely absorbed by the fight to abolish slavery? Historians have been remarkably reticent on this question. In the 1920s and 1930s, Mathieson,[16] Klingberg,[17] and Coupland[18] provided narrative accounts of the anti-slavery campaign in England but gave no indication that abolitionists might have had long-term expectations for the free Caribbean. L.J. Ragatz was also silent on the question.[19] Excellent studies of the post-emancipation Caribbean by a new generation of historians

– Hall,[20] Adamson,[21] Wood,[22] and Levy[23] – have not addressed the point. Curtin remarked only that British abolitionists seemed to hope the slaves would be 'transformed overnight' into English agricultural labourers.[24] Eric Williams, on the other hand, had much to say on the point: 'The emancipation Act', he declared, 'marked the end of the abolitionist efforts', adding that it did not occur to the 'Saints' that the 'Negro's freedom could be only nominal if the sugar plantation was allowed to endure'.[25]

Williams' verdict was mistaken all round. British emancipation was not the end of abolitionists' efforts;[26] moreover, the 'Saints' deliberately advocated retaining the plantation system and the hierarchical order of colonial society. British abolitionists were themselves products of a paternal and hierarchical social system, and as we have noted they had precise ideas about religious truth and proper personal decorum. Their responsibilities extended beyond merely freeing the slaves: they intended to enlighten them, to Christianise them, and to liberate them from 'degraded' habits and superstitions. In cultural terms, the success of the emancipation experiment would be determined by the extent to which Christian religion and British habits of behaviour were adopted by freedmen. Economically, it would be judged in terms of the ability of emancipated labour to preserve and enhance existing plantation economies.

Realistically, the cultural aims of emancipationists hinged on the success of export economies in the free Caribbean. Schools, chapels, roads, bridges, and the human resources requited to administer what the British in the nineteenth century uniformly considered a progressive society could not have been achieved without a strong export sector. The changing terms of international trade had rendered the West Indies increasingly dependent on their major staple, sugar.[27] There appeared no ready alternative to plantation production except scattered peasant agriculture of an essentially subsistence variety, and no broad body of reforming British abolitionists in the 1830s was inclined to argue that tropically situated peasant societies, comprising transplanted Africans brutalised by slavery, could secure a fertile social environment for their moral and redemptive work.[28] Furthermore, British abolitionists had a worldwide mission for which the West Indies constituted a decisive test case. If developments in those colonies could demonstrate to slave-owners throughout the Americas that emancipation could be undertaken without threat to the social order or destruction to private property, then the rational defences of the slaveocracies would be breached and bondage might quickly give way to freedom throughout the Atlantic basin.

Abolitionist propaganda gave firm assurances that Caribbean freedmen would pass the test. It condemned slavery for its inefficiency as well as its cruelty. Men worked best, abolitionists declared, when they worked in their own interest, and slavery precluded self-interested labour. Because slave-masters used people as brute beasts, they had no incentive to employ labour-saving, cost-efficient machinery or techniques. It was clear: free labour was cheaper than slave labour.[29] Only malignant perversity could have induced planters to persist so long in a system manifestly opposed to their own economic interests. Abolitionists thought it intolerable that British tariff regulations should give preference to West Indian sugar since such tariffs obliged the whole nation to subsidise a brutal and inefficient slave-owning class.[30]

After years of repetition, the slogans of anti-slavery became tenets of faith. The most zealous abolitionists seemed unaware that they were laying for themselves a political minefield; nor did they anticipate the contradictions which would arise between their strong advocacy of the superior merits of free labour and their determination to achieve full civil liberty for ex-slaves. Some of the conflicts abiding in these views derived from the special nature of the sugar industry and the deep-seated resistance of emancipated people to full-time dependency on estate labour. Sugar production was both seasonal and labour intensive. Regularity in the performance of agricultural and industrial tasks was critical to the efficient operation of a plantation, and estates could not function efficiently – and in some cases not at all – unless they could depend in advance on a sufficient body of workmen. Planters were convinced that freedmen would not provide the consistent labour they needed in critical seasons of the agricultural year unless they were coerced by law or obliged to work on estates because of the absence of an alternative source of livelihood. In the larger Caribbean colonies and throughout the Windward Islands there was abundant land available for peasant cultivation; in fact, slaves had already become proto-peasants through their cultivation of provision grounds allotted them by the planters.[31] Women and children were certain to leave plantation service in large numbers after emancipation. If men could earn their living, albeit a meagre one, beyond the estates, why should they endure the agonising labour of cane fields and boiling houses? Because the estates paid money wages, they could induce even the most independent freedmen to supplement their private earnings with occasional estate labour, but sugar properties could not hope to remain profitable in a competitive commercial environment without reliable work crews.

Abolitionists were not ignorant of these problems. All anti-slavery witnesses before the 1832 Parliamentary Select Committee on emancipation acknowledged the situation,[32] and the most explicit abolitionist text advocating the superior merits of free labour insisted that freedmen should be forbidden to settle on Crown Lands and that avenues to vagrancy and migration should be closed through judicious use of police measures.[33] Every draft of the Emancipation Bill took account of these problems, and when the legal structure for a free society was prepared at the end of the apprenticeship, planter assemblies, the Colonial Office, and abolitionist societies were fully aware that laws dealing with vagrancy, contracts, and other matters influencing the relations between employers and workers would have to restrain the freedmen's mobility and encourage them to perform regular estate labour.

How severe should such laws be? If the primary object of emancipation was to exhibit the greater efficiency and productivity of non-servile labour, then stern regulations binding ex-slaves to the estates might be preferred. Although planter assemblies were wont to adopt that type of legislation, draconian labour laws would only have substituted one form of coercion for another, a cruel deception which neither the Colonial Office nor the abolitionists could tolerate. The Colonial Office hoped to achieve a reasonable balance between the production requirements of the estates and the civil liberties of the freedmen. The commanding figure at Downing Street during the critical years when post-emancipation legislation was being drafted was James Stephen, an evangelical permanent under-secretary whose father and brother had been leading forces in the anti-slavery crusade.[34] Because a judicious balance between production and liberty was difficult to gauge – particularly since colonial law would be administered by the planter elite – Stephen chose to err on the side of liberty. Abolitionist bodies were even more determined that colonial law should scrupulously prevent planters from abusing their authority. They regarded themselves as the watchdogs of colonial legislation, and they frequently petitioned and occasionally visited the Colonial Office to represent their views on legislative, juridical, and other matters involving relationships between West India planters and the emancipated class.[35] In the transition from slave labour to free, the anti-slavery movement gave priority to freedom, not production. As Temperley observed, the most radical abolitionists possessed a 'dedication to moral principle so unwavering as to take precedence over every other consideration, including sometimes the achievement of the object sought'.[36]

Between 1837 and 1839 the dominant tone of British anti-slavery passed from the moderate posture of Fowell Buxton to that of Joseph Sturge, an uncompromising radical whose British and Foreign Anti-Slavery Society sent the old Anti-Slavery Society into humble dissolution.[37] In 1836, Sturge toured the colonies provoking the anger of planters and the irritation of governors[38] while accumulating evidence of planter excesses to be used in a successful national campaign to terminate the apprenticeship prematurely in 1838. During the next two years, emancipated people left the estates in large numbers; production fell; sugar supplies dwindled; prices rose; and the metropolitan government grew increasingly concerned for the future of the emancipation experiment.

The British government took three actions in response to these problems. It revised colonial laws which regulated relations between masters and servants in the interest of the planters; it initiated indentured immigration from Africa and the East Indies to bolster plantation work forces;[39] and it reduced, then eliminated, preferential tariffs on West Indian sugar. The first two were intended to correct a perceived imbalance between the productive requirements of the estates and the civil liberties of freedom. Attacks on the sugar duties were initially occasioned by high prices and widespread shortages,[40] but the 1846 elimination of preference was dictated by a dramatic popular shift in national policy.

Anti-slavery forces opposed stiffening colonial legislation, and they were generally hostile to immigration, condemning it as an unwarranted device for lowering the wages of freedmen. Declining colonial production was blamed on malevolent and obstinate planters who bullied and alienated the workers, managed their properties poorly, and refused to adopt labour-saving machinery.[41] Despite sobering production figures and the warnings of well-informed colleagues, the delegates attending an international anti-slavery convention in London in June 1840 declared that 'the superior cheapness of free-labour has been incontestably proved' in the West India colonies.[42] These same delegates insisted, however, that under no condition should the British government permit the 'introduction of slave grown sugar into the British market', a direct contradiction of their pre-emancipation position on protection and an apparent equivocation on their free labour versus slave labour maxim.[43]

By 1842 it appeared that British consumers were the parties most needful of protection. Reports from the colonies indicated that freedmen were enjoying substantially more leisure, luxuries, and access to freehold property than the working poor of Britain. By 1842, 200 free villages had been established in Jamaica involving over 8,000 individual holdings; in British Guiana, there were at least 4,000 freehold properties,[44] and combinations of freedmen were purchasing estates for as much as $50,000.[45] The Governor of Jamaica considered the peasantry 'remarkably comfortable, with money in plenty ... their own masters in a greater degree ... than any peasantry in the world'.[46] One cannot read the correspondence of stipendiary magistrates and Christian missionaries without being impressed by the relative well-being of the freedmen in the early 1840s.[47] When questioned whether the labourers of Jamaica were not better off than working people in Britain, William Knibb, Baptist missionary and despised enemy of the planters, answered, 'decidedly'. The Jamaican freedmen, he told a Parliamentary committee, were better paid for their labour than British workers: 'I should be very sorry to see them as badly off as the labourers here; half of them starving'.[48] Britain's free traders concluded that the material plenty of Caribbean freedmen was a direct result of monopoly-inflated sugar prices charged to the British working poor.

The controversy over sugar tariffs exposed contradictions in the abolitionists' position and demonstrated their inability to arouse continued popular support. In 1841 anti-slavery forces were strong enough to launch the Niger expedition and defeat a Government Bill to reduce sugar duties, but humanitarian reformism was taking a new turning. In August 1841, 700 clergymen of dissenting sects gathered in Manchester to denounce protection on religious and humanitarian grounds,[49] and when the second international anti-slavery convention met in 1843, a vocal minority demanded elimination of preferential tariffs as a moral duty to the British poor.[50] How could abolitionist opinion tolerate the massive importation of slave-grown cotton while excluding slave-grown sugar? If free labour was cheaper than slave labour, why should abolitionists shrink from direct competition? The British and Foreign Anti-Slavery Society held its protectionist line during the 'hungry forties', but only at the price of allying with their ancient enemies, the Caribbean planters, and alienating substantial middle and working class opinion. Defeat on the sugar duties in 1846[51] capped the steady decline of anti-slavery influence. Exeter Hall had been overwhelmed by Manchester: both had promised international peace, and both provided a missionary dimension, but by 1846 free trade had become the dynamic crusading force in Britain. It appealed to the rational self interest of the middle classes and offered some hope of relief to the working poor. Popular enthusiasm for British anti-slavery was spent. No longer could the anti-slavery leadership, itself divided, stir British consciences over the misdeeds of planters or the deprivations of colonial working people. If ex-slaves had not made good use of their freedom, the fault was considered their own.

Equalisation of the sugar duties and European depression in the late 1840s wrought havoc upon the plantation economies of the larger British colonies, particularly Jamaica, causing widespread bankruptcy and extensive abandonment of plantations.[52] Where cultivation continued, the wages of labour fell, and the prosperity enjoyed by emancipated people in the first blush of freedom disappeared. Free villages originally established in the vicinity of active estates were left isolated by abandonments; roads and bridges that coursed derelict estates fell into disrepair; taxes could not be collected; and there was little money, public or private, for schools, churches, or other civic amenities.[53] Only in communities where open land was scarce and freedmen possessed no alternative to regular estate labour, most notably Barbados, were planters able to avoid widespread insolvency.[54] The plantation economies of Trinidad and British Guiana would recover in the 1850s, but only through large infusions of East Indian indentured labour. No responsible observer examining the wreckage of the West Indian sugar industry in 1850 would have affirmed the superior productive efficiency of free labour, except under the special circumstances of a colony like Barbados.[55] American, Cuban, and Brazilian slave-owners considered themselves vindicated, not challenged, by the British experiment.

III

Even before the economic debacle of the late 1840s, British humanitarian reformers were expressing grave concern over the social and religious progress of former slaves. As we have noted, abolitionists were committed to uplifting the freedmen, inculcating in them the habits of piety, sobriety, industry, and thrift. Numerous missionaries arrived in the colonies in the decade before emancipation; many more followed during the 1830s. Although these paragons of enlightenment deplored the 'immorality' of slaves, they were confident that emancipation would encourage grateful freedmen to embrace the religious and cultural dispensations of their Christian benefactors. In this, they were bitterly disappointed.

In the first days of freedom, ex-slaves filled missionary chapels, contributed heavily to the construction of new facilities, and hastened to formalise sexual partnerships through marriage. During the 1840s, however, the number of worshippers at mission stations sharply declined, and freedmen turned increasingly to self-appointed black preachers and Afro-creole religious practitioners. European ignorance of the creole's religious traditions was almost complete, and the missionaries' cultural arrogance prevented them from appreciating the depth and resiliency of black creole culture.[56] Freedmen found evangelical Christianity unattractive: the more rigidly evangelical a missionary's ethical standards were, the less appeal he had. Methodists lost young people by forbidding them to dance,[57] and London missionaries repeatedly belaboured the unrelieved and unrepentant sinfulness of the freedmen: wife-beating, cursing, carousing, lascivious dancing, intoxication,[58] 'indecent and extravagant dress, immodest gestures and behaviour on the public roads', and, above all, fornication – the besetting sin of the colonies! By 1845, a London missionary in Demerara declared abolition a mixed blessing: liberty, he asserted, had given way to licentiousness.[59] Another expressed a widespread missionary opinion that white pastors had lost influence with the people: 'the link that bound the people to their minister ten years ago is snapped asunder ...'.[60] His colleague declared the whole missionary enterprise a failure, lamenting that it had been much easier to transform negroes from slaves to freedmen than from heathens to Christians.[61] All denominations tried to create a 'native agency' of pious, well trained creole pastors who could assume responsibility for the missions, but candidates were invariably disqualified for moral backsliding. A London missionary who strove for ten years to produce a native pastorate without a single success declared himself continuously outflanked by 'illegitimate' black preachers.[62]

Devastation in the sugar industry after 1846 reduced the money available to wage earners and impoverished missions dependent on donations. Even Baptists in Jamaica – the least demanding missionaries in matters of social comportment and theological doctrine – were leaving the island because congregations could not or would not support them. Writing at the end of 1847, James Phillippo expressed fear for the future of his society declaring that unless conditions changed dramatically it would fall to ruin.[63] Reports of magistrates and missionaries in the mid-century years are filled with anguished commentary on the extent of social demoralisation, petty crime, idleness, and disregard for marriage, for education, or for the survival of missions.[64] The Methodists echoed Phillippo: no period in the troubled history of their Caribbean missions was 'so dark and despondent'.[65] Except for Barbados and to a lesser extent the more densely populated Leeward Islands, creole society in the sugar colonies gave little encouragement to the ideas and institutions which metropolitan abolitionists and their missionary colleagues deeply esteemed.

IV

Roger Anstey once concluded, 'Everything seemed to go wrong for the abolition cause in the 1840s'.[66] He offered three reasons: failure of the Niger expedition, deep commitment to an American problem which British abolitionism could not resolve, and internal division over the sugar duties. Each of these affected British anti-slavery, but taken together they do not provide a full explanation for the declining redemptive influence of evangelical anti-slavery in the empire and Africa. The Niger expedition occurred after a string of abolitionist successes. Since abolitionists would enjoy no further victories of note, the expedition appears as a turning point in their affairs. In fact, it was only the most dramatic in a long list of British failures in the struggle against the slave trade, and it is not improbable that humanitarian leaders could have resumed their broad appeal to the nation had failure in the Niger not been accompanied by failure – or at least the perception of failure – in other regions of humanitarian outreach.

In South Africa, India, West Africa, and the West Indies, humanitarian policy seemed fraught with trouble and disappointment. The targets of British humanitarian solicitude seemed obstinately attached to their heathenish practices – to *sati*, ritual infanticide, sacrifice of the elderly, or obeah. Christian missionaries who arrived in India in large numbers during the 1820s discovered that their redemptive message appealed only to illiterate low caste Hindus, and even then to precious few.[67] The tide of reformist zeal evident at the mission stations and in the reformist administration of Lord William Bentinck, Governor General from 1828 to 1835, had ebbed substantially by the 1840s.[68] A sea change was occurring in British attitudes toward colonial dependents, and this change was coarsely punctuated by the publication of Thomas Carlyle's 'The Nigger Question' in 1849.

When this violently racist tract appeared, Britain was burdened by economic stagnation, Chartist marches, and Irish famine. Across the Atlantic, the once-flourishing sugar plantations lay prostrate while, in Carlyle's intemperate language, idle and happy freedmen sat 'yonder with their beautiful muzzles up to the ears in pumpkins ...'[69]. He drew sharp contrasts between a hard-working domestic population unable to find employment and a colonial population which, by refusing employment, had destroyed 'noble' agricultural industries. Carlyle advocated a stern, even brutal, work ethic, and he was taken to task by John Stuart Mill for his multiple excesses. But even Mill acknowledged that for a decade freedmen had enjoyed a situation in which their labour had brought so high a price that they could 'exist in comfort on the wages of a comparatively small quantity of work'.[70]

Carlyle's essay did not represent mainstream British thinking, but it touched a responsive chord and offered some portent of later imperial sentiment. If the redemptive power of British reformism and evangelical Christianity had been wasted on the black and brown peoples of the world, it had, nevertheless, borne fruit among the labouring masses of Britain. Trygve Tholfsen has argued that the union of enlightenment ideas and evangelical Christianity co-opted working class radicalism in Britain, producing a remarkably stable culture that espoused goals of self-improvement, respectability, and social harmony.[71] Growing interest in individual self-improvement led to receding concern for social injustice and inequality. Personal morality was celebrated, and the working man, having repudiated rebellion, dedicated himself to becoming worthy of his superiors' trust. If the hard-working British poor did not surrender unconditionally to middle class piety and respectability, Tholfsen believes they largely adopted the personal values and social prejudices of people of property. A society committed to these values could hardly express sustained sympathy for those who appeared to be squandering their freedom in ignorance and immorality.

Examining the sugar colonies from the perspective of mid-nineteenth century Britain, few British abolitionists could have contended that emancipation had fulfilled their high expectations. Ex-slaves might have responded similarly, but that is a wholly different matter and requires separate scholarly attention. Emancipation had been established in peace and pursued in peace. Liberty – even relatively unproductive liberty – was considered superior to tyranny. The sugar colonies had not demonstrated the superior proficiency of free labour, but more distressingly, freedmen had exhibited little sustained interest in the religious and cultural overtures of their European benefactors. These realities, in combination with social and attitudinal changes occurring in Britain, dampened enthusiasm for continued humanitarian outreach. By the 1850s, Britons of every social level were more disposed to disdain people in the colonies and beyond who, having been given opportunities for worldly enlightenment and eternal salvation, obdurately rejected both.

NOTES

1. Charles Buxton (ed.), *Memoirs of Sir Thomas Fowell Buxton* (London, 1866), p. 337.
2. The Rev. George Bridges, vituperative defender of slavery in Jamaica, declared his abhorrence of slavery in principle: 'I detest the barbarous institution as a curse'. Quoted in P. D. Curtin, *Two Jamaicas: The Role of Ideas in a Tropical Colony 1830–1865* (Cambridge, Mass., 1955), p. 41. Commenting on the literature of the emancipation era, Curtin claims never to have discovered a defence of slavery in principle. Henry Barclay, the most effective planter spokesman readily acknowledged that slavery was evil, declaring only that its elimination must be managed with greatest caution. See his *A Practical View of the Present State of Slavery in the West Indies* (2nd edition, London, 1827), p. xvii. By the late 1820s West Indians had generally recognised the inevitability of emancipation. The timing and the terms of it were their key concerns. This sentiment is apparent in H. N. Coleridge, *Six Months in the West Indies in 1825* (London, 1826), p. 308.
3. Criteria for judgment varied from one group to another, and interested parties must include West India planters, American slave-owners, European and American abolitionists, and the governments of European states having slave colonies in the Western hemisphere. For the North American community, see J. M. McPherson, 'Was British Emancipation a Success? The Abolitionist Argument during the American Civil War', *Caribbean Studies*, IV (1964), pp. 28–34.
4. The term evangelicalism is used here in its broadest context, incorporating non-conformists as well as members of the evangelical wing of the Anglican church – all those puritanical, proselytising groups having a vital approach to religion. Seymour Drescher cautions against the view that anti-slavery was merely an extension of evangelical religion, but he readily acknowledges the fundamental links between the two and the driving inspiration which the religious revival provided for anti-slavery. See his 'Public Opinion and the Destruction of British Colonial Slavery', in James Walvin (ed.), *Slavery and British Society 1776–1846* (Baton Rouge, Louisa., 1982), pp. 34–40. In the same study Drescher as well as Betty Fladeland ('"Our Cause Being One and the Same": Abolitionists and Chartism', pp. 69–99) observe the extent of artisanal and working class participation in anti-slavery, but Walvin's chapter ('The Propaganda of

Anti-Slavery') hints at a point which will be developed more fully in the final section of this paper: 'We need to recall that religion itself had been transformed, more especially among the lower orders' (p. 65).

5. Patricia Hollis, 'Anti-Slavery and British Working-Class Radicalism in the Years of Reform', in Christine Bolt and Seymour Drescher (eds.), *Anti-Slavery, Religion, and Reform: Essays in Memory of Roger Anstey* (Folkestone, 1980), pp. 294–315.
6. James Walvin, 'The Rise of British Popular Sentiment for Abolition, 1787–1832', in Bolt and Drescher (eds.), *op. cit.*, pp. 149–62.
7. E. M. Howse, *Saints in Politics: The Clapham Sect and the Growth of Freedom* (London, 1971 edition), p. 321.
8. For discussion of these points, see Jenifer Hart, 'Religion and Social Control in the Mid-Nineteenth Century', in A. P. Donajgrodzski (ed.), *Social Control in Nineteenth Century Britain* (Totawa, N. J., 1977), pp. 108–37; Standish Meacham, 'The Evangelical Inheritance', *Journal of British Studies*, 3 (1963), pp. 91–2.
9. With urging from the 'Saints', George III issued a proclamation condemning sabbath breaking, drunkenness, blasphemy, obscene literature, and immoral amusements in 1787. Slavery was considered particularly evil because it reduced men to the level of animals, because it brutalised masters as well as slaves, because it produced inordinate psychological suffering and distorted and constricted human souls. Roger Anstey stressed the connection between the redemption of the soul and the Old Testament theme of redemption from physical bondage. See his 'The Pattern of British Abolitionism in the Eighteenth and Nineteenth Centuries' in Bolt and Drescher (eds.), *op. cit.*, pp. 21–2. When the 'Saints' set out to ameliorate slavery, they began by assaulting those features of the system that violated their notions of human decency: flogging, particularly the flogging of women whose buttocks were exposed during punishment, denial of slave marriage, ignoring the sabbath and the practice of Sunday markets. *Anti-Slavery Monthly Reporter*, I (1827), p. 21.
10. The best comprehensive account of evangelicalism is Ian Bradley, *The Call to Seriousness: The Evangelical Impact on the Victorians* (London, 1976).
11. The large urban missions were established in the mid-century, several decades after the overseas missions had been in operation. Kathleen Heasman, *Evangelicals in Action: An Appraisal of Their Social Work in the Victorian Era* (London, 1962), pp. 29–47.
12. (2nd edition, New York, 1964), p. 5.
13. Elie Halévy, *A History of the English People in the Nineteenth Century*, 6 vols. (2nd revised edition, London, 1949), I, p. 450; III, p. 163.
14. Eric Stokes, *English Utilitarians in India* (Oxford, 1959), p. 28.
15. C. D. Rice, 'The Missionary Context of the British Anti-Slavery Movement', in Walvin (ed.), *Slavery and British Society*, pp. 150–51. Dates for the founding of missionaries societies are: Wesleyan, 1789; Baptist, 1792; London, 1795; Church, 1799.
16. W. L. Mathieson, *British Slavery and its Abolition 1823–1838* (London, 1926).
17. Frank Klingberg, *The Anti-Slavery Movement in England* (New Haven, 1926).
18. Sir Reginald Coupland, *The British Anti-Slavery Movement* (London, 1933; reprinted Frank Cass, 1964). This is a breezy narrative which devotes only one chapter to the abolition of slavery; it offers no documentation and appears heavily dependent on the earlier work of Mathieson.
19. See his *The Fall of the Planter Class in the British Caribbean 1763–1833* (New York, 1928); although his *A Guide for the Study of British Caribbean History, 1763–1834, including the Abolition and Emancipation Movements*

(Washington, 1932) offers a prodigious annotated bibliography of contemporary books and tracts on the slavery question, Ragatz did not, to my knowledge, publish an analytical synthesis of these materials.

20. Douglas Hall, *Free Jamaica, 1838–1865: An Economic History* (New Haven, 1959) and *Five of the Leewards, 1834–1870: The Major Problems of the Post-Emancipation Period in Antigua, Barbuda, Montserrat, Nevis, and St Kitts* (Barbados, 1971).
21. A.H. Adamson, *Sugar Without Slaves: The Political Economy of British Guiana, 1838–1904* (New Haven, 1972).
22. Donald Wood, *Trinidad in Transition: The Years after Slavery* (London, 1968).
23. Claude Levy, *Emancipation, Sugar, and Federation: Barbados and the West Indies, 1833–1876* (Gainesville, Fla., 1980).
24. Curtin, *Two Jamaicas, op. cit.*, p. 41.
25. Eric Williams, *Capitalism and Slavery* (New York, Capricorn edition, 1966), p. 191.
26. This notion was firmly put to rest by Howard Temperley's *British Anti-Slavery 1833–1870* (Columbia, S.C., 1972).
27. W.A. Green, *British Slave Emancipation: The Sugar Colonies and the Great Experiment, 1830–1865* (Oxford, 1976), pp. 44–5, 64.
28. Curtin observes that Britons in this period believed 'that Negro Africans were, at best, barbarians who had never known civilization'. In the West Indies, the deficiencies of heritage were compounded, Britons believed, by the damaging effects of slavery. P. D. Curtin, *The Image of Africa: British Ideas and Action, 1780–1850* (Madison, Wisc., 1964), p. 227.
29. This was a main staple in the abolitionist argument. At the beginning of the emancipation campaign Thomas Clarkson wrote that free labour was more productive than slave, that planters were damaging their interests by preserving slavery, that only emancipation could save them from ruin. See his *Thoughts on the Necessity of Improving the Condition of the Slaves in the British Empire with a View to their Ultimate Emancipation* (New York, 1823). These points continuously re-appeared in anti-slavery speeches and literature. The best known contemporary statement of the argument by an abolitionist was Josiah Conder's *Wages or the Whip. An Essay on the Comparative Cost and Production of Free and Slave Labour* (London, 1833).
30. From its inception, the *Anti-Slavery Monthly Reporter*, the principal organ of the Anti-Slavery Society, repeatedly attacked the preferential duties afforded to West Indian sugar. See, for example, the issues of 31 July 1825, 31 Oct. 1826, 30 Dec. 1826, 31 March 1827, and April 1828.
31. Douglas Hall and Sidney Mintz, 'The Origins of the Jamaican Internal Marketing System', in S. W. Mintz (ed.), *Papers in Caribbean Anthropology* (New Haven, 1960), pp. 3–26.
32. This point is made by David Eltis, 'Abolitionist Perceptions of Society after Slavery', in Walvin (ed.), *Slavery and British Society, op. cit.*, p. 202.
33. Conder, *Wages or the Whip, op. cit.*, pp. 82–4.
34. Stephen married the daughter of the evangelical rector at Clapham. He was deeply influenced by Wilberforce. His father, James, author of the devastating though highly partisan *The Slavery of the West India Colonies Delineated* (1824), was a leading light in the early anti-slavery movement; his brother George was a dominant force in the Agency Committee. For an account of Stephen's approach to West India policy, see W. A. Green, 'James Stephen and British West India Policy, 1834–1847', *Caribbean Studies*, XIII (1974), pp. 33–56.
35. Colonial Office records in this period contain a considerable body of anti-slavery correspondence. See, for example, P.R.O. Colonial Office Series (hereafter

C.O.) 318/134, 17 July 1838, and 318/143, 27 March 1839, Correspondence of the Negro Emancipation Committee; C.O. 137/252, Anti-Slavery Papers. Both James Stephen and a brilliant clerk in the West India department, James Spedding, were irritated by the insistence and exaggeration of the abolitionists. Writing anonymously in the *Edinburgh Review* Spedding cautioned anti-slavery zealots 'to be a little nicer as to what they believe and a little more cautious as to what they infer ...'. His article, 'The Working of Negro Apprenticeship in 1838', was reprinted in *Reviews and Discussions, Literary, Political, and Historical, not Relating to Bacon* (London, 1879).

36. Temperley, *British Anti-Slavery, op. cit.*, p. 74. The interpretation offered in this paragraph differs from that of David Eltis' 'Abolitionist Perceptions of Society', in Walvin (ed.), *Slavery and British Society, op. cit.*, pp. 204–7. Eltis makes a strong case that planters, abolitionists, and the British government were committed to 'increasing or at least maintaining pre-abolition levels of export output'. (205) A 'fine line' divided them on the subject of post-emancipation legislation, and, he contends, some of the planters' proposals 'might have been acceptable if they had come from groups with anti-slavery credentials'. (206) He suggests that abolitionists moderated their position between 1834 and 1839 and that they eventually disagreed with the government because the Colonial Office was prepared 'to put labour under a much greater degree of coercion than existed in contemporary Britain'. (206) My response to this approach involves shading more than disagreement, though the distinctions are not unimportant. As the following paragraph in this paper notes, the character of British anti-slavery changed sharply in the Apprenticeship period. When post-emancipation labour legislation was being drafted, the Colonial Office was obliged to deal with a substantially more radical abolitionist movement than had prevailed in 1834, and this radical element most decidedly placed highest emphasis on the protection of freedmen's liberty, not the maintenance of export levels. When reviewing post-emancipation colonial legislation on vagrancy, contracts, and other enactments involving employers and wage-earners, the Colonial Office insisted that such legislation be *more lenient* than that applying in the Mother Country. This legislation was modified during the 1840s, but even then it was only brought into identity with British statutes. Eltis may exaggerate the 'degree of coercion' involved in tightening labour law. West Indian practices minimised the impact of tougher legislation: in the case of contract law, for example, freedmen refused to work under contracts, and planters had no effective means of forcing them to.
37. The old society dissolved in April 1839. For the changing character of British abolitionism, see Temperley, *British Anti-Slavery, op. cit.*, pp. 62–92.
38. Sturge travelled with Thomas Harvey through the Lesser Antilles and Jamaica. Abolitionist colleagues, John Scoble and William Lloyd, toured British Guiana. On returning to Britain, Sturge and Harvey published *The West Indies in 1837* (1838). Sir Lionel Smith, the Governor of Jamaica whom the planters considered unduly well disposed toward the negroes, bitterly denounced Sturge's excesses. C.O. 137/277, 15 April 1838, Smith to Glenelg, private letter. The Lieutenant-Governor of British Guiana, like Smith a strong defender of the negroes' rights, was annoyed by Scoble's injudiciousness and want of accuracy, C.O. 111/165 no. 133, Memorandum, October 1839. Commenting on a subsequent visit by Scoble, the Governor of Barbados summarised the opinion of all West India executives: 'Travellers as Mr Scoble ... can do no good if they come as Friends, but infinite mischief if they come as enemies ...'. C.O. 28/127, no. 42, 6 April 1839, McGregor to Normanby.
39. For an analysis of the decision to initiate immigration, see W. A. Green,

'Emancipation to Indenture: A Question of Imperial Morality', *Journal of British Studies*, XXII (1984), pp. 98–121.

40. In 1841, the pre-duty price of free-grown British Caribbean sugar was double that of slave-grown Brazilian or Cuban sugar. Lord John Russell, the Colonial Secretary, determined that per capita consumption of sugar in Britain had declined 25 per cent since the end of slavery. Memorandum, Russell Papers, P.R.O. 30, 22/4A. Russell's biographer notes that a dietary necessity was fast becoming a luxury. Stories were common of British villagers watching their fruit spoil because they could not afford the sugar to preserve it. John Prest, *Lord John Russell* (Columbia, S.C., 1972), p. 173.
41. I have attempted to offer some revision of the long-standing view that West India planters were poor agriculturalists, resistant to innovation. See my 'The Planter Class and British West India Sugar Production, Before and After Emancipation', *Economic History Review*, 2nd series, XXVI (1973), pp. 448–63, and *British Slave Emancipation, op. cit.*, pp. 199–214.
42. British and Foreign Anti-Slavery Society, *Proceedings of the General Anti-Slavery Convention* (London, 1841), pp. 398–407. Dr R. R. Madden and David Turnbull, both of whom had experience in the West Indies (particularly Madden, former stipendiary magistrate in Jamaica and Superintendent of Liberated Africans in Cuba) made reasoned arguments against the simplistic nature of the convention's motion, but to no avail.
43. The growing tension in anti-slavery feeling during the early 1840s is evident in J. J. Gurney's *A Winter in the West Indies, Described in Familiar Letters to Henry Clay, of Kentucky* (London, 1840). Gurney was intent to convince Americans of the superior efficiency of free labour, but he was strongly against any reduction in the British sugar duties for fear such action would undermine the free labour experiment before the Caribbean colonies could iron out their difficulties. Conscious of declining colonial productivity, Gurney implored freedmen to undertake '*steady* attention to the cultivation' of staples. For the sake 'of the slaves in the Brazils, in Cuba, and in Porto Rico, and far above all, for the safety of untold multitudes in benighted Africa', he argued, 'let them (the freedmen) direct their energies to the extension of the cultivation of sugar and coffee' (pp. xv–xvi). Some abolitionists were either naive or brazenly dishonest in their appeals to American slave-owners. Thomas Clarkson boldly asserted that one enfranchised West Indian negro was worth two slaves, that estates were rising in value 'to an amount that is hardly credible', that American planters had not a moment to lose in freeing their slaves. He warned the Americans that they would soon 'have no market for their produce', adding that 'when the Niger expedition ... returns, measures will be immediately taken for the cultivation of cotton, rice, sugar, tobacco, etc., in Africa, on a very large scale'. *A Letter to the Clergy of Various Denominations and to the Slave-Holding Planters in the Southern Parts of the United States of America* (London, 1841), pp. 57–8.
44. Statistics on peasant freehold have been gathered in W. K. Marshall, 'Notes on Peasant Development in the West Indies since 1838', *Social and Economic Studies*, XVII (1967), pp. 252–63.
45. Rawle Farley, 'The Rise of the Peasantry in British Guiana', *Social and Economic Studies*, II (1954), p. 101. The Crown Surveyor of British Guiana determined in 1844 that there were 18,500 people living in free villages, C.O. 111/227, Report of J. Hadfield.
46. C.O. 137/248, no. 50, 30 March 1840, Metcalfe to Russell.
47. A stipendiary magistrate in Jamaica commented on the peasants' extensive possession of horses, fine clothing, and 'other superfluities'. C.O. 137/248,

no. 50, Report of Hall Pringle. John Gurney was surprised by the amount of coin in the hands of labourers. *A Winter in the West Indies, op. cit.*, pp. 103–4. Several missionaries expressed concern over the freedmen's pursuit of material wealth. C.O. 137/250, Letter of George Blyth, Oct. 1840; H.M. Waddell, *Twenty-Nine Years in the West Indies and Central Africa* (London, 1863; reprinted Frank Cass, 1971), p. 145. In Demerara, a stipendiary magistrate called the peasantry indisputably better off than 'the happiest and best paid labourers in the most fertile districts of England', *Parliamentary Papers* (1842), XII, 551, Appendix 23, p. 463.

48. *Parliamentary Papers* (1842), XIII, 479, Select Committee on the West India Colonies, evidence 6275. Even when depression descended on Jamaica, missionaries argued that poverty among freedmen was less burdensome by virtue of their possession of freeholds than it was for the British poor. London School of Oriental and African Studies, London Missionary Society Papers (hereafter LMS), 5 February 1849, Slayter to Tidman; 26 May 1851, Gardner to Tidman.
49. Norman McCord, *The Anti-Corn Law League 1838–1846* (London, 1958), pp. 104–5.
50. C.D. Rice, '"Humanity Sold for Sugar!" The British Abolitionist Response to Free Trade in Slave-Grown Sugar', *Historical Journal*, XIII (1970), pp. 412–13.
51. The Sugar Duties Act substantially reduced duties on all foreign sugar – slave-grown and free-grown – and systematically reduced the preference for colonial sugar by 1s. 6d. per year until by 1851 all duties would be equalised.
52. Green, *British Slave Emancipation, op. cit.*, pp. 234–236. Forty-nine per cent of Jamaica's plantations, 314 in number, were abandoned between 1844 and 1854. Hall, *Free Jamaica, op. cit.*, p. 82.
53. A graphic illustration of this was offered by a London missionary in British Guiana who feared his mission could not survive. The canal in his area was being neglected, was filling with silt, and was becoming impassable even for small craft. The three or four bridges over the canal were destroyed and were not likely to be repaired. He continued: 'it will soon be impossible to traverse the upper part of the district except on foot, and that through mud and rank grass', LMS, British Guiana, 21 March 1849, Charles Rattray to Tidman.
54. Even in Barbados, 13 estates suffered foreclosure in Chancery while many more heavily indebted properties were forced to sell privately. Levy, *Emancipation, Sugar and Federation, op. cit.*, p. 106.
55. Conditions similar to those prevailing in Barbados existed in St Kitts and Antigua as well.
56. Many missionaries, among others, denied that slaves had any religion other than a belief in witchcraft. For an excellent brief account of Afro-Creole religious belief, see Monica Schuler, *'Alas, Alas, Kongo': A Social History of Indentured African Immigration into Jamaica, 1841–1865* (Baltimore, 1980), pp. 32–44.
57. London School of Oriental and African Studies, Methodist Missionary Society Papers, Antigua, 6 Oct. 1840, John Hornby to General Secretary.
58. In a manner consistent wtih their actions in Britain, evangelicals tried to establish temperance societies among freedmen. Waddell, *Twenty-Nine Years, op. cit.*, pp. 114, 118.
59. LMS, British Guiana, 28 Jan. 1845, James Scott to Rev. J.J. Freedman.
60. LMS, British Guiana, 15 Aug. 1846, W.G. Barrett to A. Tidman.
61. LMS, British Guiana, 21 March 1849, Charles Rattray to A. Tidman.
62. LMS, British Guiana, 26 Jan. 1852, E.A. Wallbridge to A. Tidman. Even the most celebrated European missionaries were challenged by black competitors. In 1845, James Phillippo's Baptist congregation at Spanish Town was rent in a violent struggle that required calling out the militia. Baptist Missionary Society,

Phillippo Papers, 7 April 1845, Phillippo to Argus; Baptist Missionary Society Papers, Jamaica, 20 April 1845, Evants to Argus, 19 April 1845, Hands to Argus; *Votes of the Jamaican Assembly* (1845), Appendix LXI. Six years later Phillippo's house was stormed and pillaged, his wife wounded, and the militia called in to restore order. C.O. 137/310, 24, 28 July 1851, C.E. Grey to Earl Grey. Interestingly, a European missionary who had sided against Phillippo in the 1845 confrontation with a black minister was, ten years later, the victim of a similar invasion of his own Kingston church, with attendant rioting and calling of the militia. C.O. 137/326, 12 March 1855, Barkly to Sir George Grey.

63. E. B. Underhill, *Life of James Mursell Phillippo* (London, 1881), p. 245. This book, based on Phillippo's diaries and correspondence, provides the full canvas of experience from the buoyant and feverish days of expansion immediately after emancipation to the bitter harvest of 1852 when Phillippo wrote, 'The future is dark and gloomy. The country is increasing in poverty, and religious feeling is rapidly declining' (p. 245).
64. Social demoralisation and the rise of petty crime was intensified by the cholera epidemic of 1850.
65. G. C. Findlay and W. W. Holdsworth, *The History of the Wesleyan Methodist Missionary Society*, 5 vols. (London, 1921–4), II, p. 370.
66. Anstey, 'The Pattern of British Abolitionism', in Bolt and Drescher (eds.), *op. cit.*, p. 31.
67. There were about 340 ordained Protestant missionaries at work in India in 1851, about two-thirds of whom were sponsored by metropolitan missionary societies. G. A. Oddie, *Social Protest in India: British Protestant Missionaries and Social Reforms 1850–1900* (New Delhi, 1978), p. 9. For an evaluation of the missionaries' work, see E. D. Potts, *British Baptist Missionaries in India 1793–1837: The History of Serampore and its Missions* (Cambridge, 1967), pp. 139–68; Kenneth Ingham, *Reformers in India 1793–1833: An Account of the Work of Christian Missionaries in Behalf of Social Reform* (Cambridge, 1956).
68. The changing mood towards British India is well treated in G. D. Bearce, *British Attitudes Towards India 1784–1858* (London, 1961), pp. 153–5, 180–91, and F. G. Hutchins, *The Illusion of Permanence: British Imperialism in India* (Princeton, 1967), pp. 9–12, 54–70.
69. Thomas Carlyle, 'Occasional Discourse on the Nigger Question', reprinted with introduction by E. R. August in *The Nigger Question and the Negro Question* (New York, 1971), p. 4.
70. John Stuart Mill, 'The Negro Question', reprinted in August, *op. cit.*, p. 41.
71. T. R. Tholfsen, 'The Intellectual Origins of Mid-Victorian Stability', *Political Science Quarterly*, LXXXVI (1971), pp. 57–91.

10

Apprenticeship and Labour Relations in Four Windward Islands

W. K. MARSHALL

Various studies have indicated that the labour preservation policies pursued by planters after 1834 probably had a negative impact on labour relations during the Apprenticeship.[1] But in none of these studies nor in those on post-Apprenticeship labour conditions is there a sustained attempt either to show the nature and extent of apprentices' responses to those policies or to examine possible connections between the Apprenticeship experience and the post-Apprenticeship situation. This is surprising because the conditions which gave rise to the planters' labour policies during the Apprenticeship persisted into full emancipation, the same parties were involved and, presumably, any apprentices 'permanently alienated'[2] during 1834–8 remained so after 1838.

This paper focuses on aspects of the labour situation in four Windward Islands (Grenada, St. Lucia, St. Vincent, Tobago) mainly during 1838 – the closing months of the Apprenticeship and the first months of full emancipation. It attempts to identify some elements of continuity in the planters' strategies for the preservation and recruitment of a labour force and in the labourers' responses to them. It will be argued that the planters (like most of their counterparts in the rest of the British Caribbean) adopted a consistently tough line on labour retention and recruitment, that this had a negative impact on labour relations, and that ex-slaves' responses to post-Apprenticeship wage labour terms were in part conditioned by their Apprenticeship experience.

I

> We do solemnly protest against it [the Imperial Abolition Act], as establishing a ruinous system, which not only renders it imperative upon the owner to continue, in their fullest extent, all those privileges, indulgencies, and allowances which his slave has hitherto enjoyed, but gives to his apprentice *so large and unreasonable a portion of time as will render it impracticable for his Master to continue the profitable cultivation of the soil*; at the same time, it will superinduce in himself such habits of indolence, vagrancy and insubordination as will render him still more unfit for a state of freedom at the conclusion of his apprenticeship than he is at present.[3]

This protest of the St Vincent House of Assembly highlights the 'inveterate prejudice'[4] and fears of most planters and outlined the course they thought they had to follow in order to avoid the ruin of abolition. Severe labour loss (and therefore profits) would result from the proposed modification of slavery and, as usual, coercion would be necessary to extract labour from the blacks. Labour loss seemed unavoidable. Children under six were fully free; if their labour in the small gang was not available to the planters, adult labourers would have to substitute. Apprentices were given 'free time', about a quarter of the labour time they had been forced to give during slavery. This free time or 'extra hours' was eventually calculated at 26 full working days in each year;[5] and when the time also guaranteed to the apprentices for provision ground cultivation was taken into account, some *80 working days* were theoretically in the control of apprentices. Valuable labour time could therefore be lost by the plantation if the apprentices could not be induced or forced to sell some of it to their masters. Apprentices could purchase the unexpired portion of their apprenticeship; if many exploited the opportunity, the labour force would suffer depletion. Altogether, then, the cumulative loss might amount to about a third of the labour time which had been available during slavery, and this would disrupt the rhythm and reduce the extent of plantation agriculture.

The anticipated impact of labour loss was magnified by relatively low numbers of slaves per plantation and by slave maintenance practices. All islands were understocked with slaves. Density ranged from 57 and 100 per plantation in St Lucia and Tobago to 159 and 177 in St Vincent and Grenada. By any criteria St. Lucia and Tobago were grossly understocked. St. Vincent and Grenada were 'medium density colonies',[6] but could be shown to be short of slave labourers if St. Kitts (density of 290) and Nevis (density of 244), islands with roughly similar topography to that of St. Vincent and Grenada, are used as standards for estimating optimal slave labour density in these small mountainous islands.

Proto-peasant activity, the consequence of both the availability of much land, marginal or unsuited to plantation agriculture, and the planters' natural interest in economizing on the costs of slave maintenance, was as firmly established in these islands as in all 'home fed'[7]colonies. Cultivation of provision ground (usually mountain land) had given slaves opportunities to practise the skills of small agriculturalists and to earn quantities of cash from the sales of their surpluses in the local markets. This provision grounds/marketing complex had developed as a major element in slaves' 'adaptive patterns':[8] pride in their industry, some sense of limited independence, and an attachment to the land and small cultivation together constituted at least a partial negation of the slave regimen. The planters' legitimate fear was, therefore, that the apprentice, with 'much time on his hands',[9] might choose to devote most or all of his free time to 'a species of labour more agreeable to his taste'[10] rather than to part-time wage labour. This could restrict cultivation and, more seriously, hamper the reaping of the crop and the manufacture of sugar. Sugar factories could neither work continuously nor efficiently with a quarter or third of the gang missing. Thus it was in the planters' interests to devise measures which would emphasize their authority over their apprentices and concentrate their energies in plantation agriculture.

The local Abolition Acts as well as labour organisation practices reveal the details of the 'comprehensive system of restriction'[11] which the planters sought to put in place. Apprentices' disobedience and insubordination were deemed major offences carrying penalties of imprisonment with hard labour and whipping. Stringent prohibition against marronage, squatting, desertion and vagrancy was declared. A nine-hour work day was generally introduced to give plantations the benefit of long work shifts, and 12-hour night-time shifts in the factory were expressly permitted.[12] Task work was encouraged because it might generate additional labour time while reducing the costs of supervision. Apprentices were encouraged to contract their free time for long periods. Immigration schemes were mooted.

Specific policies designed to check and offset labour loss deserve closer attention because of their direct impact on labour relations. The obvious targets were the apprentices' opportunities for early emancipation and self-purchase, the labour time controlled by the apprentices, and whatever labour time that could be squeezed from most of those who had been customarily exempted from field labour. The chief weapons employed were sharp practice in matters of apprentices' classification and valuation, the payment of money wages, and the exercise of discretionary power over the granting of customary allowances.

False registration of apprentices could win apparent advantage. Praedial apprentices, mainly the field labourers, were required to serve six years of apprenticeship while the non-praedial, those not habitually employed in agricultural labour or sugar manufacture, were required to serve four years. Switching non-praedial apprentices (about 10 per cent of all registered slaves) to the praedial class would give planters more flexibility in the use of the total labour force and assure them of two additional years of compulsory labour from an increased labour force. Opportunities for achieving these ends were provided by the vague and misleading definition of 'praedial' in the Imperial Abolition Act and by the planters' influence over the registration process. The praedial class, according to the Imperial Act, was composed of those slaves employed in agriculture or manufacture of colonial produce for at least a year before the passing of the Act, while the non-praedial class consisted of the remaining slaves. Plantation tradesmen, many of whom could be shown to be employed in sugar manufacture, and domestics, who might have done occasional agricultural labour or who may have been 'demoted' to the field, might therefore be included in the praedial class. More importantly, planters controlled and provided the information on which registration was based. Their returns could be checked and corrected by the Registrar, and his decisions could be appealed against in the Supreme Court. But bureaucratic inertia, an identity of class interests and the 'very troublesome and delicate'[13] nature of the task of attempting to compile an accurate register encouraged collusion between planters and officials. From all territories Special Magistrates and Governors complained of 'one-sided and imperfect registration'[14] and of registries containing 'the grossest errors and mis-statements'.[15] In Grenada, planters were classifying *all* apprentices as praedial in December 1837.[16] In Tobago, the Privy Council was still insisting in March 1838 on classifying all domestics as praedial.[17] In St Lucia, the Lieutenant-Governor discovered 'many' cases of false registration, some of which had apparently been perpetrated by the Provost Marshal, the official responsible for compiling the register.[18] From St Vincent Special Magistrate Colthurst reported an example of 'cool classification': a planter had returned all his 150 apprentices as praedial with the ingenuous explanation that the domestics had been counted among the 'field negroes' because they 'often work there'![19]

Obstruction of apprentices' efforts to purchase the unexpired portion of their apprenticeship could win obvious advantage, and the procedures for the valuation of apprentices' services facilitated such obstruction. In general, valuation of apprentices' services was done by two appraisers, one each appointed by the Special Magistrate and by the owner of the apprentice's services, or by an umpire appointed by a judge of the Supreme Court. Most appraisers and umpires seem to have been either planters or individuals connected with planting interests. Moreover, they never used 'the established data'[20] like the prevailing rate of wages or the market price of sugar in determining the value of apprentices' services. Rather they relied on 'fancies',[21] the owners' grossly inflated estimates of the value of such services. The result was that invariably 'exorbitant prices'[22] were set on these services: St. Vincent apprentices, for example, paid at least a third more than they would have done if the 'proper rule' had been applied.[23]

Money wages were often offered for a portion or all of the apprentices' free time. Within a year of the start of Apprenticeship daily wages ranging from 6d. to 1s. 4d. as well as rates for hourly work, task work and contracts for work during the crop season, were established in all the islands. Wages were mainly used to attract additional labour during the crop season, the peak demand period. However, while all planters seemed agreed on the necessity to attract additional supplies of labour during the crop, not all of them seemed to agree on the best means of securing them. The Grenada planters had resolved at a public meeting at the start of Apprenticeship to support wage labour as a 'check to idleness' and 'some protection to the employer',[24] but even in this island there was a diversity of practice. Some offered a choice of wages or special food allowances; a few refused to pay the rates of wages demanded by apprentices and tried to survive without the labour increment; others paid wages when coercion failed. In November 1834, the attorney of Lataste estate in Grenada, finding that 'the generality of labourers stand out for wages', was forced to pay wages rather than risk the spoilage of the sugar which was being made.[25] By March 1835, however, he had apparently secured some additional labour time *without* the payment of wages ('12 hours with very little trouble') and could boast that his estate's sugar output was higher than that of neighbouring estates where wages of sixpence per day were being paid.[26] Payment of wages was often reluctant policy.

Discretionary power over the granting of allowances was the most potent weapon possessed by the planters because most of the allowances were securely in their control. Three types of allowances had been granted to slaves. Basic maintenance allowances consisting of shelter, provision ground or food allowance or cash equivalent, clothing, medical attention and medicine, salted fish and salt, were the first type. These were usually guaranteed by the Slave Laws and were secured to the apprentices by Section XI of the Imperial Abolition Act. Planters complied, but they refused to give the allowances to the free children; rather they stipulated that these allowances could be *earned* through labour service performed by the free children or by their mothers.[27]

Special or customary food allowances constituted the second type of allowance. These were usually distributed at Christmas and consisted of presents of fresh meat, flour, rice, sugar, tobacco and rum, 'hot liquor' during the crop and tots of rum after heavy work or after work during rain. Though these allowances were never protected by law and cannot be regarded as elements of bare subsistence, they were more than holiday fare; they were, as Lieutenant-Governor Doyle said, a large portion of 'the calculated minimum of comforts essential to keeping the people in good working condition'.[28] But because these allowances were not mentioned in the Imperial Abolition Act, many planters quickly recognized their incentive potential; the Grenada planters formally resolved that these would be given '*to such as may be found deserving*, until they are enabled to support such deficiencies from their own resources'.[29] These allowances were now termed *indulgences*, sometimes completely withheld but more usually granted or withheld at the discretion of the planters as reward or punishment.[30] In other words, planters equated them with money wages: rewards for performance of additional work. In exchange for portions of their free time, apprentices could choose to receive allowances *or* money wages. Mitchell on Lataste estate in Grenada, finding his apprentices 'very particular about their time for labour', was very clear about the necessary response:

> and I have no doubt at present, when the People will find that a number of Privileges formerly allowed them will be stopped, that they will see the necessity of coming to terms; we of course cannot grant them the normal indulgences and pay them for their extra time for labour also.[31]

Labour exemption was the third type of allowance. During slavery mothers of six children were usually exempted from all plantation labour; pregnant women and nursing mothers were exempted from labour for limited periods; and nurses and midwives were excused field labour in consideration of their responsibilities for tending the sick and caring for infant children. Some of these allowances had been guaranteed in Slave Laws as rewards and privileges but, presumably because they had not been described as allowances, they were not mentioned in the local Abolition Acts. Planters apparently agreed, as Lieutenant-Governor Darling indicated, that the allowances were justified during slavery because the planters were 'compensated by the labour of the children becoming every year more valuable',[32] but the case for their continuation had disappeared with the full emancipation of the young children and with the destruction of the masters' property interest in their labourers.

Therefore, many of them withdrew the allowances in an attempt to offset the partial loss of child labour. Long-service mothers, nursing mothers, midwives and nurses and some of the superannuated were now pressed into field labour service while pregnant women were regarded as a 'burden'[33] on the plantations.

II

Apprentices' responses cannot be determined with precision because of the legal constraints under which they lived and because of the limitations of the surviving record. The open ventilation of grievances was virtually impossible; the very high incidence of conviction for disobedience, indolence, and insolence suggests that any such expression did lead to fines, imprisonment or the treadmill, whipping, or confiscation of free time.[34] At the same time, the surviving records of punishments do not provide enough detailed information to permit identification of genuine grievance or clear legal infraction. Further, the apprentices made few violent protests through prolonged work stoppage or riot;[35] rather the indications of their responses are filtered through summary statistics and the periodic reports of the Special Magistrates. However, what these Special Magistrates reported about the apprentices' complaints, about the apprentices' disposal of the labour time they controlled and about the extent of self-purchase does allow us to draw some inferences, if not conclusions, about apprentices' sense of grievance.

The withholding of allowances, inaccurate classification and task work were subjects of frequent complaint. From all islands except St. Lucia, Special Magistrates reported 'numerous' complaints and 'dissatisfaction' directed at the 'capricious stoppage' of the special and labour exemption allowances.[36] As a result, Special Magistrate Ross of Grenada felt impelled to recommend the amendment of the local Abolition Act to ensure 'ample protection' for the aged, for pregnant women and mistreated apprentices.[37] There seems little doubt that many apprentices were shocked and angered by the reversal of customary practices which had brought not only a few comforts but also enhancement of status.[38] For those who were now forced to return to field labour, apprenticeship could not have been seen as any mitigation of slavery.

Inaccurate classification was the subject of formal appeals to the Special Magistrates and to the courts, particularly as the date for the emancipation of the non-praedial apprentices approached. Even before the Colonial Office managed, belatedly, to remove the vagueness and inaccuracy from the Abolition Act's provisions on classification,[39] apprentices had started action to secure correction of the registers. Special Magistrate Colthurst in St. Vincent was presented with 'numerous cases of appeal against the registry', and he found on investigation that 100 of the 163 appeals from 18 plantations could be sustained.[40] As it turned out, however, false or inaccurate registration neither prolonged the apprenticeship in any individual case nor brought any significant advantage to planters. Both classes of apprentice were freed in August 1838.

Task work was an issue in Grenada and St Vincent where the adoption of a Scale of Labour in 1836 had facilitated the spread of the practice. (In St Lucia and Tobago, no Scale of Labour was formulated, and the use of task work was limited to some factory operations and to the digging of cane holes on a few estates.)[41] Complaints came from both parties: employers claimed that work was not fully or efficiently performed, and apprentices protested that the labour scale was 'oppressive', or that the task had not been correctly measured.[42] Both positions reflected the suspicion and distrust which would arise in the new experiment of relatively unsupervised agricultural labour. However, some apprentices' complaints were probably justified in those cases where employers attempted to apply the scale not as a guide, as it had been intended, but as 'imperative law'[43] in conditions of widely varying terrain and types of soil. Clearly, aggrieved apprentices feared that task work in such circumstances was designed to rob them of a portion of their free time.

Apprentices guarded closely the labour time in their control. Free children's labour was never surrendered despite the inducements of the restoration of maintenance allowances and the advice of some Special Magistrates. In the four islands a grand total of *six* free children were apprentices to their former masters throughout the Apprenticeship.[44] It is probable, as some Special Magistrates asserted, that some free children grew up in virtual destitution and all in 'idleness and ignorance',[45] but parents' 'repugnance'[46] to all apprenticeship proposals was far stronger than any inducement or threat. In Grenada, some mothers even refused to accept medical attention for their children 'lest they should compromise them' or be themselves 'trapped into inconsiderate bargains'; and they responded to a Special Magistrate's suggestion that the children should be apprentices by complaining 'in great agitation that the Special Magistrate wanted them to sell their Children for slaves'![47]

Most apprentices seem to have been 'particular' about the disposal of their free time. Some of it was sold to planters during the crop season; in the first crop reaped during the Apprenticeship, planters on more than half of the St Vincent plantations had managed to conclude fixed agreements with their apprentices.[48] But judging by the Special Magistrates' comments and by the steady reduction in sugar output,[49] it is doubtful whether the planters secured as much of the apprentices' free time as they sought. Some of this free time was probably spent in leisure: some reports from Tobago and St Vincent suggested that many apprentices could be found 'lounging about the town' or 'exhibiting' their finery at negro balls.[50] Most of the free time was apparently spent in provision ground cultivation. Even in crop-time apprentices reserved Saturdays for provision ground cultivation and for the Saturday market.[51] The reasons for the preference were obvious to observers: provision ground cultivation was a more profitable and congenial activity. Some apprentices were probably encouraged by the additional time and, in some cases, additional land[52] at their disposal to extend proto-peasant activities. Others may have denied their free time to masters as a way of registering protest against the 'thousand little vexations'[53] they and their children were forced to endure. In any case, apprentices' allocation of labour which accorded low priority to plantation agriculture would have confirmed planters' worst fears about the consequences of the abolition of slavery. But such allocation also clearly indicated the apprentices' anxiety to exercise full control over their time.

Apprentices' exploitation of the opportunities for self-purchase underlined these points. Plantations lost some labourers, but of more significance were some of the attitudes associated with the drive for self-purchase. Few self-purchases were concluded during the first year of Apprenticeship: 82 apprentices paying about £30 each secured their releases through official valuations.[54] More purchases probably occurred later; by August 1836, Special Magistrate Ryan was forecasting that 'the present rate' of self-purchase would cause the abandonment of sugar cultivation in St Lucia within two years.[55] However, the indications are that no more than 10 or 15 per cent of apprentices managed to purchase their freedom; their 'general desire' for self-purchase was effectively limited by the 'large sums' demanded for their release.[56] Women were a majority of the purchasers, reflecting no doubt both a direct reaction to the withdrawal of labour exemption allowances and a growing concern for family welfare. Most of the newly-freed deserted plantation residence and labour. Artisans and domestics took employment wherever they could find it, but the former praedial apprentices sought 'more profitable' employment in small cultivation, huckstering and jobbing work in the towns.[57]

Remarkably, the incidence of self-purchase rose sharply when the early termination of the Apprenticeship became a probability. In February 1838, the desire for self-purchase was reported as 'strong to universal' in St Lucia;[58] and between mid-May and the end of July 1838, when action on early termination was taken in all islands, the Special Magistrates were deluged with applications for valuations. Though they tried to check this 'extraordinary desire' by pointing to the imminent approach of full emancipation, some of them were forced to execute deeds of release right up to the last day of Apprenticeship.[59] On the face of it, the apprentices' action made no economic (or other) sense. Action to terminate the Apprenticeship was irrevocable, and though the abbreviated term of the Apprenticeship would have brought self-purchase within the means of most apprentices, they would have been better advised to save their cash for post-Apprenticeship expenditures.

Many apprentices were clearly more interested in status considerations than in saving the money spent on self-purchase. Non-praedial apprentices, who would have been freed in any case in August 1838, sought to place social distance between themselves and the praedial apprentices whose Apprenticeship had been recently shortened. Some of them told Special Magistrate

Anderson that they did not want to be 'fuss of Augus nigger' because that would cost them the opportunity of associating with the free coloureds who had intimated that they would not mix socially with 'the "Adelaide" vulgar'![60] No doubt, too, some praedial apprentices hoped that the 'free paper' would be a passport to upward social mobility. Some apprentices wanted to savour the reward of successful self-help activity: Special Magistrate Ross detected 'a feeling of pride in procuring their release from Apprenticeship by their own means'.[61] Most important of all, many apprentices sought the best legal insurance of their freedom. Emancipation had not come in 1834 when slavery had been abolished; this doubtless created distrust of government. Masters had at first resisted the proposal to terminate the Apprenticeship; this had raised the fear that 'Buckra might change his mind and make the Apprenticeship longer', and created doubts about whether full emancipation would ever come.[62] Significantly, this attitude was more forcefully expressed in St. Lucia where there had been the greatest opposition to the early termination of the Apprenticeship and where memories of the impermanence of an earlier emancipation were still alive. Special Magistrate McLaurin reported in July 1838:

> They have much more confidence in the efficacy of a written deed of release signed by the Special Justice. This arises from the circumstance that many of the old people remember when, at the commencement of the French Revolution, all the slaves were declared free by law and, notwithstanding, were again reduced to slavery when the British took possession of the Colony.[63]

What therefore looked like 'insanity'[64] to Special Magistrate Anderson was in reality an attempt to make 'freedom more secure'.[65]

Other signs of apprentices' alienation became visible in the three months preceding full emancipation. From Tobago and St. Lucia, in particular, came reports of increased restlessness, insubordination and insolence, threats of plantation desertion and, in St. Lucia, rumours of plots by the apprentices to forcibly terminate the Apprenticeship.[66] This behaviour was obviously connected to the issue of early termination of the Apprenticeship and to announcement of the labour recruitment policies that would be pursued at full emancipation. Planters in these two islands had put up the most prolonged opposition to early termination of the Apprenticeship with the result that, when the two legislatures eventually acted, news of impending emancipation in the other Windward islands was already in wide circulation.[67] In addition, planters in these two islands decided to grant ex-slaves a maximum of three months 'gratuitous occupancy' of house and ground, in contrast to the twelve months that had been allowed in Grenada and St. Vincent. Further, the Tobago planters announced that ex-slaves would forfeit their growing crops if they refused contracts for plantation labour. In response, apprentices in one Tobago district 'discovered an intention of leaving the Estates to which they are attached as soon as they found themselves at liberty'.[68] Apprentices in two St. Lucia districts reaped their growing crops during July and destroyed 'thousands of their provision grounds'.[69] These actions suggest the beginning of industrial resistance.

More positive evidence of preparations for resistance could be found in many apprentices' increased emphasis on occupancy of 'house and ground' during the last months of Apprenticeship. Many apprentices were devoting themselves 'almost exclusively' to the cultivation of their grounds and to the repair and building of houses 'just as if they considered them to be permanent residences', and were deprecating any suggestion that they would desert the plantation at full emancipation.[70] At first sight, this behaviour might have implied an attachment by apprentices to the plantations on which they resided and an intention to accept whatever terms were offered for their labour at emancipation. But in view of the apprentices' experience of coercion and restriction during the Apprenticeship, and in view of the way in which they had allocated their free time, it is more likely that their behaviour reflected 'a deeply rooted attachment for their *native villages*',[71] an appreciation of the economic value of the grounds they occupied, and a conviction that the continued occupancy of these grounds gave them bargaining power with employers. In short, they seemed inclined to make a distinction between plantation residence and plantation labour, to the point of claiming 'possession' of house and ground;[72] and they hoped to use the provision grounds as the base from which they could defend their new rights and try to win a re-allocation of their time and labour.[73] Resistance was thus a possibility at the end of the Apprenticeship; many apprentices were preparing to 'sit down softly'[74] on provision grounds in response to the expected coercion. Occupation was replacing occupancy, thereby raising the spectre of 'an agrarian partition'.[75]

III

I have respectfully to submit to your Excellency that the object on the termination of the Apprenticeship will be to obtain, at as cheap a rate as possible, the greatest amount of combined labour on every Estate, and that inducements will be held out to the people to enter into Contracts for long terms and, with the new term of Contract Servants, the people would in fact continue Apprentices.[76]

The forecast made by Lieutenant-Governor Doyle of Grenada in early June 1838 turned out to be wholly correct. Taking no heed of apprentices' alienation, the planters elaborated a labour recruitment policy which varied only in detail from the coercive labour preservation policies they had followed during the Apprenticeship. They hastened to limit the ex-slaves' mobility as well as their choices in residence and in employment. For the compulsory labour provision they substituted the labour/rent system; in place of the subordinate legal status of slavery and the Apprenticeship they erected the summary jurisdiction of the planter-magistrate, the Justice of the Peace; and in place of the physical constraints of the Slave Codes and the local Abolition Acts they provided a variety of prohibitions on vagrancy, trespass, illegal occupation of Crown and waste land, emigration and small scale trading. Much of what they fashioned in these first months was eventually struck down by the Colonial Office because it infringed (as it was intended to do) the liberties of the individual and tended to reproduce 'many of those evils' associated with slavery.[77] But whatever modified legislation the planters were eventually forced to accept, their attitudes and most of their practices remained basically unaltered during the first years of full emancipation.

Contract Acts and new wage rates were the core of the labour recruitment policies. Two wage rates were established – one for resident labourers and the other for non-residents (or strangers). First class resident labourers were generally offered about 8d per day in addition to house and ground, the traditional allowance of salted fish, medical attention and medicine. The strangers were offered higher basic wages, ranging between 11d and 1s. 3d, and they might also be granted allowances of salted fish, rum and sugar. This higher rate was defended on the ground that non-resident labourers did not have the considerable material advantage of house and provision ground provided by the employer; but it is more likely that this rate was intended to induce some of the earlier plantation deserters to return to plantation labour. As it turned out, the rate became a source of grievance with resident labourers and a factor in the competition between employers for scarce labourers.[78]

The most important point about the wage rates, however, was that they were low in comparison to rates that had prevailed during the Apprenticeship. Resident labourers were offered at emancipation about 35 per cent less than they had received for plantation or public works labour during the Apprenticeship. Equally important, the proposed rates were at least 50 per cent below the rate which had been used in the valuation of the unexpired term of apprentices' services.[79] Planters called the rates 'fair and reasonable',[80] and they no doubt felt that the rates offered during the Apprenticeship were mainly the result of seasonal pressures on the labour market, which therefore should not determine the level of year-round wages. But it is most likely that they offered the lowest possible wages because they hoped that subsistence wages would force the free labourers into regular plantation labour.

The labour contract and conditional tenancy were the main instruments of recruitment and coercion. Ex-slaves would be bound to plantation labour by 'implied' contracts of at least a year's duration; all resident ex-slaves would be considered, in the absence of evidence to the contrary, to be under contracts of 'general hiring' which stipulated a month's notice of intention to quit. Contracts of shorter duration had to be written and witnessed before a Justice of the Peace who could exercise summary jurisdiction on the complaint of one 'credible witness'. Labourers would work a nine-hour day (in a five-day week) but employers had both the power to extend the working day in either direction and absolute discretion in awarding allowances, including house and ground. Breach of contract, absenteeism and 'ill behaviour' by the labourers would be punished by heavy fines or imprisonment with hard labour; employers offending against the labourer would be punished by the discharge of the labourer.[81]

Conditional tenancy was the companion piece to these 'one-sided' contracts. Ex-slaves could occupy or retain house and ground only if they and their families performed regular plantation labour for stipulated wages. Refusal of these terms would earn immediate eviction and forfeiture of growing crops. In essence, employers countered apprentices' squatter claims on provision grounds by emphasising *their* ownership of house and provision ground, by declaring occupancy to be both a perquisite and a portion of resident labourers' wages and by denying to the 'tenants' any of the established rights of tenancy.[82] Employers were clearly attempting to mobilise in support of the plantation the powerful factors of association and social investment that existed in the provision grounds system.

These wage labour terms were unilaterally determined and arbitrarily imposed. Employers did not discuss, far less negotiate, the terms with the ex-slaves or with any individuals who could pose as their representatives, not even with the Special Magistrates or the missionaries who were well placed to discover and transmit the ex-slaves' expectations. These new arrangements, particularly conditional occupancy, deserved full and patient explanation because they were new and because they disturbed the existing relationship between ex-slaves and the land they occupied. All explanations were, however, left to the governors who rushed around the various districts addressing groups of 300 or more ex-slaves on the intricacies of the new arrangements and new legislation.[83] Realistically, then, ex-slaves were left to guess at the meaning and extent of most of the new arrangements; and they only started to comprehend their full intent on *the first working day after full emancipation*, when many of them were peremptorily faced with the alternatives: accept the terms or quit.

The content of these terms and the manner in which they were communicated upset many, if not most of the ex-slaves, and an examination of some of their responses clearly shows the influence of recent experience as well as ex-slaves' clear perception of what constituted emancipation. Basically, there was little common ground between what ex-slaves expected or wanted and what they were offered. Their wage claim was 75 per cent to 100 per cent higher than the employers' offer: 1s. 2d. and 1s. 8d. as against 8d. Ex-slaves' claims were based on the Apprenticeship wage rates and, particularly, on the rates that had been used in valuations during the Apprenticeship. Police Magistrate Nanton of St. Vincent noted: 'it is much to be feared that *those valuations have influenced and excited the minds of the labourers, since they cannot well reconcile to themselves how their services have sustained so sudden a depreciation*'.[84] They did not want long labour contracts because these deprived them of the control of their labour and seemed a negation of emancipation; they indicated to Methodist missionary John Lee that they were 'wishful to be left to their own choice to leave [the plantations] when they please'.[85] They wanted a shorter work week for all labourers and reduced daily hours for women and children: many St. Vincent ex-slaves displayed 'an almost universal aversion to work for more than four days in the week'.[86] Clearly they wanted to extend the Apprenticeship practice by which all apprentices received one full working day in every fortnight as free time. The four-day week would provide them with a full Friday to prepare for the Saturday market. The seven-hour day for women and children could be seen as an attempt to reinstate the labour exemption allowance that had been curtailed during the Apprenticeship.

Occupancy of house and ground was naturally a major issue of contention. Ex-slaves had begun to assert claims to possession of these amenities in the closing days of the Apprenticeship, and they now met the employers' attempts to enforce conditional tenancy and labour-rent with clear statements of ownership. For example, residents on the Samaritan estate in Grenada told the magistrates and constables who tried to evict them on their refusal of the wage rates that they would not surrender their houses and grounds because these had been 'given them by the Queen'![87] The conflict sharpened when labourers discovered that they had no right to growing crops if they left the plantation residence either forcibly or voluntarily, and when they realised that severe limitations had been placed on whom they could admit to their residences.

This clash between employers' offers and labourers' expectations produced a labour crisis during the first three or four months of full emancipation. Prolonged strikes occurred in Tobago, St. Vincent and Grenada. Troops were sent to the aid of the civil authorities and to overawe labourers in districts of Grenada and St. Lucia. From every affected area there were employers' requests for military intervention and for firm executive action. Governors and magistrates (police as well as stipendiary) became very active, touring the various districts in an effort to explain the new wage labour terms and to effect reconciliation between the rival parties. Many labourers changed residence and employers.[88] Some sort of 'mutual arrangement'[89] was eventually effected because the ex-slaves' bargaining position was not very strong and because the official establishment naturally supported the planters' view that the survival of the plantation was essential to the communities' economic and social well-being. Governors, stipendiary magistrates and police magistrates, while recognising the ex-slaves' right to bargaining for wages, used reason as well as the threat of force to persuade them that they would be breaking the law if they tried to retain possession of what was not theirs; and they used their influence with employers to effect a modification of parts of the recruitment policy. The work week and work day were reduced, at least in St Vincent; contracts were shortened; evicted labourers' rights to the value of growing provisions were guaranteed; and employers conceded, at least for the time being, that labour arrangements should be discussed with labourers. Labourers' protest effected no real change on the crucial questions of wage rates and secure rights of occupancy because their tactics of withholding labour while maintaining themselves on the provision grounds were robbed of their effectiveness when they were forced to accept the legality of planters' ownership of house and ground. Since most of them were evidently not yet prepared to desert plantation residence, they were forced to accept plantation labour more or less on the employers' terms. But while this surrender eased the crisis, the factors which had created and shaped it remained unmodified. Therefore, there could only be a fragile industrial peace.

The labour crisis is evidence, then, of a deterioration in labour relations during and after the Apprenticeship. Equally important, the factors which created the crisis indicate the existence of continuities which affect the comprehension of post-slavery labour problems. Planters held fast to coercion as the means of extracting a sufficient quantity of labour from what appeared to be a reluctant labour force, and they were not deflected either by evidence of apprentices' alienation or by the creation of a wage labour force. For their part, ex-slaves, deeply influenced by participation in the provision ground/marketing complex, apparently drew the conclusion from their experience during the Apprenticeship that they could secure some insulation from coercion as well as greater rewards for their labour power by emphasising proto-peasant activity.[90] They did not recognise, however, that an effective stand could not be made on others' ground. To that extent, they, too, were victims of their past.

NOTES

1. See W. L. Burn, *Emancipation and Apprenticeship in the British West Indies* (London, 1937); D.G. Hall, 'The Apprenticeship Period in Jamaica, 1834–1838', *Caribbean Quarterly*, 3 (1953), pp. 142–67; W. A. Green, *British Slave Emancipation: the Sugar Colonies and the Great Experiment* (Oxford, 1976), pp. 129–61; W. A. Riviere, 'Labour Relations during the Apprenticeship System in the B.W.I., 1834–1838: A Comparative Analysis', unpublished paper.
2. Green, *op. cit.*, p. 133.
3. P.R.O., Colonial Office Series (hereafter C.O.) 263/7, St Vincent House of Assembly Minutes, November 1833. Emphasis added.
4. C.O. 101/85, 2 May 1838, Doyle to MacGregor, enclosed in MacGregor to Glenelg, 1 June 1838, No. 128.
5. St Lucia was an exception. Apprentices were given free time of one hour each day during a five-day work week.
6. Green, *op. cit.*, p. 193.
7. James Stephen, *The Slavery of the British West Indian Colonies Delineated*, 2 vols. (London, 1824), II, p. 261.
8. S.W. Mintz, *Caribbean Transformations* (Chicago, 1974), pp. 211–12.
9. John Anderson, Journal and Recollections, unpublished Mss, Aberdeen University Library, p. 26. Anderson was a Special Magistrate in St Vincent during 1835–8.
10. *Parliamentary Papers*, 83 (1835), p. 415.
11. Burn, *op. cit.*, p. 167.
12. In St Lucia the work day was limited to eight hours.
13. Anderson, Journal, p. 129.
14. C.O. 101/85, Report of Special Magistrate (hereafter S.M.) Ross, February 1838, enclosed in 10 April 1838, MacGregor to Glenelg.
15. W.K. Marshall (ed.), *The Colthurst Journal* (New York, 1977), p. 147; Anderson, Journal, p. 128.

16. Green, *op. cit.*, p. 133.
17. C.O. 285/46, 19 March 1838, Darling to MacGregor, enclosed in MacGregor to Glenelg, 2 April 1838, No. 88.
18. C.O. 253/64, 1 Feb. 1838, Bunbury to Glenelg. McLeod, the Provost Marshal, had apparently changed the registration of 23 apprentices from the non-praedial class to that of praedial.
19. Marshall (ed.), *Colthurst Journal, op. cit.*, p. 147. Eventually 33 apprentices on this estate made successful appeal against their classification. Colthurst also noted that some planters had falsified the registry in the hope that the British Government would award them additional compensation for the last two years of Apprenticeship rather than 'risk the public peace' by proceeding with the plan to grant earlier emancipation to the non-praedial apprentices (p. 224).
20. Marshall (ed.), *Colthurst Journal, op. cit.*, p. 152.
21. *Ibid.*, p. 154.
22. C.O. 253/64, 31 Jan. 1838, Bunbury to Glenelg.
23. Marshall (ed.), *Colthurst Journal, op. cit.*, p. 154.
24. *St. George's Chronicle*, 9 Aug. 1834.
25. 2 Nov. 1834, Mitchell to Baumer, Lataste Estate Papers, Moccas Court Collection.
26. 4 March 1835, Mitchell to Baumer, Lataste Estate Papers.
27. C.O. 101/87, Grenada S.M. Reports, 1837–8; C.O. 285/47, Tobago S.M. Reports, 1837–8.
28. C.O. 101/85, 2 May 1838, Doyle to MacGregor, enclosed in 1 June 1838, MacGregor to Glenelg.
29. *St George's Chronicle*, 9 Aug. 1834. Emphasis added.
30. C.O. 101/87, Grenada S.M. Reports; C.O. 285/47, Tobago S.M. Reports.
31. 3 Dec. 1834, Mitchell to Baumer, Lataste Estate Papers. Mitchell reinforced his policy by sending the more recalcitrant apprentices to the treadmill.
32. C.O. 285/47, 25 January 1838, Darling's summary of the Tobago S.M. Reports.
33. C.O. 285/47, Dowland's S.M. Report, March 1838; C.O. 101/87, Ross's S.M. Report, Feb. 1838.
34. For example, convictions for these offences constituted 68 per cent of all convictions of apprentices in Grenada during the first year of the Apprenticeship.
35. Work stoppages occurred on two plantations in Grenada and on another plantation in St Vincent at the inception of the Apprenticeship. In Grenada, prompt exemplary action against 'the most active and forward offenders' apparently checked the 'refractory conduct' in a short time, *St George's Chronicle*, 2, 9 Aug. 1834. In March 1836, a number of apprentices on the Fairhall estate in St Vincent were imprisoned for firing 'negro huts' on the estate. See Anderson, Journal, p. 37.
36. C.O. 101/87, Grenada S.M. Reports, 1837–8; C.O. 285/47, 25 Jan. 1838, Darling's summary of Tobago S.M. Reports.
37. C.O. 101/87, Grenada S.M. Reports, Feb. 1838.
38. Lieutenant-Governor Darling of Tobago observed in January 1838 that 'some of the women' had 'construed their exemption from labour for a time into freedom'. C.O. 285/47, Tobago S.M. Reports.
39. C.O. 854/2, 30 March 1838, Circular Despatch, No. 40; W. L. Mathieson, *British Slavery and its Abolition, 1823–1838* (London, 1926), pp. 299–300. By the new ruling *all* estate artisans whose 'ordinary employment' was that of mechanic were to be classified as non-praedial even if they did occasional agricultural labour.
40. Marshall (ed.), *Colthurst Journal, op. cit.*, pp. 150–1.
41. C.O. 285/49, Tobago S.M. Reports, November 1837; Riviere, *op. cit.*, p. 9.

42. C.O. 101/86, 30 July 1838, MacGregor to Glenelg, and Grenada S.M. Reports, July 1838; C.O. 285/47, Tobago S.M. Reports, 1837; C.O. 260/57, St Vincent S.M. Reports, May 1838.
43. C.O. 101/87, Grenada S.M. Reports, Feb. 1838.
44. C.O. 260/56, 16 March 1838, MacGregor to Glenelg; C.O. 285/46, 16 March 1838, MacGregor to Glenelg; C.O. 101/86, 30 July 1838, MacGregor to Glenelg; Riviere, *op. cit.*, p. 19. By Clause XIII of the Imperial Abolition Act, destitute free children could be apprenticed by their mothers to the mothers' masters until they reached the age of 21.
45. C.O. 285/47, Tobago S.M. Reports, December 1838 and Darling's summary, 25 Jan. 1838; C.O. 260/56, St Vincent S.M. Reports, Jan. 1838.
46. C.O. 260/56, 16 March 1838, MacGregor to Glenelg.
47. C.O. 101/85, 2 May 1838, Doyle to MacGregor, enclosed in 1 June 1838, MacGregor to Glenelg.
48. 2 November 1835, Smith to Glenelg, Parliamentary Papers, 83 (1835), p. 378.
49. Between 1835 and 1838 output declined by about 13 per cent from the 1830–4 figure.
50. C.O. 285/47, Tobago S.M. Reports, Darling's summary of S.M. Reports for December 1837; Anderson, Journal, p. 26.
51. C.O. 253/64, 4 May 1838, Mein to Glenelg, and St Lucia S.M. Reports, April 1838; C.O. 285/47, Tobago S.M. Reports, 1837–8; C.O. 101/87, Grenada S.M. Reports, 1837–8; C.O. 260/57, St Vincent S.M. Reports, May and June 1838.
52. In Tobago, the provision ground allowance was doubled (to half an acre) at the start of the Apprenticeship.
53. C.O. 101/85, 2 May 1838, Doyle to MacGregor, enclosed in 1 June 1838, MacGregor to Glenelg.
54. Parliamentary Papers, 83 (1835).
55. C.O. 253/52, 5 Sept. 1836, Hill to Glenelg and St Lucia S.M. Reports, Aug. 1836.
56. C.O. 253/64, 21 March 1838, Bunbury to Glenelg and St Lucia S.M. Reports, Feb. 1838; C.O. 260/56, St Vincent S.M. Reports, March 1838; C.O. 285/47, Tobago S.M. Reports, Nov. 1837; C.O. 101/87, Grenada S. M. Reports, Sept.–Nov. 1837.
57. C.O. 101/87, Grenada S.M. Reports, 1837–1838; C.O. 285/47, Tobago S.M. Reports, Darling's summary, 25 Jan. 1838; C.O. 253/64, 21 March 1838, Bunbury to Glenelg, St Lucia S.M. Reports, Feb. 1838.
58. C.O. 253/64, 20 Feb. 1838, Bunbury to Glenelg and St Lucia S.M. Reports, Jan. 1838.
59. C.O. 253/64 23 July, 13 Nov. 1838, Mein to Glenelg and St Lucia S.M. Reports, June 1838; C.O. 253/62, 20 Sept. 1838, MacGregor to Glenelg, and S.M. Reports, July 1838; C.O. 101/87, Grenada S.M. Reports, June and July 1838; C.O. 260/57, St Vincent S.M. Reports, May and June 1838. These reports do not support Green's conclusion: 'In all colonies the number of apprentices who appealed for valuation was relatively low, and as the time for freedom approached, the incentive to expend one's savings to purchase a premature release diminished'. (Green, *op. cit.*, p. 134).
60. Anderson, Journal, p. 135; C.O. 260/57, St Vincent S.M. Reports, May 1838.
61. C.O. 101/87, Grenada S.M. Reports, June 1838.
62. C.O. 260/57, 31 July 1838, MacGregor to Glenelg and St Vincent S.M. Reports, May 1838; Marshall (ed.), *Colthurst Journal, op. cit.*, p. 200.
63. C.O. 253/62, 20 September 1838, MacGregor to Glenelg and St Lucia S.M. Reports, July 1838.
64. C.O. 260/57, St Vincent S.M. Reports, June 1838.
65. C.O. 253/64, 12 April 1838, MacGregor to Glenelg and St Lucia S.M. Reports, March 1838.

66. C.O. 285/47, Tobago S.M. Reports, June and July 1838; C.O. 253/64, 30 June 1838, Mein to Glenelg and St Lucia S.M. Reports, May 1838; C.O. 253/62, 20 Sept. 1838, MacGregor to Glenelg and St Lucia S.M. Reports, July 1838.
67. In St Vincent and Grenada action to terminate the Apprenticeship was taken on 11 May and 25 May. In Tobago and St Lucia similar action was taken on 2 June and 13 July. See W.K. Marshall, 'The Termination of the Apprenticeship in Barbados and the Windward Islands', *Journal of Caribbean History*, 2 (1971), pp. 22–30.
68. C.O. 285/47, Reports of S.M. McIntosh, Tobago, June and July 1838.
69. C.O. 253/62, 20 Sept. 1838, MacGregor to Glenelg, No. 54 and St Lucia S.M. Reports, Johnston and Lewis, July 1838.
70. C.O. 285/47, Tobago S.M. Reports, May and June 1838; C.O. 260/57, St Vincent S.M. Reports, May and June 1838; *St George's Chronicle*, 28 May 1838, report of Grenada House of Assembly debate on the bill to terminate the Apprenticeship.
71. C.O. 285/47, Tobago S.M. Reports, May 1838.
72. *St George's Chronicle*, 23 May 1838, speeches of Lamb and Waddilove in the debate in the Grenada House of Assembly on the bill to terminate the Apprenticeship; C.O. 285/47, Tobago S.M. Reports, June 1838; 4 March 1835, Mitchell to Baumer, Lataste Estate Papers.
73. W.K. Marshall, 'Commentary One on "Slavery and the Rise of Peasantries"', *Historical Reflections*, 6 (1979), p. 246.
74. Anderson, Journal, p. 24.
75. Henry Taylor, *Autobiography of Henry Taylor, 1800–1875*, 2 vols. (London, 1885), I, p. 105. Taylor used the phrase to describe the slaves' likely response to a 'simple and immediate emancipation'.
76. C.O. 101/85, 2 May 1838, Doyle to MacGregor, enclosed in 1 June 1838, MacGregor to Glenelg. Emphasis added.
77. C.O. 261/15, 14 Aug. 1838, Glenelg to MacGregor.
78. W.K. Marshall, 'The Ex-slaves as Wage Labourers on the Sugar Estates in the British Windward Islands, 1838–1846', unpublished paper, presented at the Annual Conference of Caribbean Historians, Curaçao, 1979, pp. 18–19.
79. C.O. 101/87, Grenada S.M. Reports, April–Aug. 1838; Marshall (ed.), *Colthurst Journal, op. cit.*, p. 153. According to Colthurst, the level of valuations seemed to assume a wage rate of at least 1s. 6d.
80. C.O. 260/58, St Vincent House of Assembly comments on Glenelg's criticisms of the Act to terminate the Apprenticeship, enclosed in 31 Jan. 1839, MacGregor to Glenelg.
81. These provisions could be found in the Master/Servant Acts adopted in Grenada, St Vincent and Tobago.
82. C.O. 261/15, 14 Aug. 1838, Glenelg to MacGregor.
83. Marshall (ed.), *Colthurst Journal, op. cit.*, pp. 218–23.
84. C.O. 260/57, 22 Aug. 1838, MacGregor to Glenelg. Emphasis added.
85. London School of Oriental and African Studies, Methodist Missionary Society, Box 140, No. 154, 2 Aug. 1838, John Lee to General Secretaries.
86. C.O. 263/8, St Vincent House of Assembly Minutes, 3 Sept. 1838, Report of Police Magistrate Ross.
87. C.O. 101/86, 18 Sept. 1838, MacGregor to Glenelg, enclosures.
88. See Marshall, 'Ex-slaves as Wage Labourers', *op. cit.*, pp. 21–3.
89. Methodist Missionary Society, Box 140, No. 82, 20 Nov. 1838, Cullingford to General Secretaries.
90. Marshall, 'Commentary', *op. cit.*, p. 247.

11

Economic Change and Contract Labour in the British Caribbean: The End of Slavery and the Adjustment to Emancipation

S. L. ENGERMAN

I

The adjustments to the end of slavery, and the transition to new forms of labour organisation, differed considerably among the various parts of the British West Indies. That they would do so was not unexpected. In the long discussions preceding emancipation there was great attention paid to the questions of creating a 'free' labour force and the appropriate policies in regard to land and labour required to bring about a relatively smooth adjustment within the sugar economy. These discussions often involved considerations of the impact of the ratio of labour to land upon the expected changes, and long before the more formal statement of what economic historians have come to call the Domar–Nieboer model, its basic contentions had become widely examined.[1]

The differences in responses among the British slave colonies were perhaps most clearly (and familiarly) presented by Herman Merivale, first writing in 1841, who divided them 'into three classes, as respects their economical situation'.[2] A key point, to Merivale, was the land–labour ratio, but he also brought in considerations of relative fertility of soil at the time of emancipation. The three classes were:

1. 'The oldest of our settlements, established in the smaller Antilles.' 'They were those in which the land was nearly all occupied, population extremely thick, cultivation ancient, and capital accumulated.' They included Barbados and Antigua, and 'possibly', among others, St Vincent and Dominica. On these islands no additional labour was seen to be required, and it was expected that they would suffer little or not at all from emancipation.

2. 'Colonies in which the fertile or advantageously situated soil was all cultivated, and becoming exhausted; but there remained much unoccupied soil, of a less valuable description, and the population was not dense in proportion to the whole surface.' These included some of the smaller Antilles and, 'most conspicuously', Jamaica. These had been suffering declines in 'prosperity' prior to emancipation, and the adjustment to emancipation would be quite difficult.

3. Colonies, 'in some of which the fertility of the cultivated soil is as yet unexhausted, in others there is abundance of fertile and unoccupied land'. These included Mauritius, Trinidad, and, 'in a far higher degree', Guiana. These were areas in which the ex-slaves could avoid plantation labour but in which, unlike those areas in the other two categories, immigration would be feasible economically and could be the basis of future prosperity.

Similar distinctions among the sugar colonies had been made in earlier debates. These differences among the colonies had an important influence upon the policies discussed at the time of emancipation. In addition, attention to these differences can be of help in understanding the subsequent adjustments in forms of labour organisation, including the rise of contract labour. While the magnitude and availability of arable land were not determined independently of political and legal factors, the extent of unsettled land did play a major role in determining the post-emancipation responses in regard to both land and labour policy. This paper will discuss some aspects of the differences in the transition among the colonies, both as reflected in debates and expectations at the time of emancipation and as seen in the actual adjustments made in the latter parts of the nineteenth century.

II

A major concern in the discussions about the desirability and expected effects of ending slavery was the maintenance of a labour force to produce sugar on plantations. To the abolitionists this, of course, was not seen as a problem since their arguments about the greater efficiency of free than slave labour implied that ending slavery would increase sugar output.[3] To the slave-owners, and to those in the Colonial Office involved with the drafting of policies to ameliorate and then end slavery, this was a critical issue. While few may have disputed the contention that in similar work and for equivalent time free labour would be more productive than slave, most argued that where land was freely available there would be a strong preference to avoid plantation wage work. This contention was based upon a belief in the universal distaste for wage labour (observed in Europe, the Americas, and elsewhere, not just among West Indian ex-slaves) and, of immediate concern, was held to have been demonstrated by the behaviour of manumitted blacks in the colonies.[4] It was argued that few freed blacks worked on plantations, and, indeed, this point became the pivot around which a debate on the evaluation of slaves who could purchase their freedom under compulsory manumission laws in the crown colonies in the 1820s centred: whether it should be the market price of a slave within an ongoing slave system or else the cost to replace that slave by a free worker – an issue that would become practically, not just theoretically, important when the entire slave population was to be freed.[5]

The concern about the possible limited amount of wage labour was not, at this time, strictly racist. Most argued that the desire to avoid wage work for others was universal, and as the frequent comparison between Europe and the white-settled colonies indicated, the existence of wage workers was attributed to population density rather than to taste differences. That parts of the West Indies would soon confront the same difficulties seen 'in the Western States of America; in the British North American Provinces; in the colony of the Cape of Good Hope, and in the Australian settlements' where 'the facility of procuring land has invariably created a proportionate difficulty in obtaining hired labourers', was anticipated.[6] It was argued that with Irish population densities there would be no wage-labour problem (and, correspondingly, that at colonial population densities the Irish would avoid wage work).[7] It was understood that the withdrawal from plantation labour would increase leisure and hold down material consumption, but the existence of a general desire to own land and to produce for one's own (minimal) desires was a widely held belief.[8]

Given the belief that wage work would be avoided, where possible, and the important role attributed to population density, it is not surprising that a diversity of response was expected to result from slave emancipation. Nor was it unexpected that Parliamentary debates included discussions of measures to reduce the availability of land (by various restrictions on, and high prices for, land to be sold, and by taxation of small farms) or to increase the labour force (by immigration, by restrictions of land availability, by taxation of land, and by raising the price of subsistence by taxes on imports).[9] The 'appropriate' policy for each colony could differ, since there might be different prospects for the immediate creation of a 'free labour' market based, in large measure, upon the population density at the time of emancipation.

The expectations of differing responses of the ex-slave population played a major role in several of the debates about the provisions of the Slave Emancipation Act. Slave-owners were aware that the prospects for continuing the plantation system were not the same in all islands, and that the magnitude of the declines in labour supply and in land values would vary. These variations were expected, and differences in policies argued for, based on differences in land availability and fertility, as well as in the economic conditions in the period prior to emancipation. The relative roles of these different factors can be seen in some of the disagreements about policy that arose among slave-owners in different colonies. There was, for example, some split in the colonial ranks on the principles of compensation, the older areas advocating a scheme of payment based upon the number of slaves, while the then expanding areas argued for payments based upon the market value of the slaves prior to emancipation.[10] The arguments among the colonies were based, in part, on the presumed nature of 'just compensation', but underlying this was, as expressed by the Jamaica agents, a sense that for other areas – both those densely settled and those expanding – the losses due to ending slavery would necessarily be less than they would be for Jamaica.[11] The argument for per capita payment was, however, not based solely on considerations of population density. This is demonstrated by the claim of the agent of the most densely settled of the islands, Barbados, who argued that the lower prices there reflected the natural increase of the slave population, and thus that Barbadian planters were, in effect, being penalised for their more favourable treatment of their chattels.[12] The split on this issue was clear, and can be seen in the harsh comments of the Jamaica agents about planters in the expanding, high slave price colonies of Trinidad and British Guiana, and in their concern about their economic plight relative to those in the more densely populated islands of Barbados and Antigua. The immediate emancipation in Antigua, without the period of apprenticeship that characterised all but one of the other colonies (Bermuda), was influenced by the planter belief that the labour–land ratio there was so high that they would not confront the same difficulties in obtaining plantation labour as would planters in other colonies.[13]

As noted, in understanding both the abolition debates and the adjustments to the end of slavery, the land–labour ratio is not the only consideration. Also important were the economic circumstances in the decade just prior to abolition when marked differences developed between the islands earlier settled and those developed only in the early nineteenth century, whose expansions were just getting underway when the British introduced the sequence of policies culminating in the end of slavery. A comparison of trends in slave prices will help place the British West Indian debate on the economics of slavery and emancipation in perspective, and highlight the quite divergent economic circumstances within the British West Indies.

Published records provide information, collected for purposes of setting slave compensation, on the average prices of slaves in the different areas in the period 1823–1830 (see Table 2, column 1). Compensation was to be based upon prices in that period, presumably representative of a more typical pattern of slave prices, not directly influenced by the emancipation debate.[14] Differences across islands were sharp, with noticeably higher prices in Trinidad and British Guiana than in the older areas of the Caribbean. These are average prices over an eight-year period, and contain, as shown in Table 1, sharply divergent movements within the period between the newer and the older colonies.

The slave prices of 1823 to 1830 were used as the basis of allocating compensation among the colonies, with the compensation paid to planters being roughly 45 per cent of the market value in each colony.[15] Nevertheless, it was argued by the planters that the sale prices between 1823 and 1830 were not based on 'normal' market conditions, but included the declines in values that occurred once the final drive to end slavery had begun in 1823.[16] The uncertainty generated, and the various restrictions proposed and implemented as part of the amelioration campaign, seemed to have left an impact. Slave prices in each of the areas included in Table 1 show a decline between 1823 and 1825. For Jamaica this decline occurred after more than a decade of price stability, while it is probable that there had been increased, or unchanged, prices elsewhere.[17] What is striking, however, is the quite marked differences in price movements from 1825 to 1830 between the older areas (Jamaica, St. Kitts, Antigua, and Barbados) and the newer areas (Trinidad and British Guiana). While in the older areas slave prices continued to decline, in the newer areas slave prices increased. By 1830 slave prices in Trinidad and British Guiana were about one-third greater than they had been in 1823, while in the older areas of Barbados, Antigua, and Jamaica slave prices had fallen by at least one-third. This difference in price patterns (not the last time that Trinidad and British Guiana would react differently than would the other West Indian colonies) was based on their fertile soil and scarcity of labour at a time when restrictions on the inter-island slave trade effectively separated the slave economies of the different colonies.[18] These differences in trend make clear the differing economic circumstances in the West Indies at the time of emancipation, differences that were to continue into the post-slavery era and to shape the responses to the end of slavery.

III

The varying reactions in the British West Indian colonies and in Mauritius to the end of slavery and apprenticeship are shown in Table 2, comparing the changes in sugar output after the end of apprenticeship with that in the last decade of slavery, the length of time required before the level of sugar production achieved under slavery was recovered, and, to indicate the long-term responses, the ratio of sugar production at the end of the nineteenth century to that after the end of Apprenticeship.[19] As Merivale pointed out, areas with high levels of labour to land suffered no declines in sugar output. Those colonies with land availability initially suffered very sharp declines, Trinidad's mild decline after Apprenticeship being an atypical outcome. The case of Mauritius was also unusual, in that the end of slavery led to an expansion of labour inflows from India that soon came to dominate the plantation labour force.[20] Where possible the ex-slaves left the plantation, and in none of the cases in which large-scale withdrawal took place did a predominantly black plantation labour force re-emerge in the nineteenth century.

The problem of ex-slave dispersal from the plantation was solved first, and most easily, on the British Indian Ocean island of Mauritius. The initial decline in labour was offset by the importation of labour under contract from India, a migration not without its concerns in India and the Colonial Office. Nevertheless, this beginning became the basis of a widespread outflow from India to the rest of the world in subsequent decades. Down to 1865, however, Mauritius was the major recipient of Indian contract labour, receiving about three-quarters of the gross outflow.[21] And, in the period from 1834 to 1865 sugar output on Mauritius more than tripled, the largest increase in any of the British colonies.

In the West Indies, the widely proclaimed 'successful' adjustment of Barbados, with the continuation of black plantation labour, was frequently pointed to, even while there was an outflow of labour from that island, mainly to Trinidad and British Guiana.[22] Trinidad and British Guiana, where land-labour ratios were highest, as well as Jamaica, initially sought to attract labour from elsewhere – Europe, the Portuguese islands, the United States, India, China, Africa – to expand the plantation labour force. There were attempts to attract 'free' labour, as well as the re-introduction of a form of labour organisation widely utilised for British North American and West Indian settlement in the seventeenth and eighteenth centuries – indentured or contract labour.[23] The nature of the contracts, as well as the possibilities of recruiting in different parts of the world, became major Colonial Office concerns, and there were detailed studies and debates about what forms of labour migration would be permitted into the West Indies (as well as Mauritius).[24]

The period prior to about 1850 was one of experimentation with differing sources of labour supply in the West Indies, without there being one dominant supplying region. Through 1845 the largest source of contract migrants was Africa, and it was only after 1850 that the numbers from India and also from the Portuguese Atlantic Ocean islands exceeded the Africans.[25] Through 1850, Jamaica was an important recipient of migrant labour, accounting for about one-fifth of the inter-continental movement, basically its last unsuccessful attempt to compete in the sugar economy.[26]

After a series of debates on several continents, large-scale controlled emigration of contract labour from India to the West Indies was permitted. India soon became the major source of supply of immigrants into the West Indies, the Indian migration accounting for nine-tenths of the inter-continental immigrants between 1850 and the end of the Indian contract labour system in 1917. Despite the great interest and attention paid to other possible sources, Chinese migration was quite limited in amount, while the restrictions on African migration limited these to less than 3 per cent of the post-1850 inflow, none being recorded after 1867.[27] The British West Indies became the major recipient for the Indian inter-continental contract labour outflow, between 1865 and 1895 accounting for about one-half of the gross outflow, the share falling to about one-third after 1895 with the increased flow to emerging sugar-producing areas in Natal and Fiji.[28] With the return flow of Indians amounting only to about one-quarter of the total inflow, the Indian share of the population in Trinidad and British Guiana rose dramatically, and those Indians who remained after the expiration of their indenture became an important component of the plantation labour force.[29]

After the mid-1840s, the two major West Indian areas of expanding sugar production prior to the end of slavery, Trinidad and British Guiana, accounted for over four-fifths of the labour in-migration. British Guiana received about one-half of all contract labour coming to the British Caribbean, with Trinidad receiving about 30 per cent.[30] The economic recovery of British Guiana was relatively late, sugar production taking about three decades to achieve the pre-emancipation levels. With the continued inflow of Indian plantation workers, by the last decades of the nineteenth century sugar production reached levels more than double those in the last decade of slavery.[31] Trinidad had suffered a smaller decline with emancipation, but rapid increases in sugar output awaited the large-scale inflow of plantation labourers from India.[32] The labour inflows to the other islands were small in amount and intermittent, and in few cases did they provide an important basis for sugar production.

The direction of movement of contract labour within the West Indies had been predictable on the basis of changes in the sugar economy at the time of slave emancipation, being greatest where the land-to-labour ratio had been greatest and where slave prices had been high and rising, and where freedmen's wages after emancipation were highest.[33] In this sense, the post-emancipation movement of labour and of sugar production continued the geographic mobility of the sugar economy that had characterised the period of slavery. Despite the magnitude of the contract labour movements, however, the pattern of relative wage differentials did not change over this period, and Trinidad and British Guiana continued to import contract labour from India until this was legally barred, due to Indian pressure, in 1917.[34]

IV

The story of indentured labour and its implications are well known, and it will be useful here only to mention several points to place the movement in perspective. Contract labour was intended to solve two problems at the same time: the short-run problem of estate labour, arising with the end of slavery, and the longer-term problem of labour force adjustment created by the emancipation. Presumably, with population growth due to in-migration of labour as well as natural increase, the colonies would ultimately be able to end immigration without any difficulties – there was still a belief in the effects of an increased number of labourers per unit of land – but, of course, such a time never emerged before the legislated end of Indian contract labour. The short-term problem was perceived as the need for 'continuous' plantation labour for sugar (and, later in Trinidad, also cocoa) production, and the contractual binding for a period of years in exchange for transport was to ensure that workers would provide steady work for that term. The longer-term problem was expected to be solved by having the time-expired workers remain as settlers. Settlement would presumably increase the plantation labour force, possibly directly by providing plantation workers, and, more probably, indirectly even if settlers did not work on plantations, as a result of the increased labour-to-land ratio. That increase would reduce the amount of available land and, if settlers grew their own food crops, reduce the incomes of the freedmen. It would also mean a lowering of wage rates which, given the widespread belief in the backward-bending supply curve of labour, would lead to an increased labour force participation by the freedmen.

The attempts to solve both long- and short-term problems with a single measure led to a number of policy debates among planters, and between planters and the Colonial Office, in regard to arrangements for paying for labour imports, provisions in regard to return passage, incentives to influence repatriations, and the sex ratio of the imported labour.[35] In Trinidad and British Guiana the burden of costs for the imported labour was split between general revenues, special taxes on the planter class (in British Guiana based on acreage in plantation crops, in Trinidad on plantation crop exports), and the individual planter utilising the indentured worker during the period of the initial contract. Provisions to defer free return for five years after the indenture expired were introduced, as were various grants of cash and/or land to encourage permanent settlement in the colonies.[36] While the time-expired Indian immigrants did work on estates more frequently than did the freedmen, the planters never felt that the available labour force for plantations was adequate, and their requests for more labour from India continued until the Indian government terminated the outflow.[37]

The timing of the expansion of contract labour in the West Indies and its ultimate termination were greatly influenced by political as well as by economic factors. Clearly there was a differential between incomes to be earned in India and in the British West Indies, while the costs of transport were high enough that a large-scale movement of non-contract labour was not possible.[38] Nevertheless the movement to the West Indies was only a part of the movement out of India, both contract and free, and India represented only one of the several sources of contract labour in the late nineteenth century.[39] The specific date of the rise of large-scale movement was determined by the policies set by the Colonial Office.[40] Fares from Africa and the Portuguese islands to the West Indies were below those from India, while the costs of moving labour from India to Natal and to Mauritius were below those to the West Indies. The costs of acquiring and shipping contract labour from India to the West Indies showed little trend in the interval from the 1840s to the early twentieth century. Until the first decade of the twentieth century migration from India to the West Indies was almost exclusively on sailing ships, and there was little change in average sailing time. While mortality rates on board declined, and the later transition to steamships cut sailing time in half, the overall costs of attracting labour to the West Indies from India changed little during the nearly three-quarters of a century that the migration lasted.[41]

The West Indies were not the only recipients of Indian migrants, and their relative share in this migration varied over time. The variation in West Indian receipts was linked to demand (based on sugar production) and to the availability of supply from India. The factors which influenced the overall outflow were related to conditions within India, and the reduced availability of potential migrants in times of improved economic conditions in India was a frequent complaint.[42] Nevertheless, unlike the free migration from Europe to the Americas which increased dramatically in the late nineteenth century, the total outflow of contract labour from India peaked in the 1850s and early 1860s and, while the amount remained at close to peak levels in the later nineteenth century, the outflow did not accelerate. And, despite increased populations, and the later stagnation of sugar production in Trinidad and British Guiana, as well as in Mauritius, the demand for contract labour remained high until the system was ended.

V

The adjustments to emancipation in the West Indies involved quite distinct transitions in the nature of the labour force in different colonies.[43] In some areas the plantation system remained, with black labourers; in others, the plantation system was severely weakened as blacks left the plantation economy but economic conditions precluded a large-scale importation of contract (or free) labour from elsewhere; and, in some areas – those expanding at the end of the era of slavery – the plantation system persisted. In the last case, however, the use of contract labour, mainly from India, and of those labourers who remained after their contracts had expired, meant that the black population provided only a small component of the plantation labour force.[44] Central to understanding the different patterns of adjustment and the demand for contract labour immigrants was the ratio of land to labour at the time of emancipation. However, while this simple ratio can be an important aid in explaining the debates prior to slave emancipation and the economic changes subsequent to the ending of slavery, the need to consider other influences is indicated by the role of political factors in determining the permitted institutional basis of the plantation labour force.

TABLE 1

Prices of Slaves Sold, 1823–1830, Selected West Indian Colonies[1]

(a) (1823 = 100 for each colony)

	British Guiana[2]	*Antigua*[3]	*Barbados*[4]	*Jamaica*[5]	*Trinidad*[6]
1823	100	100	100	100	100
1824	84	84	80	88	91
1825	99	100	81	75	92
1826	116	71	82	76	121
1827	118	88	78	73	124
1828	115	72	68	64	134
1829	145	79	69	67	151
1830	139	55	57	62	129

(b) (1823–4 = 100)

	St. Kitts[7]
1823–4	100
1825–27	90
1828–30	79

1. These are based upon the prices of slaves sold between 1823 and 1830, as recorded for the Slave Compensation Commission. The materials collected did not differentiate slaves by age and sex, but the trends seem sufficiently sharp that it is doubtful that the composition of slaves sold could have changed sufficiently to have altered the pattern. There were several different types of sales recorded but where possible the information utilised was for slaves sold separately (not as part of estates), and not under judicial order. There were minor adjustments needed in most cases to provide these estimates, but the basic patterns are not affected. Details are given in notes 2–7.
2. Based on the Sales of Slaves Sold in Public Vendue Unmixed With Other Property, for Demerara and Essequibo and for Berbice. There were, on average, data for over 1,000 slaves per year.
3. Based on the Returns of Sales of Slaves, with deduction made for those sold with land. This deduction reduced the average number of slaves with price data from 246 per year to 87, and may account for the greater fluctuation observed in the Antigua ratios.
4. Based on Class A, Slaves Sold Alone. There were, on average, data for about 200 slaves per year.
5. Based on Schedule A, which includes slaves sold 'unmixed with other property and which appear to have been sold for valuable consideration'. Because of the manner in which the Jamaica data were recorded (and analysed by me), there is some imprecision in assigning prices to specific years. Some sales were entered out of order, and, rather than re-do the entire collection process, some crude breakdowns to get annual estimates were made. Tests indicate that these have not distorted the basic pattern of change within the period. There were, on average, data for over 1,900 slaves per year.
6. Based upon the sums of the unadjusted data recorded in Protocol A, Protocol B, and Judicial Sales. In Trinidad the data used were for slaves sold with land and estates. The estimaters presumed slaves accounted for one half the value of slaves and estates over this period. There were, on average, data on over 1,250 slaves per year.
7. Based upon List no. 1, Sales of Slaves Alone. The data were recorded for blocks of years, but the pattern of change is clear. There were, on average, data for about 106 slaves per year.

Source: P.R.O., Treasury, T 71/1537, 1542, 1544, 1548, 1549.

TABLE 2

Slave Prices, Land–Labour Ratios, and Changes in Sugar Production in the British Slave Colonies Prior to and After Emancipation

	(1) *Average Slave Prices 1823 to 1830 (£)*	*(2)* *Land/Labour Ratio (Square Miles per Thousand Total Population)*	*(3)* *Percentage Change in Average Annual Sugar Production 1824–1833 to 1839–1846*	*(4)* *Period in Which Pre-Emancipation Level of Sugar Production Regained*	*(5)* *Ratio of Sugar Production in 1887–1896 to Sugar Production in 1839–1846*
1. Antigua	33	3.1	+ 8.7%	–	1.5
Barbados	47	1.7	+ 5.5	–	3.5
St. Kitts	36	2.9	+ 3.8	–	2.7 ‹3›
2. Trinidad	105	47.7	+21.7 ‹1›	–	3.0 ‹2›
British Guiana	115	832.4	–43.0	1857–1866	3.4
Mauritius	70	8.0	+54.3	–	3.1
3. Dominica	43	16.3	– 6.4	1847–1856	0.7
St. Lucia	57	15.5	–21.8	1857–1866	1.7
Nevis	39	5.0	–43.1	1867–1876	‹3›
Montserrat	37	4.6	–43.7	1867–1876	2.5
St. Vincent	58	5.7	–47.3	never	0.7
Tobago	46	8.8	–47.5	‹2›	‹2›
Jamaica	45	12.2	–51.2	1930's	0.6
Grenada	59	6.3	–55.9	never	‹4›

Notes:

1. Trinidad output did decline slightly after the end of the Apprenticeship, and it was not until 1845 that the 1834 level was regained.
2. Tobago data merged with Trinidad after 1891. The 1877–1886 level of sugar production in Tobago was two-thirds that of 1824–1833.
3. Nevis data merged with St. Kitts after 1882.
4. No sugar output shown after 1888, a year in which only 77 tons were recorded.

Sources:

Column (1) Parliamentary Papers (1837–1838) XLVIII, p. 329. The values of those slaves designated 'praedial attached' present a somewhat similar ranking, although there are some differences. See the table in Merivale, *op. cit.*, p. 333. See also p. 312.

(2) Population from the Statistical Chart in the front of R. M. Martin, *History of the Colonies of the British Empire* (London, 1843). Areas from *Worldmark Encyclopedia of the Nations* (New York, 1960), pp. 1038, 1049, 1155. For the ratio of slaves per square mile in 1834, see Green, *Slave Emancipation, op. cit.*, p. 193.

(3) Deerr, *History of Sugar, op. cit.*, p. 377. The periods are those shown by Deerr. Any alternative sets of years would show a similar comparison.

(4) Deerr, *op. cit.*, pp. 377, 199–200, 203–4. Again, the periods shown by Deerr were utilised, but any alternative sets of years would show a similar comparison.

(5) Deerr, *op. cit.*, pp. 377, 196, 199, 203–4. As before, the periods shown by Deerr were utilised, but any other set of years would show a similar pattern.

NOTES

* A slightly different version of this paper was published in *Explorations in Economic History*, 21 (1984), pp. 133–50.

1. See E. D. Domar, 'The Causes of Slavery or Serfdom: A Hypothesis', *Journal of Economic History*, 30 (1970), pp. 18–32 and H. J. Nieboer, *Slavery as an Industrial System* (The Hague, 1900). For critiques of this approach, see Orlando Patterson, 'The Structural Origins of Slavery: A Critique of the Nieboer–Domar Hypothesis from a Comparative Perspective', in Vera Rubin and Arthur Tuden (eds.) *Comparative Perspectives on Slavery in New World Plantation Societies*, New York Academy of Sciences, vol. 292 (N.Y., 1977), pp. 12–34, and O. N. Bolland, 'Systems of Domination after Slavery: The Control of Land and Labor in the British West Indies after 1838', *Comparative Studies in Society and History*, 23 (1981), pp. 591–619. For an application of the Nieboer analysis to post-slavery societies see W. Kloosterboer, *Involuntary Labour since the Abolition of Slavery* (Leiden, 1960). The key aspect of the hypothesis discussed in regard to the nineteenth-century West Indies was the problem created by 'free land' for obtaining a wage labour force. Some observers pointed to the effects of an increasing population in ultimately resolving this problem. A related issue, the impact of population expansion in ending the profitability of slavery, was frequently discussed in the United States in the first half of the nineteenth century.
2. See Herman Merivale, *Lectures on Colonization and Colonies* (2nd edition, London, 1861), pp. 300–48, which includes the basic 'predictions' made in the 1841 edition, as well as data on sugar production and emigration after emancipation and an appendix (dated 1860) discussing the post-emancipation pattern.
3. Some abolitionists undoubtedly believed that ending slavery would raise sugar output and not just improve the overall welfare of the ex-slave population. That others would also argue that point was perhaps understandable tactically, but such contentions posed subsequent problems in accounting for the outcome of emancipation. The output of other plantation crops declined even more than did sugar production in most colonies. The most frequent possibilities discussed for post-emancipation agriculture were staple-producing plantations based on wage labour or non-staple-producing family farms, the prospect for family-farm production of export staples being less frequently considered. See David Eltis, 'The Traffic in Slaves between the British West Indian Colonies, 1807–1833', *Economic History Review*, 2nd series, 25 (1972), pp. 55–64.
4. See, for example, Parliamentary Papers (1829), XXV, Slave Trade: Slaves in Demerara, etc. pp. 30–5 where it was claimed 'that the Colonies of Demerara and Berbice do not afford one instance of a Slave made free, or a free-born negro ever having worked as a hired labourer in the cultivation of the soil'. There were frequent discussions of the possible withdrawal from plantation labour by freed slaves in the 1832 Parliamentary hearings on slavery.
5. See, for example, the extended discussion of the 1826 Trinidad case of Pamela Munro, with the most complete examination to be found in P.R.O. Colonial Office Series (hereafter C.O.), 320/1, nos. 107–24. See also the correspondence reproduced in Parliamentary Papers (1826–1827), XXVI, State Papers: The Slave Population, Trinidad, pp. 77–83.
6. See C.O. 320/8, 'Heads of a Plan for the Abolition of Negro Slavery, and for the securing of the continued Cultivation of the Estates by the manumitted Slaves'. The same volume includes a memo on the proposed legislation, dated 7 January 1833, that makes many of the same points in almost identical wording. Also of interest is the Colonial Office, Memo for the Cabinet, January 1833,

written by Henry Taylor (C.O. 884/1, no. 2). This expected difficulty in developing a wage labour-force also influenced colonial reformers such as Edward Wakefield, who directed their attentions to the colonies of white settlement.

7. 'The free negro, if transferred into a population as dense as that of Ireland, or the Irishman, if migrating to a country as thinly peopled as Jamaica, would each be found to reverse his present habits in this respect – the one anxiously seeking for the wages which he had previously refused, the other despising the hired service which he had formerly solicited.' 'Heads of a Plan', C.O. 320/8.
8. See the sources cited in footnote 6. Note that it seemed generally believed that land ownership would mean restricted participation in the market, particularly in the production of export crops.
9. For useful presentations of the various proposals related to emancipation see W.L. Burn, *Emancipation and Apprenticeship in the British West Indies* (London, 1937) and W.A. Green, *British Slave Emancipation: The Sugar Colonies and the Great Experiment, 1830–1865* (Oxford, 1976).
10. See, for example, the letters of 12, 13 and 26 June, 18 July and 21 Aug. in Jamaica Archives, 1B/5, Agents Letter Books, vol. 6. See also the discussion in the House of Lords on 15 Aug. 1833. *Hansard's Parliamentary Debates*, XX (1833b), pp. 627–31. These reflect a split in the colonial interests, it being contended by the Jamaica planters that those in Trinidad and British Guiana were so concerned with obtaining high levels of compensation that they did not attack the emancipation proposals as strongly as they should have.
11. It was argued that emancipation 'will be less mischievous to other Colonies than ours. For instance, in Barbados and Antigua and several other Islands the liberated Slaves must work for wages or want the necessaries of life, those Islands being so fully peopled and occupied that, as in England, the Choice of the lower order lies between work and starvation'. Letter of Richard Barrett and Abraham Hodgson, 18 July 1833, in Jamaica Archives, Agents Letter Books, vol. 6. In the Parliamentary debates, Colonel Torrens pointed out that 'in the old colonies circumstanced like Barbados, instantaneous emancipation, without intermediate apprenticeship or preparation might take place', in contrast with the situation expected in Jamaica, Trinidad, Berbice, and Demerara. *Hansard's Parliamentary Debates*, XIX (1833a), pp. 1263–6.
12. B. M. Taylor, 'Our Man in London: John Pollard Mayers, Agent for Barbados, and the British Abolition Act, 1832–1834', *Caribbean Studies*, 16 (1976–77), pp. 60–84. A similar point was also made in Parliamentary debate by Viscount St Vincent, see *Hansard's Parliamentary Debates*, XX (1833b), p. 631.
13. While there was some concern expressed about the impact of emancipation on the number of field labourers in Antigua (C.O. 7/38, no. 99, Blue Book for 1833), a letter from Nicholas Nugent, Speaker of the Assembly, to Sir Evan J. Murray MacGregor pointed out that conditions for slave emancipation were more favourable in Antigua than elsewhere because of 'the all important and paramount one of an utter dependence, from peculiarity of climate and the absence of unoccupied Lands except those of absolute sterility, of the labourer on the Proprietor and Capitalist for the means of procuring food'. C.O. 7/37, letter of 2 Nov. 1833. The Antigua Blue Book for 1833 is also of interest in its statements relating emancipation to the possibility of separating the 'growing' and the 'making' of sugar, thus improving the productivity of both and permitting the development of a yeomanry.
14. For a discussion of the compensation process, including details on the information collected, see R. E. P. Wastell, 'The History of Slave Compensation, 1833 to 1845' (unpublished MA thesis, University of London, 1932). The choice of period to be used to set compensation was itself not without considerable

debate. The Jamaica agents argued (for obvious reasons relating to the impact of the slave revolt of 1831) 'that the average of the value of Slaves should be taken from the year 1822 to 1830 instead of from 1822 to 1832' – the latter being the period originally proposed. See letter of Richard Barrett and Abraham Hodgson, 21 Aug. 1833, in Jamaica Archives, Agents Letter Books, vol. 6.

15. For a discussion of the economics of the compensation scheme see R. W. Fogel and S. L. Engerman, 'Philanthropy at Bargain Prices: Notes on the Economics of Gradual Emancipation', *Journal of Legal Studies*, 3 (1974), pp. 377–401. It was also understood that the period of Apprenticeship would serve as an additional compensation to the slave-owners, reducing their losses. See, for example, the comments of Buckingham and of Lushington in *Hansard's Parliamentary Debates*, XIX (1833a), pp. 1066–9, 1260–2.

16. This theme of earlier price decline featured extensively in the Parliamentary hearings on slavery of 1832, as well as the Parliamentary debates on slave emancipation, and was a recurrent theme in subsequent years. Typical is the comment of Simon Taylor, dating the onset of uncertainty and 'distrust', leading to a depreciation in slave values after 1823: 'I consider that it commenced in 1823, soon after the publication of the Resolutions which were then passed in the House of Commons upon the subject'. Parliamentary Papers (1831–1832), XX, pp. 745–6. A dating of the onset of decline one year earlier, attributed to the 'constant agitation' on the slave question, is given by R. H. Schomburgk, *The History of Barbados* (London, 1848), pp. 458–9. It was claimed in 1828 by A. Colville that from the 'first discussion' of the question there 'was an indisposition, on the part of all those who were not already engaged in the colonies, and whose property was not engaged in the colonies, to vest capital in the colonies'. Parliamentary Papers (1828a), XXV, p. 492.

17. The price data for Jamaica from 1808 to 1827 are in Parliamentary Papers (1828b), XXVI, Slave Trade: Jamaica Slaves, pp. 25–9. They are referred to in Seymour Drescher, 'Public Opinion and the Destruction of British Colonial Slavery', in James Walvin (ed.), *Slavery and British Society 1776–1846* (London, 1982), pp. 45–6. See also the comments by Stanley in *Hansard's Parliamentary Debates*, XX (1833b), pp. 132–5. The discussion of the value of manumitted slaves in Trinidad after 1821 describes an increase in the price of slaves from about £65 in 1821–1824 to £100 in 1824–1827, attributed to 'the operation of the Consolidation Slave Act, which prevents the importation of plantation slaves from the old colonies, where their value daily decreases'. Parliamentary Papers (1828c), XXVII, State Papers: The Slave Population, Trinidad, pp. 212–16.

18. The impact of the restrictions on the inter-island slave trade upon slave prices had been noted by the planters at the time, and there was some interest in its re-opening (as well as a fear by the Jamaicans that this might be attempted). In 1848 it was pointed out, by the authors of a draft report to a Select Committee concerned with West Indian problems, that:

> The grievances alleged by the Planters of the British West Indies are, first, that by a series of Legislative Enactments, carried against their will, the Imperial Government commenced, in 1823, by depreciating the sale price of their slave property by various restrictions, prohibiting their transfer by sale of Negroes from one estate to another by a condition imposed, that families or reputed families should not be separated. Humane, just, and moral as were these regulations, it cannot be disputed that they were an invasion of the strict rights of property, and brought down the *'sale price'*, as contra-distinguished from the *intrinsic value when attached to Sugar Plantations,*

> *and taken in connexion with the value of land*, from 50 to 70 per cent. Thus whilst previous to these regulations the sale price of slaves ruled high, and was nearly equal throughout the colonies, in the latter years previous to emancipation the public sales fell 50 and 70 per cent in Jamaica, Antigua, and Barbados, as compared with the sale-price value of slaves in the Sugar-planting States of the United States, and even as compared with the market price of slaves in British Guiana and Trinidad.

Parliamentary Papers (1847–1848), XXIII, Report from the Select Committee on Sugar and Coffee Planting, Part 4, p. 43. While, as Table 1 indicates, planters were correct in regard to the relative prices among the islands, in the United States slave prices did not rise as dramatically as claimed within that period. The sharp rise in slave prices in British Guiana and Trinidad between 1825 and 1830 raises some questions about the expectations of planters there about the timing of emancipation. On the inter-island trade, see Eltis, 'Traffic in Slaves', *op. cit.* For some indication of the difficulties raised for a proposed transfer of slaves from the Bahamas to Trinidad, including a scheme for gradual emancipation of those born after the migration, see an undated letter (written sometime in 1826 or 1827) discussing Lord Rolle's slaves, in C.O. 320/5.

19. For a longer discussion of these issues, see S. L. Engerman, 'Economic Adjustments to Emancipation in the United States and British West Indies', *Journal of Interdisciplinary History*, 12 (1982), pp. 191–220. The pattern during the period of apprenticeship was also diverse, although for most colonies there were either increases in sugar output or, where sugar output declined, it did so by a lesser amount than it would after the end of apprenticeship. Particularly hard hit by the end of the apprenticeship controls were Jamaica and British Guiana. See Noel Deerr, *The History of Sugar*, 2 vols. (London, 1949–50), p. 377.
20. For the most complete discussion of the origins and development of Indian contract labour, see Hugh Tinker, *A New System of Slavery* (London, 1974). The rapid transition in the ethnic composition of the Mauritius labour force on sugar estates, the Indians amounting to an estimated share of 85 per cent by 1844, is described in C.O. 170/21, Council of Government Minutes and Proceedings, Appendix. This includes an estimate that Indian workers were about three-fourths as productive as were the slaves. By 1846 about 96 per cent of the labour force on sugar estates was Indian. See John Macgregor, *Commercial Statistics*, 5 vols. (London, 1850), V, p. 128.
21. Computed from Imre Ferenczi and W. F. Willcox, *International Migrations*, 2 vols. (N.Y., 1929), I, pp. 904–5. For a discussion of the role of contract labour in the nineteenth century, see S. L. Engerman, 'Contract Labor, Sugar and Technology in the Nineteenth Century', *Journal of Economic History*, 43 (1983), pp. 635–59.
22. In addition to the frequency of such comments about Barbadian 'success' in the Parliamentary reports of 1842 and 1847–8, see John Davy, *The West Indies Before and Since Slave Emancipation* (London, 1854; reprinted Frank Cass, 1971) and W. G. Sewell, *The Ordeal of Free Labor in the British West Indies* (N.Y., 1861; reprinted Frank Cass, 1968). For a discussion of the out-migration from Barbados, see G. W. Roberts' 'Emigration from the Island of Barbados', *Social and Economic Studies*, 4 (1955), pp. 245–88.
23. See the discussion (and literature cited) in S. L. Engerman, 'Servants to Slaves to Servants: Contract Labor and European Expansion', in Ernst van den Boogaart and P. C. Emmer (eds.), *Colonialism and Migration: Indentured Labour Before and After Slavery* (The Hague, 1985 forthcoming). Particularly

useful on West Indian contract labour is K. O. Laurence, *Immigration into the West Indies in the Nineteenth Century* (St Lawrence, 1971) and the articles cited therein.

24. For an examination of these discussions, see Green, *op. cit.* and Tinker, *op. cit.*
25. This discussion is based upon the data in G. W. Roberts and J. Byrne, 'Summary Statistics on Indenture and Associated Migration affecting the West Indies, 1834–1918', *Population Studies*, 20 (1966), pp. 125–34. The very high level of labour demand after the end of slavery is reflected by the fact that the quinquennium 1846–50 had the highest level of contract labour migration in the nineteenth century, even though Indian immigration was restricted for part of the period. The early date of large inflows has obvious implications for examining the impact of the closing of the slave trade, while the importance of British Guiana and Trinidad as recipient areas is another indication of the importance of the restrictions on the inter-island slave movements.
26. Jamaica differed from most other colonies in that there was a continued decline in sugar production after 1846. See P. D. Curtin, *Two Jamaicas* (Cambridge, Mass., 1955) and Douglas Hall, *Free Jamaica, 1838–1865* (New Haven, 1955).
27. Computed from Roberts and Byrne, 'Summary Statistics', *op. cit.* On the migration of African contract labour to the West Indies, see J. U. J. Asiegbu, *Slavery and the Politics of Liberation, 1787–1861* (London, 1969) and Monica Schuler, *'Alas, Alas, Kongo'* (Baltimore, 1980).
28. Computed from Ferenczi and Wilcox, *op. cit.*, I, pp. 904–5. Because of the greater return flow from Mauritius than from the West Indies, the share of net outflow to the West Indies was relatively greater than was its share of the gross movement. See also Kingsley Davis, *The Population of India and Pakistan* (Princeton, 1951), pp. 98–106.
29. See Roberts and Byrne, 'Summary Statistics', *op. cit.*
30. Computed from Ferenczi and Willcox, *op. cit.* These give the same breakdown as do the estimates in Roberts and Byrne, 'Summary Statistics', *op. cit.*
31. On British Guiana, see A. H. Adamson, *Sugar without Slaves* (New Haven, 1972); J. R. Mandle, *The Plantation Economy* (Philadelphia, 1973); and Walter Rodney, *A History of the Guyanese Working People, 1881–1905* (Baltimore, 1981). This doubling of output, however, occurred with a more than doubling of the population, an indication of the movement off the sugar estates.
32. On Trinidad, see Bridget Brereton, *A History of Modern Trinidad, 1783–1962* (Kingston, 1981) and Donald Wood, *Trinidad in Transition* (London, 1968).
33. See W. E. Riviere, 'Labour Shortage in the British West Indies after Emancipation', *Journal of Caribbean History*, 4 (1972), pp. 1–30, which draws together wage data from various sources. For an anticipation of the relative wages that could be paid after the end of apprenticeship, see James MacQueen, *General Statistics of the British Empire* (London, 1836), pp. 190–7.
34. The basic argument was that the continuation of contract labour emigration was an affront to India's national dignity and, in addition to the effects upon the labourers, had 'a debasing or degrading influence on the estimation in which India is held by outside nations'. See Tinker, *op. cit.*, pp. 334–66. There were some attempts to introduce a system of non-contract migration from India to the West Indies during World War I, but these were not successful.
35. The question of the sex ratio among the imported labourers was long a concern of the Colonial Office, and from the start of the discussion of importing Indian and Chinese labour this was one of the major factors discussed. There are many comments on this issue in the letters in C.O. 386 and other sources, and even earlier this issue was raised in a discussion of the possibility of importing labour

from China. See Parliamentary Papers (1810–1811), II, Reports from Committee: West India Free Labourers, pp. 409–10.

36. For a description of the changing provisions in British Guiana, see, in addition to the sources cited in footnote 31, Dwarka Nath, *A History of Indians in British Guiana* (London, 1950). The provisions for return passage were a constant source of discussion both within the colonies and between the colonies and the Colonial Office.
37. For British Guiana the census data on the ethnic composition of the sugar estate population between 1861 and 1891 is conveniently brought together in G. W. Roberts and M. A. Johnson, 'Factors Involved in Immigration and Movements in the Working Force of British Guiana in the Nineteenth Century', *Social and Economic Studies*, 23 (1974), pp. 69–83. See also Rodney, *op. cit.*, p. 231, for data based on the Annual Reports of the Immigration Agent-General. In 1891 it was estimated that about 80 per cent of the resident sugar estate population was East Indian, about 30 per cent of the immigrant adults being under indenture. For Trinidad, in 1890, of the adults working on estates, 82.3% were Indian immigrants, of whom 38.4% were under their original indentures. C.O. 298/47, no. 68, Report of the Protector of Immigrants for the Year 1890.
38. D. W. Galenson, 'The Rise and Fall of Indentured Servitude in the Americas: An Economic Analysis' (unpublished paper).
39. Engerman, 'Contract Labor, Sugar and Technology', *op. cit.*
40. See, for example, Laurence, *op. cit.* and Tinker, *op. cit.*
41. These statements are based upon ship data from the Colonial Land and Emigration Commission (C.O. 386), the reports of the Immigration Agents in the receiving colonies, and the *Annual Report on Emigration from the Port of Calcutta to British and Foreign Colonies*. For a presentation of the data on sailing times and types of ships taking labour to British Guiana, see Nath, *op. cit.*, pp. 181–3. The initial costs of transport were less than one-half of the total expenditures upon indentured labour, there being costs of collection and provisioning in India, return passage, medical costs after arrival, etc. See, for example, C.O. 298/47, no. 38, Immigration Account, 1 Oct.–31 Dec. 1890.
42. See, for example, the wistful comments of the Trinidad Government Emigration Agent in Calcutta: 'Recruiting conditions and prospects at present are abnormally bad in almost every district. The recent good harvest has done away with the chief inducement of the labouring classes to emigrate and recruits are almost unobtainable'. C.O. 295/430, letter of 10 March 1904. The minutes of 22 Dec. 1904 noted that: 'It is unfortunate that the Emigration Agencies must view with alarm a good harvest in India'. For an earlier comment on this pattern, see G. A. Grierson, *Report on Colonial Emigration from the Bengal Presidency* (Calcutta, 1883).
43. For an excellent discussion of these different transitions, see S. W. Mintz, 'Slavery and the Rise of Peasantries', *Historical Reflections*, 6 (1979), pp. 213–42.
44. At the end of the nineteenth century, even while contract labour inflows continued, Trinidad and British Guiana responded differently to the technological developments in sugar production. In Trinidad there emerged a system of small-scale cane farming for the large central mills, while in British Guiana the plantation remained the basis of sugar production. By the first decade of the twentieth century about one-quarter of the cane in Trinidad came from cane-farmers, whereas in British Guiana only about 3% of sugar acreage was on cane farms. H. C. Prinsen Geerligs, *The World's Cane Sugar Industry* (N.Y., 1912), pp. 216–19, 256–63.

12

The Great Escape: The Migration of Female Indentured Servants from British India to Surinam 1873–1916*

P.C. EMMER

I

In moving to the colonies Europeans tended to improve their living standards as well as their social status with the exception of those who fled their homeland because of religious, political or judicial persecution. Some Europeans settled overseas because of economic reasons. They were attracted by the possibility of earning higher incomes than they had been making at home. Some were looking for more leisure or a degree of independence, which could only be supported by the ownership of land.[1]

By selecting a colony of white settlement, European migrants hoped to find a society in which their attempts at improving their social and economic position would not be frustrated by established hereditary barriers of land-ownership. In temporarily choosing a tropical colony the European migrants also expected to improve their professional career, and to obtain a higher income while experiencing a social hierarchy which was completely different from the one at home.[2] After their stay in a tropical colony, the European migrants usually expected to have saved enough money to allow them to spend the rest of their lives as pensioners at home.

In the historiography on European emigration to the colonies of white settlement there is usually little compassion for the majority of migrants. The traditional view depicted the migrants as social refugees from their country of origin, who used emigration overseas as a chance to improve themselves. The same motives were attributed to the lower echelons of the personnel of the colonial governments and trading companies in the tropical colonies. The 'colonial escape hatch' offered European migrants a chance to improve their lot.[3]

Recent research on the social background of European migrants to North America has changed the view that only poor and almost destitute people were willing to work or settle overseas. Their social mix was much more balanced than has previously been assumed.[4] In addition, new data have been produced on the development of the economies of the colonies of white settlement, indicating that income levels indeed were higher overseas and that settlers experienced lower mortality, higher life expectancy and larger families. On material grounds many of the European migrants seem to have made the right choice: by leaving their homes they improved their chances of living a longer and more prosperous life and having a larger family than they would have been able to have at home.[5]

The historiography dealing with the nineteenth century emigration of indentured labourers from British India is written from a completely different perspective from that of the history of European emigration. The title of a recent comprehensive survey of this emigration is revealing: *A New System of Slavery*. In fact, in none of the studies on the Indian overseas diaspora is a comparison made with the simultaneous emigration from Europe. The author of *A New System of Slavery*, Hugh Tinker, seems to have poured all his indignation about the system of migrating indentureds into the following lines when criticising the opinion of some nineteenth century colonial officials in India that emigration was 'an active search for a rewarding life'.[6] Tinker writes:

> This view of emigration – which one might describe as the 'American dream' version – as an escape to opportunity, was genuinely held by some enlightened and humane observers, British and Indian; but it did not accord with the reality of the exile into bondage which was the experience of the great majority of the emigrants during the ninety years, 1830–1920. Some, indeed, did live to attain better material conditions, though many found they had exchanged one form of poverty and servitude for another,

and many more found only death and disease in the new life. But what weighed most in the balance of benefit and affliction was that Indians exchanged a society and a living community (though unequal and degrading to many, tiresome and tedious to most), for a lifeless *system* in which human values always mattered less than the drive for production, for exploitation. It was the system that demanded the emigration of Indian workers overseas and stamped its mark upon the coolies as a 'peculiar people' for so many years to come.[7]

This paper will argue that emigration did provide an opportunity for many Indian emigrants to improve themselves not only in a material way – as Tinker reluctantly concedes – but also in creating their own social and cultural environment with fewer social barriers than existed back home. This applied in particular to the female indentureds who migrated to the colonies. In this paper, those Indian women who went to Surinam will be studied in detail. Their situation was apparently more or less similar to that in the other Caribbean sugar colonies which recruited contract-labour from India. Paradoxically, during the era of Indian indentured emigration, the treatment of female indentureds was always used by the opponents of contract labour in order to attack the 'system'.[8] Thus, it was pointed out that many Indian women were deceived by the recruiting-agents when registering for employment abroad. It will be argued in this paper that the cases of obvious deception were few and that the majority of the women were aware of their overseas destination especially as the practice of indentured emigration became a well-established system.[9] It has also been claimed that many of the female recruits were unfit for manual agricultural labour because of deceptive recruitment. This paper intends to show that the majority of the migrating women had in fact undertaken agricultural work in India and that their shipment to Surinam actually gave many women a chance to choose whether to work in the fields to earn money or to work at home.

In addition, it will be argued that Indian women enjoyed a great deal more personal freedom than they did in India. This was true in particular for those Indian women without a family who had been widowed or wanted to escape their pre-arranged marriage. For them, more than for any other category of Indian migrants, moving to Surinam opened the door to a new, independent future without the many sanctions Indian society exercised upon women who had infringed established customs.

It is clear that those women who chose to work at home caring for their family had a good chance to obtain a better standard of living in Surinam. The birth-rate was certainly not lower than in India and the incomes earned by their (common law) husbands enabled many wives to stay away from fieldwork.[10] In addition, the education provided in the colony opened opportunities for their offspring – both male and female – which did not exist in India. The fact that only a small number of Indian children were sent to school in Surinam was not a fault of the system of indentured labour but reflected instead the persistence of an Indian tradition.[11]

In describing the condition of female Indian indentured servants in Surinam, it will become clear that more women than men used the system of contract labour as it operated in the Caribbean in order to increase their social status and to emancipate themselves from an illiberal, inhibiting and very hierarchical social system in India. The existing body of historical writing about the system of Indian indentured emigration seems to have followed the traditional historiography on slavery in failing to compare conditions experienced by unfree labour with conditions of free labour elsewhere at the same time. By keeping in mind the recurrent bad harvests in India and the ensuing marginal physical condition of large sections of the Indian population, indentured emigration can be viewed as a perhaps desperate escape from hunger and starvation. And by analysing the position of women – particularly single women – in India, indentured emigration can also be regarded as a vehicle of female emancipation.

II

In India, the recruitment of indentured labourers for Surinam had been regulated in exactly the same way as the recruitment for other colonies which imported Indian labour. An agent in Calcutta was appointed to supervise recruitment for Surinam and a network of a head recruiter, sub-recruiters, recruiters and assistant recruiters carried out the actual work.

Recruiting women constituted one of the main problems for these agencies. After 1860 all colonies importing Indian labour had to comply with the rule that 40 per cent of the recruited labourers had to be women. This figure had been agreed upon after careful consideration by the British authorities in both London and India. During the period 1840–1860, the emigration on long-term contracts of mainly male Indians had proved to be very unsatisfactory because it failed to create the stable labour force that planters were looking for. Left to the laws of demand and supply, the number of women leaving India on a contract would have been less than half of that required by the emigration laws.[12] In spite of the difficulties in contracting enough women to emigrate, neither the British colonies nor the foreign governments with recruiting rights in India ever protested against the obligation to recruit a compulsory number of women. As far as Surinam was concerned, the authorities there were probably in complete accord with the required proportion of women, since the very small number of women among the Chinese indentured emigrants to Surinam in previous years had caused men to leave the plantations as soon as possible.[13] In fact, the 40 per cent target was adopted when the Dutch started to recruit indentured labour on Java despite the fact that in this case no foreign power could dictate these rules.[14]

Protests against the 40 per cent rule arose only from recruitment agents in Calcutta for they had to pay considerably more commission to the recruiters in order to obtain women. There were also instances in which ships ready to sail had to wait in order to fill the required quota of women. These delays were not only costly, but also detrimental to the morale of the labourers who had usually already been waiting for several weeks in the Calcutta depot. Married women accompanied by their children were also expensive, since they made intensive use of the medical facilities of the depot. Sometimes good, able-bodied men had to be turned away, because their wives and children were sickly and unfit for the voyage and the labour ahead of them. In short, the required proportion of women complicated the process of recruitment.

The colonial agents in Calcutta supported their aversion against female indentureds by using moral arguments. They argued that many of the recruited women had been prostitutes and were infested with veneral diseases. According to the Dutch agent in Calcutta women were 'worse than useless' and 'a curse for the men'.[15] The female coolies were mainly 'widows who have gone astray' and suffer from syphilis, according to Count Van Hogendorp, who had been commissioned by the colonial government of the Dutch East Indies to study the governmental structure of British India.[16] In fact the colonial agents in Calcutta managed to obtain some relaxation by the colonial authorities of their annual target percentages of women; usually the agents were allowed to make up the shortage of female recruits in one season during the course of the next one.[17] However, the British Indian government strictly adhered to the rule with the exception of the emigration to Mauritius, where the percentage of women indentureds from India was set each year according to the actual sex ratio among the Indian indentured community in that colony.

In contrast to the opinion on female recruits as expressed by the recruitment agencies, it is possible to provide a more balanced view on the emigration of female indentureds based on the data provided by the yearly reports of the Protector of Emigrants in Calcutta. These reports show, first of all, that the forced emigration of women provided a possibility for married couples to emigrate together. Were emigration left to the individual's preference, the majority of the male indentureds would have left their families behind. Now, both men and women as well as their children had a chance to improve their lot by emigration as was the case in the nineteenth century emigration from Europe. About half the women emigrating to Surinam were married.[18] For those not married, emigration meant more personal freedom and an escape from a culture which was hostile to single women. It seems that in India the word 'prostitute' was loosely used and applied to women who had casual relationships with one or more men, had committed adultery or simply had not settled down in one of those marriages which were arranged in India at a very early age.

One other category of women should be mentioned. These were women who were looking for a divorce and were intending to live permanently with another man. If the registering magistrates did not find out about their formal attachments, these women would be able to register as 'married' to their male companions. Obviously this possibility to elope became well known and in the course of the indentured emigration system the Indian magistrates were reluctant to register women who were suspected of having left their husband and children. The recruiters resented this delay and the colonial agents complained about it.[19] Recruiters who had 'enticed' those women to sign an indenture had their licence taken away.[20]

In criticising the recruitment of indentured labour liberal anti-slavery campaigners in Europe and Indian nationalists joined forces in asserting that fraud and deception were the sole basis of the emigration movement. The recruiters of contract labourers in India were never able to completely free themselves from suspicion and were frequently seen as pimps. In campaigning against indentured emigration, Indian nationalists made good use of this notion. During this campaign, Sital Persad, the chief interpreter at the Paramaribo Immigration Department, was sent back in 1914 to his native village in India in order to reassure the population about the position of Indian immigrants in Surinam. Aside from inquiries into the financial side of emigration the main doubts about the system concerned the position of single Indian women in the colony.[21] In a last bid to save the emigration of Indian labourers, the assembled colonies which employed Indian indentured labour proposed to assist only Indian families to emigrate in the future and specifically agreed to seek to stop the emigration of single women.[22]

The majority of Indian women who emigrated were not the victims of deception, fraud or proverbial female innocence, but used the system of indentured labour to escape hunger and misery and to seek more personal freedom. In this respect, Indian women did not differ from their European counterparts who emigrated during the same period to the colonies of white settlement.

Firstly, the escape from hunger and starvation should be mentioned. In this respect recruitment seemed to have been of special importance for women according to a report on indentured emigration of 1883: 'Women who often come to the sub-depot in a state bordering on nudity are in such cases clothed by the sub-agent'.[23] In his yearly reports, the Protector of Emigrants at Calcutta repeatedly confirmed the life-saving aspects of the system of colonial recruitment: 'Although the scarcity in the North Western Provinces and Oudh had not reached the more acute stage of famine, it was still sufficiently severe to urge crowds of half starved adults and emaciated children to the different recruiting centres with the result that the Calcutta depots eventually became asylums for a large number of people in a more or less anaemic and unhealthy condition'.[24] Dismissal from the depot was sometimes postponed, because the rejected emigrants would have been sent to a certain death.

Secondly, the emigration system was a means of escape from low earnings. Over time the emigration to Surinam showed an increase in the number of people who had done agricultural labour in India and intended to do the same type of work overseas. Still, it took some time to get recruits with the right occupational background. Writing on the recruitment for the 'season' 1877–1878, the agent for Surinam wrote about the female recruits: 'Their number was considerably augmented by a batch of dancing-girls and women of a similar description with their male attendants. These people laughed at the idea of labouring as agriculturalists'.[25] However, over time the recruiters for Surinam managed to raise the percentage of men and women from the agricultural sector in India to 93 per cent of the total.[26]

Thirdly, the emigration system was used in order to escape 'personal problems' which would not be solved within Indian society. The plight of single women has already been mentioned as well as the virtually insurmountable social barriers for divorcees. The recruitment system for labour far away from home provided an alternative to degradation and rejection. Within India, the recruitment system was blamed for stimulating women to run away from their families; few contemporaries indicated that the system served to alleviate the deficiencies of Indian society which hardly allowed women any personal freedom.

There is only one indication that women were recruited from a specific geographical area. On 14 December 1880, the Dutch agent in Calcutta was urging the Protector of Emigrants for a speedy clearance of his ship destined for Surinam. Not only had the recruits become impatient and one case of cholera occurred, but the required percentage of women proved difficult to achieve in spite of the high commission paid to the recruiters 'since food prices had dropped considerably in Tirhoot, where many women come from'.[27]

In their attempts to escape hunger, disease and personal misery female emigrants no doubt were subject to fraud and deception. The paragraphs on recruiters' licences in the annual reports of the Protector of Emigrants provide ample evidence of this. Each year recruiters stole jewelry and money from the women they recruited. Rape and illegal detention in the recruiters' depots occurred. Sometimes, female recruits were transferred from their home district to another one making it difficult to check the information given to the magistrate supervising the registration. However, the number of licences withdrawn for the mistreatment of women diminished over time.[28] The call for female recruiters – possibly ex-indentureds themselves – who could do a better job in getting the right type of women to emigrate, as expressed in many reports on indentured emigration, was no longer heard by 1914.

In using the innocent, misguided female recruit as their main weapon against the emigration system both the liberal abolitionists in Europe as well as the Indian nationalists overlooked the possibilities for personal improvement which the recruitment system provided. However, several of the colonial civil servants writing on the recruitment of indentured labour were well aware of the escape hatch provided by emigration overseas: 'women might benefit more than men' and 'women have rights too and if an alienated wife was determined to go, no officer had the right to stop her'.[29]

III

The difficulties in recruiting the required percentage of female indentureds enable us to obtain the most elaborate information on women as a separate category during the process of recruitment. Information is available on the death-rate and birth-rate of female indentureds after they had embarked, but there exists no specific information regarding their participation in rebellion, education, labour law complaints and possession of money and property. Within the system of indentured labour women ceased to be a special problem after they had been recruited.

But even if we had more statistical information on the female indentured labourers, it would certainly be impossible to document the feelings of uncertainty and bewilderment which must have overcome these women from India upon their arrival in Surinam. Those women who were married and were accompanied by their husbands as well as those women who were single when recruited but who had started a formal relationship with a man either at the depot in Calcutta, aboard ship or in the depot in Paramaribo could share their anxieties about the future with someone from whom they were not to be separated by the procedure of allotment. There is no information on the allotment of single women to the plantations, but they always constituted a small minority on any plantation.[30]

The difference between men and women in the official hierarchy on the West Indian plantation was probably less than in Indian society, and the unofficial code of slave society did not compare at all with the relatively inferior position of women in India. In the slave quarters, women were able to acquire a position equal to that of the men. Within the West African value system which slaves had brought with them, a woman had a right to possess land and to have an income separate from that of her husband. Marriages might be arranged, but both men and women had the right to obtain a divorce and to look for another partner. On the plantation, slave women obtained their rations and provisions on an individual basis independently from their male partners. Furthermore, both men and women could equally obtain extra social status within the slave community because of special gifts within the domain of religion and native medicine.[31] All this was alien to Indian society.[32]

It is impossible to prove that female indentureds from British India actually enjoyed new personal freedoms and independence in Surinam. However, there are several indications that indentured women had indeed succeeded in improving their situation. To begin with, their life expectancy seems to have been no worse and may well have improved compared to India. Details of the British India indentured population of Surinam from 1873 to 1916, and of associated births and deaths, are set out in appendices 1–3. Unfortunately, data are not available to compare closely the demographic performance of the British Indians in Surinam to that of a similar segment of the population in India.

Furthermore, the female part of the population cannot be distinguished from the rest of the population in either Surinam or India. Nevertheless, the death-rate of the Indian indentured immigrants in Surinam was much lower than that of the population in India: 27.4 per 1000 in Surinam compared to 42.76 per 1000 in India.[33] However, it should be noted that emigrants from India did not constitute a random sample of the Indian population. They had been selected because of their relative superior physical condition. Also men and women older than 40 years of age were usually not recruited. Separate figures for the death-rate of men and women do not exist for India, but in Surinam that difference was very slight: 22.6 per 1000 for men against 24.6 per 1000 for women.

Turning to the birth-rate, the particular demographic characteristics of the indentured servants make it difficult to compare statistics for Surinam with those for India. The birth-rate among the Surinam indentureds from India was lower because of the unequal sex-balance: only 30 to 40 per cent of the indentured population consisted of women. However, the relatively low death-rate in Surinam caused the indentured immigrant population to increase more rapidly than the population in India, as is indicated in Table 1.

Of course, it is possible to explain the lower birth-rate among the indentured Indians in Surinam as a sign of protest against the conditions in that colony as has been done in studies of slave

TABLE 1

Natural Increase in Population in Surinam and India 1878–1902

In Surinam (indentured)				In India			
period	birth-rate per 1000	death-rate per 1000	natural increase per 1000	period	birth-rate per 1000	death-rate per 1000	natural increase per 1000
1878–1882	31.74	28.45	+ 3.3	1881–1891	48.9	41.3	+7.6
1892–1902	37.33	18.58	+18.75	1891–1901	45.8	44.4	+1.6

Source: P.C. Emmer, 'The Importation of British Indians into Surinam (Dutch Guiana), 1873–1916' in: Shula Marks and Peter Richardson (eds.), *International Labour Migration: Historical Perspectives* (London, 1984), table 1; Kingsley Davis, *The Population of India and Pakistan* (Princeton, 1951), p.85.

societies. Tinker suggests that Indian indentured women gave birth to proportionally low numbers of children and had relatively large numbers of still-born babies due to such diseases as malaria and syphilis.[34] Tinker's views are, however, not supported by statistical evidence. In Surinam the number of births per 1000 women aged 15 to 39 during the period 1878–1906 compared favourably with the number of births of women of a similar age group in India around 1930. In Surinam 155 children were born per 1000 women yearly from 1878 to 1906 compared to 119 per 1000 in the Indian cities of Bombay, Calcutta and Madras and 154 per 1000 in the countryside around these cities in 1930.[35] This number of births per year in Surinam is strikingly high when we recall that only about half the women were married when recruited. In addition to being an indication of the improved living standards of indentured Indian women, this relatively high number of births per 1000 women suggests too that a considerable number of single women found a male partner after they had been recruited.

In spite of the possibility of earning an independent income many Indian indentured women preferred household work and rearing a family to offering to work for wages on plantations as their contracts of indenture required. The number of women who re-indentured after the expiration of the first contract was relatively low. Of the total of 21,237 men landed in Surinam between 1878 and 1916, 7,221 or 34 per cent re-indentured, while only 1,173 or 13.75 per cent of the total of 8,527 women did so. A second indenture was usually considered as a last option for the Indian immigrants. Where possible immigrant workers, men and women alike, tried to return home with the savings from their first indenture or to settle down in the colony as small farmers or as free labourers.[36] Whilst their contracts lasted, however, women in general seem to have accepted the condition of indentured labour more readily than men. In all 286 indentured Indian men deserted the colony (or 1.35 per cent of the total number of indentured men) between 1878 and 1916 compared to only 28 (or 0.3 per cent) women. Of the deserters, 100 men (or 35 per cent of deserters) and 17 women (or 60 per cent) returned.[37]

Another indication of the quality of life of female indentureds in Surinam can be deduced from the sex distribution of returnees who used their right to a free return passage to India after the expiration of their five year contract. As indicated earlier, the proportion of female to total indentured recruits was set after 1860 at 40 per cent. During the years 1878–1891, however, returning emigrants were 72 per cent male and 28 per cent female, while the male domination increased further during the period 1890–1931, when 77 per cent of the returnees were male and only 23 per cent female.[38]

In summing up the position of the female indentureds it should be remembered that the system of indentured emigration offered many opportunities to women for emancipation, but in reality many of these were not used. The norms and values regarding the role of women within Indian society continued to have an important impact on the decisions made by indentured women about their life in Surinam.

Under the system of indentured labour, each adult female was provided with a separate contract and thus with the possibility of earning an income as an individual, paid to her in money. However, the average number of days worked per year by women was between a quarter and a third less than men.[39] Adopting the role of housewife came most naturally to those female indentureds who had emigrated with their husbands and children. However, even the women who had left India as unmarried or widowed generally became housewives and reared children. There are many indications that virtually all Indian women found a male partner in Surinam. Dr Comins, the Inspector of Emigrants at Calcutta, specifically mentioned the relatively low level of female participation in plantation work because of family obligations.[40] Furthermore, according to Comins, plantation managers were well advised not to demand labour from females after three years of their indentures had expired.

Another problem for the emancipation of female indentureds was the relatively heavy workload per day. In time only sugar plantations could afford to import indentured labour and such plantations offered only a limited number of jobs besides fieldwork. However, the system did provide workers, both male and female, with a minimum: if an indentured labourer was unable to earn half the minimum wage, he or she would not receive money, but only food rations.[41]

Nevertheless, if she really so desired, the female indentured could survive by herself.

IV

A review of the evidence regarding the emigration of female indentureds from India to Surinam supports the contention that this migration not only enabled Indian women to earn more than at home, but also provided an opportunity for single or widowed women to escape their degrading position in Indian society. There is no clear evidence that wages for indentured labourers overseas were consistently higher than at home.[42] However, the continued supply of labour for employment overseas does suggest that wages were competitive at least with the wages earned by migrant labourers within India itself, and this seems to have applied equally to men and women.[43] Evidence on the living standards of Indian indentured servants in Surinam after 1878 is sparse but indirect indications suggest that they were an improvement over conditions in India itself. Birth-rates of indentured servants were higher than that of the Indian population whilst death-rates were lower. Furthermore, despite the availability of free return passages to India at the expiration of contracts, most indentureds chose to remain in Surinam. All in all about two-thirds of the Indian immigrants remained in the colony, disproportionately more women than men.[44] The relatively low percentages of female indentureds deserting the colony and re-indenturing themselves suggest that the majority of these women were satisfied to make Surinam their permanent home.

In view of this, the disfavour with which the migration of indentured labour was regarded by groups in Western Europe and India, and its abolition in 1916, has to be explained. It is true that the migration was surrounded by difficulties such as deception in recruitment, loss of cultural values, and the problems of adapting to new life styles but in the context of European migration to the Americas from the sixteenth to the nineteenth century such drawbacks were usually seen as unavoidable side-effects of the migrants' drive to improve themselves. In the case of Indian indentured migration, however, they were used as central arguments to stop all regulated emigration to the West Indies in 1916. In spite of protests from the British Indian community in Surinam itself this ban was never removed, even though the far more important and unregulated migration from India to Ceylon and the Straits went unchallenged.[45]

The problem with Indian indentured migration was that it was an affront to both European liberals and Indian nationalists (including Gandhi). For liberals in Europe, indentured labour was 'unfree' labour and as such a continuation of slavery. For these opponents it did not matter that indentured labourers in some respects seemed to enjoy better working conditions than contemporary free labour in Europe. From the very beginning the maximum hours of work per day were set at seven to ten, while Sunday was set aside as a day of rest, as were 32 days of Hindu festivals and 16 days for Islamic religious holidays. In principle equal pay was given to indentured labourers of both sexes for equal work. However, the 'penal sanctions' by which the colonial state could force indentured labourers to honour their contracts offended opponents of the system.[46] A comparison of the actual working conditions of labourers in the colonial West Indies and Western Europe, much less India, was never made.[47] In India, the nationalists exploited popular antipathy for indentured emigration overseas. The 1914 report by McNeill and Chimmam Lal on the conditions of indentured Indians overseas made a special point of showing that the majority of the women who migrated were not prostitutes but common housewives and agricultural labourers. But this report was quickly discarded and among Indian nationalists the suppression of the indentured labour system continued to be seen, amongst other things, as a measure to protect innocent Indian women.[48] The Great Escape was over.

NOTES

* An earlier version of this paper was presented to the Colloque Franco-Néerlandais: 'Les femmes à la situation coloniale', at Groningen, The Netherlands, in September 1982. A different version of the paper has also been published in Dutch in *OSO, Tijdschrift Voor Surinamse Taalkunde Letterkunde en Geschiedenis*, 2, no. 2 (December 1983), pp. 149–63.

1. Charles Tilly, 'Migration in Modern European History', W. H. McNeill and R. S. Adams (eds.), *Human Migration: Patterns and Policies* (Bloomington,

Indiana, 1978), pp. 48–72; and David Eltis, 'Free and Coerced Transatlantic Migrations: Some Comparisons', *American Historical Review*, 88 (1983), p. 257.
2. Louis Hartz, *The Founding of New Societies: Studies in the History of the United States, Latin America, South Africa, Canada, and Australia* (New York, 1964), pp. 11–16; Jean Meyer, *Les Européens et les Autres de Cortès à Washington* (Paris, 1975), pp. 149–57.
3. K. G. Davies, *The North Atlantic World in the Seventeenth Century* (London, 1974), pp. 63–108.
4. David Souden, '"Rogues, Whores and Vagabonds?" Indentured Servant Emigrants to North America and the Case of mid-seventeenth-century Bristol', *Social History*, III (1978), pp. 23–41.
5. G. M. Walton and J. F. Shepherd, *The Economy of Early America* (Cambridge, 1979), pp. 52–5, 142–51.
6. A. A. Yang, 'Peasants on the Move: A Study of Internal Migration in India', *Journal of Interdisciplinary History*, X (1979), p. 37.
7. Hugh Tinker, *A New System of Slavery: The Export of Indian Labour Overseas, 1830–1920* (Oxford, 1974), p. 60.
8. India Office Records (hereafter I.O.R.) London, Proceedings 9270, pp. 335–6; Tinker, *op. cit.*, p. 341.
9. P. C. Emmer, '"The Meek Hindu": The Recruitment of Indian Indentured Labourers for Service Overseas, 1870–1916', paper presented to the VIth Workshop of the Centre for the History of European Expansion on 'Colonialism and Migration: Indentured Labour Before and After Emancipation', 21–23 April 1982.
10. James McNeill and Chimmam Lal, *Report to the Government of India on the Conditions of Indian Immigrants in Four British Colonies and Surinam* (London, 1915), pp. 313–14.
11. D. W. D. Comins, *Note on the Emigration from the East Indies to Surinam or Dutch Guiana* (Calcutta, 1892), p. 33.
12. Tinker, *op. cit.*, pp. 88–89.
13. J. Ankum-Houwink, 'Chinese Contract Migrants in Surinam Between 1853 and 1870', *Boletin de Estudios Latinoamericanos y del Caribe*, XVII (1974), p. 47.
14. Rudolf van Lier, *Samenleving in een Grensgebied: een Sociaal-Historische Studie van Suriname* (Amsterdam, 1977), p. 162.
15. I.O.R., Emigration Proceedings (hereafter E.P.), 2526 (1885), pp. 475–82.
16. Algemeen Rijksarchief (General State Archives, hereafter A.R.A.), Buitenlandse Zaken A 135, box 278, 17 June 1876.
17. I.O.R., E.P., 5666 (1899), pp. 627–8.
18. Emmer, 'The Meek Hindu ...', *op. cit.*, p. 11.
19. I.O.R., E.P., 1862 (1882), pp. 1241–68.
20. *Annual Report on Emigration from the Port of Calcutta to British and Foreign Colonies*, by the Protector of Emigrants, 1871 to 1917.
21. A.R.A., Buitenlandse Zaken, A 135, box 282, 21 Feb. 1914.
22. I.O.R., E.P., 10219 (1914), pp. 489–94. Report of the Inter-Departmental Conference on Assisted Emigration from India to British Guiana, Trinidad, Jamaica and Fiji.
23. G. A. Grierson, *Report on the Colonial Emigration from the Bengal Presidency* (Calcutta, 1883), p. 8.
24. Protector of Emigrants, *Report 1883–4, op. cit.*
25. Protector of Emigrants, *Report 1877–8, op. cit.*
26. Emmer, 'The Meek Hindu', *op. cit.*, p. 4; C. J. M. de Klerk, *De Immigratie der Hindostanen in Suriname* (Amsterdam, 1953), pp. 104–13.

27. I.O.R., E.P., 1662 (1881), pp. 51–8.
28. Based on the Annual Reports of the Protector of Emigrants, 1898 to 1914.
29. Tinker, *op. cit.*, pp. 267–8, quoting Pitcher, Lyall and Grierson.
30. *Koloniale Verslagen, Surinam*, 1873–1916, The Hague.
31. Barbara Bush, 'Defiance or Submission? The Role of the Slave Woman in Slave Resistance in the British Caribbean', *Immigrants and Minorities*, I (1982), pp. 29–31.
32. In order to explain the inferior position women held in Indian society the Immigration Department in Surinam issued a brochure about the plight of women in India: C.v.D.[rimmelen], *Iets over de Hindoe-vrouw; Bijdrage tot de Kennis van het Leven, de Zeden en de Gewoonten van het Volk, Waartoe de Britsch-Indische Immigranten in Suriname Behooren* (Paramaribo, 1912).
33. P. C. Emmer, 'The Importation of British Indians into Surinam (Dutch Guiana), 1873–1916' in Shula Marks and Peter Richardson (eds.), *International Labour Migration: Historical Perspectives* (London, 1984), table 1 and Kingsley Davis, *The Population of India and Pakistan* (Princeton, 1951), p. 36.
34. Tinker, *op. cit.*, p. 205.
35. Davis, *op. cit.*, p. 70; *Koloniale Verslagen Surinam* (yearly).
36. Comins, *op. cit.*, p. 21. See Appendix 4 for details of re-indentures.
37. See Appendix 5.
38. Comins, *op. cit.*, p. 31; McNeill and Chimmam Lal, *Report, op. cit.*, p. 332 (Appendix C).
39. Emmer, 'The Importation of British Indians', in Marks and Richardson (eds.), *op. cit.*, Table 2.
40. Comins, *op. cit.*, p. 19; *Report of the Committee on Emigration from India to the Crown Colonies and Protectorates (Sanderson Report)* (London, 1910), question 654.
41. Emmer, 'The Importation of British Indians', in Marks and Richardson (eds.), *op. cit.*, p. 130.
42. Emmer, 'The Meek Hindu ...', *op. cit.*, p. 12.
43. Yang, 'Peasants on the Move ...', *op. cit.*, p. 49 mentions a maximum of 'over 5 annas a day', which is about 25 Dutch cents. In Surinam the minimum was 60 Dutch cents.
44. de Klerk, *op. cit.*, pp. 146, 159.
45. Emmer, 'The Meek Hindu', *op. cit.*, pp. 14, 15.
46. For the contents of contracts of emigrants bound for Surinam, see McNeill and Chimmam Lal, *Report, op. cit.*, pp. 187–9; I.O.R., Confidential Proceedings, 29 (1917), pp. 273–8.
47. A. T. Yarwood, 'The Overseas Indians as a Problem in Indian and Imperial Politics at the End of World War One', *Australian Journal of Politics and History*, XIV (1968), pp. 204–18.
48. For the suppression of the Report of McNeill and Chimmam Lal see, I.O.R., Confidential Proceedings, 29 (1917), pp. 34, 35.

STATISTICAL APPENDICES

Sources: All data in these Appendices are from either the *Koloniale Verslagen, Surinam* 1873–1916 or the yearly Immigration Abstracts sent to the F.O. in London by the British Consul at Paramaribo, Surinam (in the I.O.R., Emigration Proceedings: J + P files, and in the P.R.O. Foreign Office Papers, F.O. 37, Holland and Netherlands)

Appendix 1: British Indians Under Indenture in Surinam 1873–1916

Year	Men	Women	Boys	Girls	Total
1873	1,525	572	214	137	2,448
1874	1,782	714	357	232	3,085
1875	1,682	666	372	239	2,959
1876	1,647	656	389	248	2,940
1877	1,813	718	403	281	3,215
1878	1,820	687	380	273	3,160
1879	1,657	602	345	269	2,873
1880	2,175	765	441	347	3,728
1881	2,406	863	488	399	4,156
1882	2,499	933	557	439	4,428
1883	2,575	939	508	424	4,446
1884	3,653	1,359	662	555	6,229
1885	3,565	1,243	695	575	6,078
1886	3,281	1,234	710	605	5,830
1887	3,203	1,156	718	618	5,695
1888	2,406	852	560	493	4,311
1889	2,524	789	473	418	4,204
1890	3,213	966	567	464	5,210
1891	3,441	1,073	641	554	5,709
1892	3,781	1,245	711	599	6,336
1893	4,235	1,460	822	716	7,233
1894	3,856	1,308	624	562	6,350
1895	4,040	1,405	591	556	6,592
1896	4,369	1,547	604	546	7,066
1897	3,671	1,268	514	466	5,919
1898	3,409	1,185	500	435	5,529
1899	3,090	1,053	471	444	5,058
1900	2,400	704	317	306	3,727
1901	1,970	446	215	214	2,845
1902	2,637	763	308	303	4,011
1903	2,367	678	294	272	3,611
1904	1,920	580	248	255	3,003
1905	1,739	576	244	257	2,816
1906	2,180	689	328	311	3,508
1907	2,474	838	303	282	3,897
1908	3,173	1,163	347	352	5,035
1909	3,695	1,408	378	398	5,879
1910	3,742	1,439	460	478	6,119
1911	3,513	1,338	520	505	5,876
1912	2,850	1,045	402	372	4,669
1913	2,805	939	362	325	4,431
1914	2,890	971	348	278	4,487
1915	2,578	840	346	259	4,023
1916	2,694	882	405	303	4,284
Total	122,945	42,557	20,142	17,364	203,008

Appendix 2: Deaths of British Indian Indentureds in Surinam 1873–1916

						Deaths per 1000		
Year	Men	Women	Boys	Girls	Total	Total	Women	Men
1873	77	31	14	16	138	56	54.1	50.5
1874	389	146	47	59	641	171.4	204	218.2
1875	97	46	11	13	167	56	69	57.6
1876	47	23	19	30	119	37	35	28.5
1877	46	24	33	16	119	36.6	33	25
1878	34	22	13	15	84	26.5	32	18.6
1879	19	10	17	14	60	20.8	16.6	11.4
1880	22	14	14	9	59	15.8	18.3	10.1
1881	75	20	20	15	130	31.2	23.1	31.1
1882	59	28	21	18	126	28.4	30	23.6
1883	92	20	17	16	145	32.6	21.2	35.7
1884	85	34	33	32	184	29.5	25	23.2
1885	77	31	30	26	164	26.5	24.9	21.6
1886	56	23	24	27	130	22.2	18.6	17.1
1887	53	23	18	13	107	18.7	19.9	16.5
1888	35	14	26	14	89	20.6	16.4	14.5
1889	31	16	11	9	67	15.9	20.3	12.3
1890	48	9	19	15	91	21.8	9.3	15
1891	85	33	43	25	186	26.6	30.7	24.7
1892	81	29	32	29	171	27	23.2	21.4
1893	79	28	26	30	163	22.5	19.1	18.7
1894	84	27	33	29	173	27.2	20.6	21.7
1895	65	20	28	29	142	21.5	14.2	16.1
1896	64	20	46	33	163	23	13	14.6
1897	51	25	49	40	165	27.9	19.7	13.9
1898	51	16	27	29	123	22	13.5	15
1899	39	7	16	16	78	15.4	6.6	12.6
1900	28	9	18	20	75	20.1	12.8	11.7
1901	22	8	8	8	46	16.1	17.9	11.2
1902	59	19	11	19	108	26.9	24.9	22.4
1903	33	24	16	18	91	25.2	35.4	13.9
1904	24	8	9	5	46	15.3	13.8	12.5
1905	21	7	5	10	43	15.3	12.2	12
1906	15	2	9	12	38	10.8	2.9	6.9
1907	32	9	18	16	75	19.2	10.7	13
1908	36	12	32	20	100	19.9	10.3	11.3
1909	61	26	34	31	152	25.8	18.5	16.5
1910	41	26	27	45	139	22.7	18.1	11
1911					126	21.4		
1912	23	11	38	32	104	22.2	10.5	8
1913	18	11	29	38	96	21.7	11.7	6.4
1914	24	10	26	31	91	20.3	10.2	8.3
1915	10	6	7	15	38	9.4	7.1	3.8
1916	15	11	12	14	52	12.1	12.5	5.6

Appendix 3: Births to British Indian Indentureds in Surinam, 1873–1916

Year	Boys	Girls	Total	Births per 1000 women
1873	8	12	20	30
1874	16	15	31	40
1875	38	32	70	100
1876	55	39	94	140
1877	33	35	68	90
1878	38	33	71	100
1879	58	54	112	190
1880	84	63	147	190
1881	55	61	116	130
1882	81	60	141	150
1883	64	66	130	140
1884	76	74	150	110
1885	138	105	243	190
1886	107	104	211	170
1887	94	81	175	150
1888	104	102	206	240
1889	51	53	104	130
1890	63	51	114	120
1891	75	77	152	140
1892	71	69	140	110
1893	100	100	200	140
1894	83	69	152	120
1895	78	82	160	110
1896	111	75	186	120
1897	124	110	234	180
1898	100	94	194	160
1899	109	125	234	220
1900	78	80	158	220
1901	52	68	120	270
1902	40	36	76	100
1903	58	71	129	190
1904	41	62	103	180
1905	39	45	84	150
1906	57	39	96	140
1907	36	52	88	110
1908	83	79	162	140
1909	116	106	222	160
1910	124	139	263	180
1911			244	180
1912	105	112	217	210
1913	73	90	163	170
1914	76	87	163	170
1915	57	60	117	140
1916	70	59	129	150

Appendix 4: Re-Indentures Among British Indian Immigrants, Surinam 1873–1916

Year	Men	Women	Boys	Girls	Total
1873					
1874					
1875					
1876					
1877					
1878	602	198	89	57	946
1879	429	165	126	84	804
1880	–				
1881	–				
1882	62	10	7	8	87
1883	512	153	131	109	905
1884	371	133	101	77	682
1885	87	17	11	7	122
1886	129	31	12	14	186
1887	39	7	1	8	55
1888	137	30	23	27	217
1889	581	106	82	85	854
1890	429	32	25	20	506
1891	116	17	21	12	166
1892	65	4	3	1	73
1893	77		2		79
1894	218	17	14	21	270
1895	197	14	12	10	233
1896	80	3		2	85
1897	63	1	1		65
1898	52	3	2	2	59
1899	215	17	15	10	257
1900	427	43	37	25	532
1901	372	39	19	23	453
1902	119				119
1903	38				38
1904	45	8	4	5	62
1905	39	3	3	1	46
1906	308				308
1907	234	32	7	10	283
1908	104	3	2	2	111
1909	60				60
1910	79	5	3	1	88
1911					
1912	146	6	5		157
1913	107	34	9	14	164
1914	143	19	7	5	174
1915	207	17	12	6	242
1916	229	6	1	1	237
Total	7,118	1,173	787	647	9,725

Appendix 5: Desertions Among British Indian Immigrants, Surinam 1873–1916

	Missing/Deserted					Returned			
Year	Men	Women	Boys	Girls	Total	Men	Women	Boys	Total*
1873	–					–			
1874	–					–			
1875	–				2	–			
1876	2				2	–			
1877	1				1	–			
1878	3				3	–			
1879	14				14	4			4
1880	5			2	7	6	3	3	12
1881	1				1	–			
1882	4	1	1	1	7	–			
1883	4				4	1			1
1884	12	2	1		15	2			2
1885	23	1			24	3			3
1886	10	2			12	3			3
1887	12				12	2			2
1888	17	2	3	2	24	3		1	4
1889	15	1			16	7			7
1890	16	1			17	7	2		9
1891	4	2			6	6	1		7
1892	23	2	2	1	28	5			5
1893	6	2			8	5	1		6
1894	3	2			5	3		1	4
1895	14	1			15	4	1		5
1896	5	1			6	3			3
1897	6	1			7	5	1		6
1898	5				5	3			3
1899	4	1			5	2			2
1900	6	1			7	3			3
1901	2				2	2			2
1902	1				1	–			
1903	1				1	–			
1904	3				3	1			1
1905	18				18	2			2
1906	–					–			
1907	1				1	–			
1908	–					–			
1909	–					–			
1910	6				6	–			
1911	–					–			
1912	–					7			7
1913	14	3			17	1	1		2
1914	12	1			13	9	7		16
1915	–								
1916	11	1			12	1			1
Total	286	28	7	6	327	100	17	5	122

*There were no girls recorded as returned.

13

Comments on the Papers by Green, Marshall, Engerman and Emmer

K.O. LAURENCE

Professor Green has argued convincingly that the abolitionists did have a vision of the kind of free society they wanted. Broadly, one of their aims was to make the freedmen into committed Christians with English habits, while another was to maintain the plantation system through the use of genuinely free labour. Indeed the re-acculturation of the people seemed to hinge on maintaining a successful export economy. Thus the abolitionists had relatively little use for the peasant sector.

Green himself indicates the contradiction between the parallel aims of achieving genuinely free labour and sustaining the plantation system. I wish to suggest that the aim of Christianisation and re-acculturation likewise contained an inherent difficulty which he has not quite exposed. Success with this project required the continuance and broadening of the missionaries' position as guides and mentors of black and coloured people. But these people, now being free, were tasting a new element of self-consciousness, a new freedom, and so were no longer content in the 1840s and 1850s to absorb missionary precepts and injunctions quite so easily as during slavery. If the missionaries were to retain and expand their influence they would have to treat the now emancipated people with more flexibility than before, in a sense with more respect. An effort was needed to evaluate and accommodate initiatives from below, even perhaps to tolerate cultural manifestations of creole rather than European character.

Green says that the freedmen found evangelical Christianity unattractive. Probably its unattractiveness was enhanced by a failure to consider that the freedmen of the 1840s needed more delicate handling than slaves had done. The heavily paternal attitude of the missionaries was no longer appropriate. I suggest that many missionaries found it impossible to come to terms with this. An arrogance entrenched before 1838, combined with the belief in the absolute validity of their own behavioural patterns, allowed them only to persist with the assumption that their flocks must follow blindly where they led. Those flocks reacted with grateful gestures in 1838–9, when there occurred a sudden increase in the number of weddings, but soon showed antipathy to the assumption that they were mere sheep. When their views and initiatives were given scant attention, they reacted by moving in the direction of the black preachers. This picture is worth pondering, at least for Jamaica. The missionaries sometimes seem to have been more successful elsewhere. The work and attitudes of the missions after 1838 is a subject still badly in need of further research.

Finally, if I myself were seeking to explain the anti-slavery decline after 1838 I would probably place more emphasis on the triumph of material self-interest among the British public and less on the inner contradictions and other difficulties which the movement suffered as well as on the general decline in popular enthusiasm for a seemingly obsolete cause. I think that the phrase 'Exeter Hall had been overwhelmed by Manchester' strikes a truer chord than the careful account of anti-slavery's own failures, when one comes to sum up.

Professor Marshall gives us a picture of planter attitudes during Apprenticeship which is generally familiar, but I was struck by the use of indulgences not merely as a weapon but specifically as an alternative to paying wages which the planters apparently found more attractive. I am not wholly clear why the planters were so much more reluctant to pay in money than in kind, though a shortage of small coin was no doubt involved.

The movement for task work in Grenada and St Vincent even during Apprenticeship raises many interesting questions. Why only in two of the four islands under consideration? How widespread was it in those two? How far did the trend persist after 1838? And exactly why was task work so great a source of complaint? Certainly the system might be so manipulated as to rob the apprentices of some of their free time and the atmosphere of distrust and suspicion was important. But this was also true of British Guiana where task work gave much less trouble. Here there seems room for further comparative research.

Also noteworthy is the account of the apprentices' determination to purchase freedom rather than receive it as a gift. Not only did it thus seem more secure. The argument that quest for social status was an important factor can be supported with reference to other colonies: both in Trinidad and in Jamaica the expression 'fuss of Augus nigger' was used by old freedmen to distance themselves from the masses who were freed in 1838.

The picture of a progressive deterioration in labour relations throughout Apprenticeship, culminating in the last months with rumours of violence, is also striking. Marshall indeed suggests that there was a real possibility of general resistance by the time Apprenticeship came to an end. In particular one notes a contrast with the view that in some colonies relations improved somewhat during 1835 and possibly later.

In the light of the suggestion that mid-1838 saw the beginnings of industrial resistance in the face of anticipated coercion, and of Marshall's general picture of the attitudes of employers and labourers, the question arises why in the event was full freedom achieved with so little violence. For while a number of difficulties have been cited the transition still seems to have been relatively peaceful. It is a question which seems to merit new attention. Certainly, the picture of embryonic industrial resistance, the coercive attitudes of employers, and their failure to explain the terms of the new contract law must affect the general assessment of the behaviour of the people after Apprenticeship ended. A three-month crisis seems a very muted reaction to the conditions here depicted. Governors, stipendiary magistrates and police magistrates must have had to work very hard in the last months of 1838 to avert graver trouble by explanations and by securing modification of some of the employers' demands.

In sum, Marshall has shown that the continuities, as he calls them, between Apprenticeship and freedom, require deliberate and careful attention.

Professor Engerman gives us a summary account of the background to the system of contract labour, stressing that in discussions and debates preceding the 1833 Act, the fact that varying population densities in the colonies would produce varying responses to emancipation was fully recognised. This point is not exactly new, but it still deserves to be pondered. If the fact that emancipation would bring different problems was widely recognised, how did the British Government come to impose an Apprenticeship System which was essentially the same in all colonies? To say that the Government wished to be quickly rid of the emancipation problem in order to proceed to other business, so that haste was the order of the day, is no doubt sound as far as it goes. But it suggests a really staggering level of irresponsibility within the government. Were there perhaps factors involved which have received too little attention?

In the latter part of his paper Engerman sees two purposes behind the constant demand for contract labour: a short-term demand for estate labour after 1838 and a long-term problem which he calls 'labour force adjustment', which would partly be solved when immigrants became permanent settlers. In fact, however, the concept of permanent settlement by Indian contract labour hardly emerged before 1870. In my view it never really gained much currency as a deliberate method of solving the problem of estate labour. If it had, efforts to promote settlement would have been less trivial, for trivial is what they were.

As time passed new factors emerged to prompt the continuance of the indenture system. First, there was the factor of habit, plus a disinclination to face any change. Second, a clearer concentration on the fact that contract labour was unfree, relatively docile, easily directed. Contract labour was sought because it was unfree, rather than because a new labour force was needed, by the late nineteenth century. This is a principal reason for the longevity of indenture and it raises the question of what the planters really meant when they spoke of their labour force as inadequate. It may be surmised that they would have deemed the labour force inadequate as long as they were not able to command as much labour as they chose for whatever wage they chose. Such conditions, of course, never appeared.

Engerman says that the variation in the supply of contract labour was linked to demand and availability, and links demand to the state of sugar production. In my view demand really had little to do with the matter since it invariably exceeded the supply of available immigrants. And demand was based not so much on sugar production, which only rarely affected the requisitions, as on the planters' desire to improve their command of the labour market even when they already commanded it for all practical purposes, tempered by Imperial concern for the total size of the public subsidy. The Imperial government sometimes intervened to limit the requisition for immigrants on financial grounds.

Engerman says that British Guiana and Trinidad responded differently to new technological developments in sugar production because British Guiana never made much use of cane farming. I find it difficult to see this as a matter of differentiated response. Rather did both colonies respond by creating larger catchments for modernised manufactures. For excellent local reasons relating to the condition of the land, cane farming was not an option generally open to the Guianese.

I have some sympathy with Dr Emmer's view of the system of Indian indentured immigration. I support his contention that Tinker underestimates the extent to which emigrants improved their material conditions by emigrating. As for the system of recruiting in general, Tinker believes that many earlier writers were 'reluctant to pursue the sordid far enough'. I think more recent pursuits of the sordid have sometimes led the pursuers beyond the safety barrier. I also support Emmer's comment that much of the historical writing on Indian immigration has failed to keep firmly in view the conditions surrounding both contract and free labour generally in the nineteenth century.

At the same time I think Emmer sometimes sees too optimistic a picture. On the question of deception by recruiting agents, I have no doubt most women emigrants knew the name of their destination. But it is unconvincing to say simply that cases of genuine deception were few. So far as the British West Indies were concerned many people were not adequately informed about the enterprise on which they set out, and the several agencies were too closely modelled on each other for the Dutch to have been significantly different. We must also beware of discounting too largely the talk about prostitutes. Not all the stories of the behaviour in the depot carry a tone of malicious invention.

I am not sure how Emmer estimates that half the women were married. In the British West Indies couples who attached themselves to each other on board ship were commonly recorded as *married* in the immigration registers if they so desired. Our information on how many married women left India is not complete and 50 per cent seems a very high figure, at least until the final decade of the emigration. Again it is clear that many male emigrants left their wives behind. Emmer gives the impression that the emphasis on recruiting women, and sometimes whole families, averted this.

The picture of indentured emigration as a means of escape from 'personal problems', especially those of the single woman or widow, may be reinforced from several quarters. It was a fairly well used avenue of such escape. But this did not mean that the alternative life offered by emigration was positively attractive, and again I think that Emmer's picture may be overdrawn. Since women generally appear to have preferred household positions to employment and nearly all who arrived single were quickly married, I think that there is a certain unreality about the notion of greater employment opportunity in the West Indies. In this context I doubt if much importance attaches to the fact that relatively few women returned to India. Single men tended to return, the married to stay. Most women were married to men who did not return. Whether or not their wives were happy in the West Indies may not have played a decisive part in that decision.

The view that Indian women enjoyed more personal freedom in the West Indies than in India seems in a general way likely to be sound. But a cautionary note is needed. Any such increase in freedom must rest on the weakening of traditional family organisation and social custom among the immigrants. To some extent this did happen in the course of the emigration, but these forces still retained much strength, and in later decades, as numbers grew, they began to recover strength. In the Indian immigrant societies in the Caribbean in the early twentieth century there must have been extremely strong pressures against the assertion of a new personal freedom by recently arrived women. Probably most continued to live lives not very far removed from those typical of India.

Altogether Emmer has provided a useful qualification of

the common picture of indentured immigration as merely exploitative, though he does seem to overdraw the picture of benefit to the immigrants.

INDEX